Vitra Design Museum

Antibodies
Antikörper
Fernando
& Humberto
Campana
1989–2009

Humberto and Fernando
Campana in the courtyard of
their studio in São Paulo, 2005.
Humberto und Fernando
Campana im Innenhof ihres
Ateliers in São Paulo, 2005.

Mathias Schwartz-Clauss

Thanks!

Presenting the work of living artists is always fascinating, as the oeuvre continues to evolve and forge new unanticipated connections with the project. With the one-off installation that Fernando and Humberto Campana designed for our *Antibodies* exhibition, with their collages that comment on our grouping of the exhibits, and with the paper objects that we developed together, an exceptional number of new works were produced especially for this exhibition and catalogue. A great and unexpected gift has also been the personal friendship that has developed between us. I will never forget how the two brothers welcomed me in Brazil! For their engagement and trust, their patience and understanding, and their steadfast enthusiasm, I shall always be grateful.

During the preparations for the exhibition, Lélia Arruda and Leo Kim of Estúdio Campana acted as the extended arms and duplicated eyes of the Campanas and were indispensable in the development of the content and administration of the project. No matter how often I kept them waiting and pestered and peppered them with questions, they always remained calm and cheerful and with a ready sense of humour. I offer my heartfelt thanks to them as well as to their colleagues – Luiza Albuquerque, Eduardo Wolk, Dorival Pereira Barbosa, and Cristina Esther – who spared no effort to assist us. Another tremendous source of support was Fernando Laszlo, who photographed most of the objects for this catalogue in São Paulo; I hope to meet him face to face some day in order to thank him in person.

My gratitude also goes to the authors – to Massimo Morozzi, for his refreshing essay on the building of furniture and other adventures with the Campanas; to Maria Helena Estrada, who drew from her decades of friendship with the brothers; and to Adélia Borges, the grande dame of Brazilian design – as well as to the translators and editors for navigating the many hurdles with aplomb.

Special thanks is owed to those who generously loaned objects to the exhibition: Adriana Adam, the Albion Gallery in London, the Ballet National de Marseille, Dorival Pereira Barbosa, Bernardaud SA in Limoges, José Alberto Campana and Mariangela Martinez Campana, Edra spa in Perignano Pisa, Claudio Elisabetzky, Dan Fialdini, Paulo Sergio Brito Furtado, Christian Heymes, Leo Kim, Lumsden Ltd. in London, José Roberto Moreira do Valle, Moss Gallery in New York, Craig Robins and Ambra Medda of Design Miami, Beth Rudin DeWoody, Jacqueline Terpins, Pedro Useche, and Alexander von Vegesack. Above all, I am especially grateful to Robert Wasilewski, who provided us with many important early works of the Campanas, and of course to Estúdio Campana itself, without whose loans the exhibition would have been simply unimaginable. The studio also played a key role in contacting most of the lenders and encouraging trust and belief in our project.

Realizing the exhibition and catalogue together with the groenland-basel design office– with Matthias Schnegg, Dorothea Weishaupt, Bernhard Schweizer, and Matthias Huber – was a new and exceedingly positive experience. I thank them all for their wonderful ideas and designs and their collaboration!

Finally, I owe special thanks to Daniel Kern, who assisted me with his tremendous imagination, precision and energy, as well as to all the others who helped carry out the project here on location: Stefani Fricker, Gregor Bielser and the technical team of our museum, Alexa Tepen, Esmeralda Hernandez, Kilian Jost, Marine Gallian, Anneliese Gastel, Marianne Goebel, Harry Schöpflin and Jörn Strüker, Richard Adler, Bogusław Ubik-Perski, Reiner Packeiser and Isabel Serbeto, Yvonne Radecker, Mateo Kries, and finally Alexander von Vegesack, who through his workshops at the Domaine de Boisbuchet made my personal contact with Fernando and Humberto Campana possible in the first place.

Danke!

Das Werk lebender Künstler zu präsentieren, ist immer aufregend, weil es unablässig wächst und neue, unerwartete Beziehungen zum Projekt aufbaut. Mit der einmaligen Installation, die Fernando und Humberto Campana für unsere *Antikörper*-Ausstellung entwarfen, mit ihren Collagen, die unsere Zusammenstellung der Exponate kommentieren, und mit den Objekten aus Papier, die wir gemeinsam entwickelten, entstanden ungewöhnlich viele neue Arbeiten eigens für die Ausstellung und diesen Katalog. Als großes, unerwartetes Geschenk empfinde ich auch die Freundschaft, die sich zwischen uns entwickelte. Ich werde nie vergessen, wie mich die beiden Brüder in Brasilien empfangen haben! Für dieses Engagement und Vertrauen, für Geduld und Verständnis und für ihren unerschütterlichen Enthusiasmus bin ich ihnen stets dankbar.

Lélia Arruda und Leo Kim vom Estúdio Campana waren während der Ausstellungsvorbereitung sozusagen die verlängerten Arme und die vervielfachten Augen der Campanas und unverzichtbar für die inhaltliche Ausarbeitung und administrative Begleitung des Projekts. Wie oft habe ich sie hingehalten, gestört und bedrängt – sie sind immer ruhig und herzlich geblieben und haben mich oft zum Lachen gebracht. Ihnen und ihren Mitarbeitern Luiza Albuquerque, Eduardo Wolk, Dorival Pereira Barbosa und Cristina Esther, die keine Mühe gescheut haben, uns zu unterstützen, bin ich von ganzem Herzen dankbar. Großartig war auch Fernando Laszlo, der in São Paulo die meisten Objekte für den vorliegenden Katalog fotografiert hat; ich hoffe, dass ich ihm eines Tages persönlich begegne und ihm danken kann.

Mein Dank geht auch an die Autoren – an Massimo Morozzi für seinen erfrischenden Essay über das Bauen von Möbeln und andere Abenteuer mit den Campanas, an Maria Helena Estrada, die aus ihrer jahrzehntelangen Freundschaft mit den Brüdern schöpfte, und an Adélia Borges als Grande Dame des brasilianischen Designs – sowie an die Übersetzer und Lektoren, die so einige Hürden souverän zu nehmen wussten.

Ein besonderer Dank gebührt den Leihgebern: Adriana Adam, der Albion Gallery in London, dem Ballet National de Marseille, Dorival Pereira Barbosa, der Bernardaud SA in Limoges, José Alberto Campana und Mariangela Martinez Campana, der Edra spa in Perignano, Claudio Elisabetzky, Dan Fialdini, Paulo Sergio Brito Furtado, Christian Heymes, Leo Kim, der Lumsden Ltd. in London, José Roberto Moreira do Valle, der Moss Gallery in New York, Craig Robins und Ambra Medda von Design Miami, Beth Rudin DeWoody, Jacqueline Terpins, Pedro Useche und Alexander von Vegesack. Mein größter Dank gilt an dieser Stelle Robert Wasilewski, der uns viele wichtige frühe Arbeiten der Campanas zur Verfügung stellte, und natürlich dem Estúdio Campana selbst, ohne dessen Leihgaben die Ausstellung schlicht undenkbar wäre und das den Kontakt zu den meisten Leihgebern hergestellt und dort mit viel Engagement um Vertrauen für unser Projekt geworben hat.

Die Ausstellung und den Katalog zusammen mit dem Designbüro groenland-basel zu realisieren – mit Matthias Schnegg, Dorothea Weishaupt, Bernhard Schweizer und Matthias Huber – war eine ganz neue und überaus erfreuliche, schöne Erfahrung. Für ihre wunderbaren Ideen und Entwürfe und die Zusammenarbeit danke ich ihnen allen sehr herzlich!

Mein besonders großer Dank gilt schließlich Daniel Kern, der mich mit viel Phantasie, Präzision und Energie eng begleitet hat, sowie all den anderen, mit denen ich das Projekt hier vor Ort durchgeführt habe: Stefani Fricker, Gregor Bielser und dem technischen Team unseres Museums, Alexa Tepen, Esmeralda Hernandez, Kilian Jost, Marine Gallian, Anneliese Gastel, Marianne Goebel, Harry Schöpflin und Jörn Strüker, Richard Adler, Bogusław Ubik-Perski, Reiner Packeiser und Isabel Serbeto, Yvonne Radecker, Mateo Kries und Alexander von Vegesack, der mir mit seinen Workshops auf der Domaine de Boisbuchet den persönlichen Kontakt zu Fernando und Humberto Campana überhaupt erst ermöglichte.

armchair Armsessel
Favela (Slum Elendsviertel)
one-off piece Unikat
2009
85 × 74 × 65 cm

Mateo Kries

Chief Curator/Deputy Director Chefkurator/Stellvertretender Direktor
Vitra Design Museum

Preface

Now in its twentieth year of existence, the Vitra Design Museum is proud to present *Antibodies: The Works of Fernando and Humberto Campana, 1989–2009.* In marking our anniversary, we could not have chosen a better exhibition, for it calls to mind important aspects of our work and offers an excellent opportunity to compare some of our original goals with what has been achieved throughout the years.

Among the themes we have explored since our very beginning are the tendencies of globalization that traverse contemporary design. In this regard, numerous projects – some dating back to the 1990s – have taken us to Latin America. In 1995, for instance, we acquired the estate of Mexican architect Luis Barragán and later organized a retrospective, which travelled around the globe, based on the materials we accrued. At the same time, we began to show travelling exhibitions in Caracas, Bogotá, Santiago de Chile, and other cities throughout the continent. Thus, in our explorations of the Brazilian design scene, we came upon Fernando and Humberto Campana – long before they had risen to become international shooting stars. It quickly became apparent that there are few designers of their rank who draw ideas and inspirations so directly from the culture of their homeland and yet manage to transcribe them so effectively into the global language of contemporary design.

Thanks to their crossing of cultural borders, the Campanas also manage to present oft-discussed environmental issues in a new light. They embrace seemingly worthless objects with an observant, confident, and playful approach that elicits undreamt-of creative possibilities; and they utilize these objects by questioning conventional understandings of precious or valuable materials, revitalizing the principles of collage and objet trouvé, and finding unusual metaphors of nature.

The light-hearted way by which they tackle serious topics, such as globalization and sustainability, seemingly predestined the Campanas to lead summer workshops at the Domaine de Boisbuchet, our educational centre in France. Over the years, they have enthused and inspired students from all over the world with their charm, imagination, and curiosity. The experiences from this collaboration helped bring focus to the idea of dedicating a show to the works of the brothers; and thanks to his personal relationship with them, curator Mathias Schwartz-Clauss managed to attain numerous key works that have never been shown before.

The oeuvre of the Campanas reflects a tendency that has crystallized with ever-greater clarity since the founding of our museum in 1989: the confluence of art and design. This development is especially notable, for it was neither intended nor foreseeable when our institution was first established. On the contrary, along with the Design Museum London, likewise inaugurated in 1989, we placed ourselves – being the very first museums specializing in design – squarely within the modernist tradition that seeks to clarify the interrelations of form, function, and industry.

Today, twenty years later, the picture has changed considerably. Of course, the significance of mass-produced design has continued to grow incessantly and we hope we have managed to inform audiences worldwide about the multilayered developments of our discipline. Yet, at the same time, a powerful complex, whose dimensions were impossible for us to predict, has emerged at the interface between design and art. Through our success as a museum, it is very well possible that we have given designers the incentive to produce directly for the art market and to turn away from the ideal of simple, functional objects intended for the general public. Have our aspirations fallen victim to our own success? Perhaps. Yet, the *Antibodies* exhibition shows that this new intersection of art and design also bears within it vast potential to generate important technical and aesthetic innovations.

Vorwort

Das Vitra Design Museum zeigt die Ausstellung *Antikörper. Arbeiten von Fernando und Humberto Campana 1989–2009* im zwanzigsten Jahr seines Bestehens. Für unser Jubiläum hätten wir keine bessere Ausstellung finden können, denn sie ruft wichtige Aspekte unserer Arbeit in Erinnerung und bietet einen hervorragenden Anlass, einige ursprüngliche Ziele mit dem Erreichten zu vergleichen.

Von Anfang an haben uns beispielsweise Tendenzen der Globalisierung im Design beschäftigt, was schon in den 1990er Jahren zu mehreren Projekten in Lateinamerika führte: 1995 übernahmen wir den Nachlass des mexikanischen Architekten Luis Barragán und organisierten daraus eine international reisende Retrospektive. Zur gleichen Zeit begannen wir, Wanderausstellungen in Caracas, Bogotá, Santiago de Chile und anderen Städten des Kontinents zu zeigen. Bei unseren Erkundungen der dortigen Designszene stießen wir auch auf Fernando und Humberto Campana – lange bevor sie zu Shooting-Stars avancierten. Wie kaum andere Designer dieses Ranges beziehen sie ihre Anregungen aus der kulturellen Identität ihrer Heimat und übertragen diese dennoch in die globale Sprache des heutigen Designs.

Dank ihrer kulturellen Grenzgänge schaffen es die Campanas auch, den heute so viel diskutierten Umweltbegriff in ein neues Licht zu stellen. Mit Gegenständen und Werkstoffen, die uns wertlos erscheinen, gehen sie selbstverständlich, ja spielerisch um und entlocken ihnen ungeahnte gestalterische Möglichkeiten. Sie nutzen sie, indem sie unser gängiges Verständnis von edlen oder hochwertigen Materialien in Frage stellen, die Prinzipien der Collage oder des Objet Trouvé neu beleben und völlig neue Naturmetaphern finden.

Ihr unbeschwerter Zugang zu dennoch ernsten, aktuellen Themen wie Globalisierung und Nachhaltigkeit war es auch, der die Campanas dazu prädestinierte, in unserem edukativen Zentrum in Frankreich, der Domaine de Boisbuchet, immer wieder Sommerworkshops zu leiten. Dort begeistern sie mit Charme, Phantasie und Neugier Studenten aus aller Welt. Nicht zuletzt aus diesen Erfahrungen unserer Zusammenarbeit entstand auch der Gedanke, den beiden eine Werkschau zu widmen. Dank seiner persönlichen Beziehung gelang es dem Kurator Mathias Schwartz-Clauss schließlich, etliche Werke für die Ausstellung zu gewinnen, die noch nie öffentlich gezeigt wurden.

Mit ihrer Arbeit sind die Campanas kennzeichnend für eine Entwicklung, die seit der Gründung unseres Museums 1989 von zentraler Bedeutung ist: das Zusammenwachsen von Kunst und Design. Diese Entwicklung ist insofern bemerkenswert, als sie bei der Gründung unseres Hauses noch überhaupt nicht absehbar war. Im Gegenteil: zusammen mit dem ebenfalls 1989 gegründeten Designmuseum London standen wir – als die ersten beiden spezialisierten Designmuseen überhaupt – noch ganz in einer Tradition der Moderne, die über die Zusammenhänge von Form, Funktion und Industrie aufklären will. Heute, 20 Jahre später, sieht alles ganz anders aus. Zwar hat die Bedeutung von Design auch für die Massenmärkte weiter rasant zugenommen – und sicher haben auch wir dazu beigetragen, ein weltweites Publikum über die vielschichtigen Entwicklungen unserer Disziplin zu informieren. Doch zugleich ist ein mächtiger Komplex von Design an der Schnittstelle zur Kunst entstanden, dessen Dimensionen wir nicht vorhersehen konnten. Womöglich haben wir als Museum durch unseren Erfolg gerade erst den Anreiz für Designer geschaffen, direkt für den Kunstmarkt zu produzieren und sich vom Ideal einfacher, funktionaler Objekte für die breite Masse abzuwenden. Sind unsere Ansprüche also Opfer ihres Erfolgs geworden? Vielleicht. Doch die Ausstellung *Antikörper* zeigt, dass auch die neue Verbindung von Kunst und Design für technische und ästhetische Innovationen zentrale Bedeutung hat.

stage prop Bühnenrequisite
Peter and the Wolf; Wolf
(Peter und der Wolf; Wolf)
one-off piece Unikat
2008
70×46×144 cm

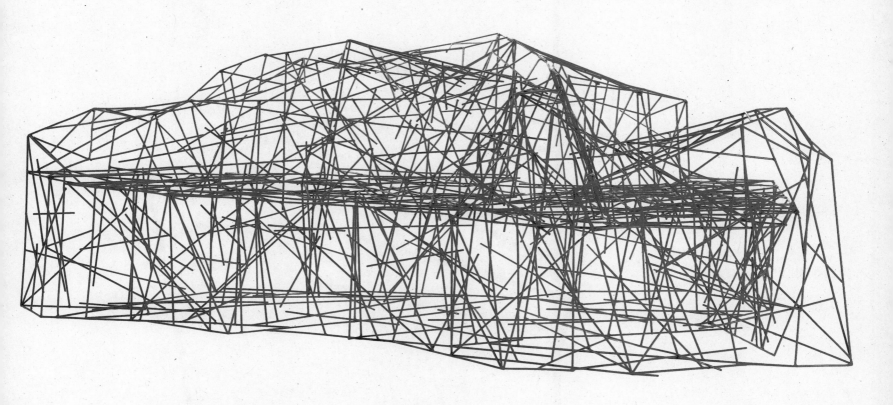

bench Sitzbank
Pedra (Rock Fels)
limited edition of 10 copies (prototype)
limitierte Auflage von 10 Exemplaren (Prototyp)
2004
80 × 301 × 190 cm

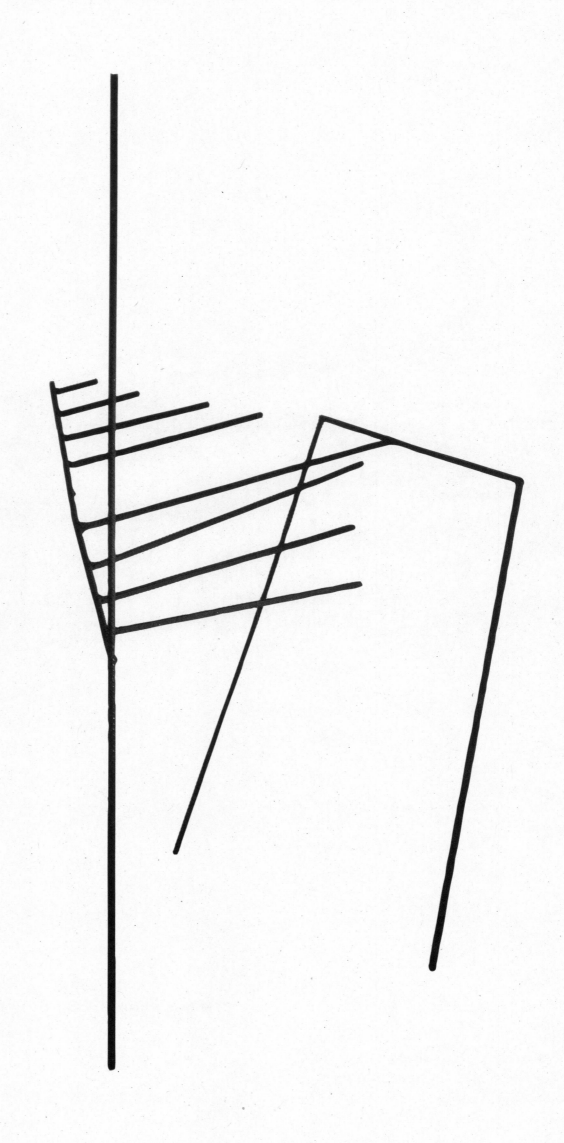

Humberto Campana
sculpture Plastik
Grelha (Grill Rost)
one-off piece Unikat
1987
164 × 70 × 110 cm

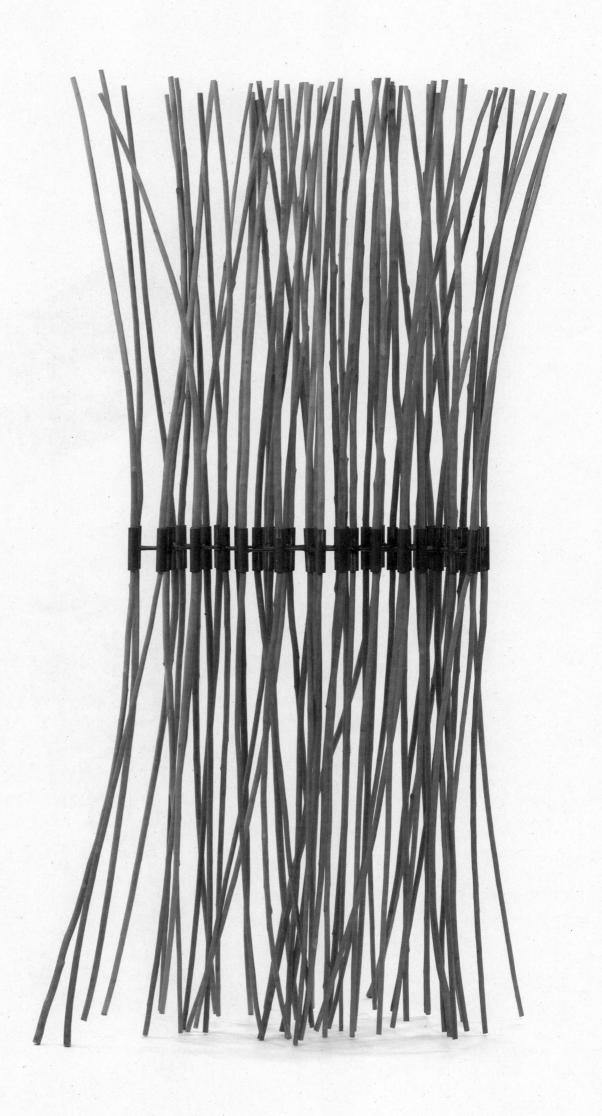

screen Wandschirm
Cerca II (Fence II Zaun II)
one-off piece Unikat
1994
204×90×36 cm

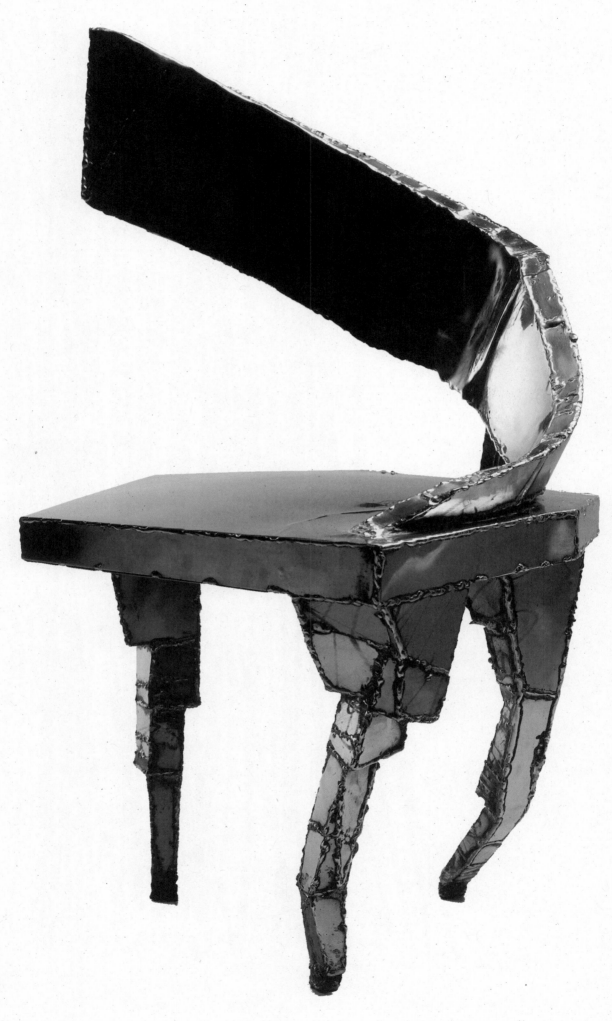

chair Stuhl
Untitled Ohne Titel
one-off piece Unikat
1989
106 × 55 × 66 cm

chair Stuhl
Harumaki (detail Detail)
unlimited edition,
numbered per year
(prototype)
unlimitierte Auflage,
numeriert pro Jahr
(Prototyp)
2004
92 × 66 × 55 cm

armchair Armsessel
Sushi
serial model Serienmodell:
Edra spa, Perignano
2002
60×95×85 cm

Humberto Campana
chair Stuhl (detail Detail)
Negativo (Negative Negativ)
one-off piece Unikat
1988
110×50×50 cm

Mathias Schwartz-Clauss

Antibodies. The Works of Fernando and Humberto Campana 1989–2009 Antikörper. Arbeiten von Fernando und Humberto Campana 1989–2009

seating landscape Sitzlandschaft
Diamantina III (detail Detail)
one-off piece Unikat (commissioned by Design
Miami on the occasion of the Designer
of the Year Award, 2008 Auftragsarbeit für
Design Miami, anlässlich der Auszeichnung
als Designer des Jahres 2008)
2008
466×206×175 cm

Fernando and Humberto Campana consider themselves designers rather than artists because they 'make things people are supposed to use.'[1] And yet what sets them apart from other designers is the decidedly artistic nature of their work. Already evident in Humberto Campana's early work, this merging of disciplines has been accentuated time and again over the course of the brothers' joint career. In this respect, over the past twenty years they have developed a distinctive and visually opulent language that lends a unique voice to our times. In their furniture pieces, accessory items, and large-scale installations, the brothers make the familiar seem foreign by building up a poetic tension between contradictory realities. On the one hand, this aspect of their work emerges through their contrasting personalities and talents,[2] but on the other hand, it stems from their mutual commitment to examining and embracing Brazilian culture. The following essay seeks to illuminate this cultural approach and the integration of design and art that is inherent in it.

In conferences and presentations across the world as well as in interviews, the Campanas frequently profess a strong connection to their native country. This always meets with great sympathy, not only because globalization-era audiences have learnt to appreciate regional and national identities but also because of the authenticity with which the brothers convey their relationship to Brazil. In September 2008, they presented their work at the Folk Futures international design seminar in the Norwegian town of Stavanger and portrayed Brazil as their key source of inspiration. After showing a map in order to illustrate the size of the country, they surprised the audience with a historical depiction of a cannibalistic feast by recounting the tale of Pedro Fernandes Sardinha, the first bishop of Bahia. In 1556, barely half a century after the country was 'discovered' by European explorers, Sardinha was captured by natives, roasted over a fire, and eaten. 'These', explained Humberto with a laugh, 'are the origins of our Brazilian civilization.'

Tree fungi in the Amazon rainforest in the state of Pará, photographed by Fernando Campana, 2005.
Baumpilze im Amazonas-Urwald im Bundesstaat Pará, fotografiert von Fernando Campana, 2005.

From Folk Art to Postmodernism

During the remainder of their presentation, the Campanas did not dwell further on the complex significance of this historical reference, but it is central to their self-conception as purveyors of culture in Brazil. The stark contrasts that permeate Brazilian life represent an enduring legacy of the nation's colonial past. The Campanas process these differences from a viewpoint that has its origins in the late beginnings of modernism in Brazil and has since developed a tradition of its own in the country.

First and foremost, it harkens back to the ideas of Oswald de Andrade and his *Manifesto Antropófago* (Cannibal Manifesto), which he formulated in 1928 as one of the founding fathers of Brazilian modernism. In this treatise, Andrade calls on artists to act in the manner of cannibals and unashamedly 'swallow' the methods of the European avant-garde in order to elevate and reinvigorate native themes. In particular, his influential manifesto paved the way for the practice of Cubism, Surrealism, and Dada in Brazil, which were practically predestined to integrate the myths and customs of the country's Native Indians and the Africans who had arrived to it as slaves.

Since their school days, the Campanas have been well acquainted with the *Manifesto,* as it was during Andrade's times that Brazil first began 'to define its cultural, political, and artistic identity

1 Fernando Campana, interview by the author, May 2008.
2 See Maria Helena Estrada, 'Intuition as Guidance, Hands for Tools', in this catalogue.

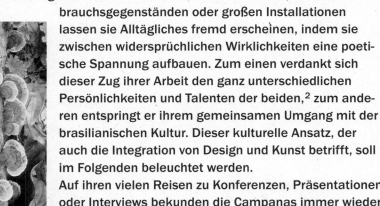

Fernando und Humberto Campana sehen sich als Designer und nicht als Künstler, weil sie »Dinge schaffen, die man benutzen soll«.[1] Und doch zeichnet sie vor anderen Designern gerade der entschieden künstlerische Charakter ihrer Arbeit aus. Die Überschreitung beider Disziplinen ist schon in Humberto Campanas Frühwerk angelegt, und im Verlauf der gemeinsamen Karriere der Brüder wurde sie immer wieder akzentuiert. So entwickelten sie in den vergangenen zwanzig Jahren eine bildreiche, unverwechselbare Sprache, die unserer Zeit einen eigenen Ausdruck verleiht. In ihren Möbeln, kleinen Gebrauchsgegenständen oder großen Installationen lassen sie Alltägliches fremd erscheinen, indem sie zwischen widersprüchlichen Wirklichkeiten eine poetische Spannung aufbauen. Zum einen verdankt sich dieser Zug ihrer Arbeit den ganz unterschiedlichen Persönlichkeiten und Talenten der beiden,[2] zum anderen entspringt er ihrem gemeinsamen Umgang mit der brasilianischen Kultur. Dieser kulturelle Ansatz, der auch die Integration von Design und Kunst betrifft, soll im Folgenden beleuchtet werden.

Auf ihren vielen Reisen zu Konferenzen, Präsentationen oder Interviews bekunden die Campanas immer wieder die Verbundenheit mit ihrer Heimat. Damit treffen sie stets auf große Sympathie, nicht nur weil man in Zeiten der Globalisierung die regionalen Identitäten zu schätzen gelernt hat, sondern weil die Brüder ihre Beziehung zu Brasilien authentisch und glaubhaft vermitteln. Zuletzt zogen sie beim internationalen Designseminar *Folk Futures* im norwegischen Stavanger im September 2008 ein Resümee ihrer Arbeit und schilderten Brasilien als die entscheidende Quelle ihrer Inspiration. Nachdem sie anhand einer Karte die enormen Ausmaße des Landes illustriert hatten, zeigten sie zur Überraschung des Publikums die historische Darstellung eines kannibalistischen Gelages und erzählten von Pedro Fernandes Sardinha, dem ersten Bischof von Bahia. Im Jahr 1556, gut fünfzig Jahre nach der Entdeckung des Landes, war er als Schiffbrüchiger in die Hände von Indios geraten, über dem Feuer gebraten und verspeist worden. »Dies«, so Humberto lachend, »sind die Ursprünge unserer brasilianischen Zivilisation.«

Von der Volkskunst zur Postmoderne

Auf die komplexe Bedeutung ihres Verweises gingen die Campanas nicht weiter ein, für ihr Selbstverständnis als Kulturschaffende ihres Landes ist sie aber zentral. Die krassen, allgegenwärtigen Gegensätze des brasilianischen Lebens sind das bis heute wirksame Erbe der Kolonialisierung. Von den Campanas werden diese Unterschiede aus einer Haltung heraus verarbeitet, die in Brasilien seit dem späten Beginn seiner Moderne eine eigene Tradition entwickelt hat. Sie geht vor allem zurück auf die Ideen Oswald de Andrades und dessen *Manifesto Antropófago* (Kannibalistisches Manifest), das er 1928 als Mitbegründer des brasilianischen Modernismo formulierte. Darin fordert er die Künstler dazu auf, gleich Menschenfressern die Methoden der europäischen Avantgarde zu »verschlingen«, um mit deren Hilfe die einheimischen Themenschätze zu heben und neu zu beleben.

De Andrades einflussreiches Manifest bereitete vor allem den avantgardistischen Praktiken von Kubismus, Surrealismus und Dada den Weg, denn sie waren geradezu prädestiniert dafür, die Mythen und Bräuche der einheimischen Indianer und der als Sklaven ins Land geholten Afrikaner zu integrieren. Den Campanas ist das *Manifesto* seit ihrer Schulzeit ein Begriff, immerhin fing Brasilien zu Andrades Zeiten erst an, »seine kulturelle, politische und künstlerische Identität zu definieren und den politischen, anthropologischen

1 Fernando Campana, Humberto und Fernando Campana im Interview mit dem Autor im Mai 2008.
2 Siehe dazu den Artikel »Die Intuition als Wegweiser, die Hände als Instrumente« von Maria Helena Estrada in diesem Katalog.

and gave carte blanche to political, anthropological, and creative thinkers.'[3] The tracing of their own cultural roots, the integration of foreign influences, the techniques of intuition and dream, assemblage and accumulation – all these are, in fact, themes and techniques that the Campanas continually and confidently employ in their processing of popular and everyday culture, albeit not necessarily with a deliberate consciousness of art history. The fact that they do this not as artists but as self-taught designers distinguishes them from many others and is one of the reasons for their unique success.

Cultural Assemblage

Brazil is a country that first vigorously suppressed and then gradually rediscovered its Native Indian roots. Over the course of the twentieth century, it worked very self-consciously on its identity, developing in the meantime many strategies for the tolerant coexistence of people from all corners of the earth. In São Paulo – the largest metropolitan area in the southern hemisphere, with some twenty million inhabitants – the population features a colourful mix of European, African, Native Indian, and Asian ethnicities. Rich and poor nearly always live in spatial isolation from one another, and indeed many neighbourhoods are dominated by individual ethnic communities. Fernando, for instance, refers to the Avenida Angélica, which he crosses on the way from his apartment to the studio, as 'the Gaza Strip' because it forms the dividing line between an affluent neighbourhood founded by Jews of European origin and an adjoining district inhabited by Lebanese and other less well-off ethnic groups. Yet for all intents and purposes, the heterogeneous population of this subtropical city has made it impossible to allocate residents to clearly defined ethnic communities. Public life plays out on urban plazas and in the streets, marked by an incessant and lively exchange and collision of contradictory fragments of reality that create downright surreal situations.

The subtropical climate and, in particular, the African and Native Indian heritage of the inhabitants are to thank for São Paulo's extreme vitality and extroversion; and despite its widely renowned criminality a European outsider cannot help but marvel at the 'emotional generosity'[4] of the people. It manifests itself in the emphasis they place on the body as well as in the wholly unselfconscious manner of their interactions. 'It's the spirit of the natives wanting to touch the colonizers that we still keep alive in different ways,'[5] explains Humberto. As a result, people not only like to put themselves on display but also seek to show off what they have and what they want to sell. The humble shops in the neighbourhood in which the Campanas' studio is located are wide open to the street and chock-a-block with merchandise, displays spilling over to the sidewalk and street hawkers joining the fray and peddling their wares.

One of the many high-rise buildings in downtown São Paulo whose facades are sprayed with graffiti right up to the roof's edge, photographed by Fernando Campana.
Eines von vielen Hochhäusern in der Innenstadt von São Paulo, deren Fassaden bis unter die Dachkante mit Graffiti übersät sind, fotografiert von Fernando Campana.

Stuffed ox heads in the neighbourhood surrounding Estúdio Campana, photographed by Humberto Campana, 1996.
Ausgestopfte Ochsenköpfe in der Nachbarschaft des Estúdio Campana, fotografiert von Humberto Campana, 1996.

3 Fernando and Humberto Campana, interview, Design Museum London, http://www.designmuseum.org/design/fernando-humberto-campana.

4 Humberto Campana, interview by Vik Muniz, 'Campana Brothers', *Bomb* 102 (Winter 2008), p. 27.

5 Ibid.

und schöpferischen Denkern einen Freibrief zu geben«.[3] Das Aufspüren der eigenen kulturellen Wurzeln, die Integration fremder Einflüsse, die Techniken von Intuition und Traum, Assemblage und Akkumulation – all dies sind tatsächlich Themen und Verfahren, die die Campanas, wenn auch nicht unbedingt mit kunsthistorischem Bewusstsein, so doch selbstverständlich und stetig einsetzen, um Populär- und Alltagskultur zu verarbeiten. Dass sie dies nicht als Künstler, sondern als autodidaktische Designer tun, unterscheidet sie von vielen anderen und ist einer der Gründe für ihren einzigartigen Erfolg.

Kulturelle Assemblage

Brasilien ist ein Land, das seine indianischen Wurzeln zunächst rigoros verdrängt und dann allmählich wieder entdeckt hat. Im Verlauf des 20. Jahrhunderts hat es sehr bewusst an seiner Identität gearbeitet und mittlerweile viele Strategien im toleranten Zusammenleben von Menschen aus allen Erdteilen entwickelt. In São Paulo, der mit etwa 20 Millionen Einwohnern größten Agglomeration auf der südlichen Halbkugel, herrscht ein buntes Gemisch von europäischen, afrikanischen, indianischen und asiatischen Einflüssen. Reich und Arm wohnen fast immer räumlich voneinander getrennt, und tatsächlich sind viele Viertel von einzelnen Ethnien dominiert. So nennt Fernando die Avenida Angélica, die er auf dem Weg von seiner Wohnung ins Atelier überquert, den »Gazastreifen«, weil sie die Trennlinie bildet zwischen einem wohlhabenden Viertel, das Juden europäischer Herkunft gründeten, und einem, das von libanesischen und anderen ärmeren Volksgruppen bewohnt wird. Doch im Grunde hat das Gemenge in dieser subtropischen Stadt dazu geführt, dass eine klare ethnische Zuordnung der Bewohner nicht mehr möglich ist. Das Leben spielt sich in der Öffentlichkeit auf Plätzen und Straßen ab, wo es einen ständigen, lebhaften Austausch gibt und wo das Aufeinanderprallen gegensätzlicher Wirklichkeitsfetzen geradezu surreale Situationen hervorbringt.

Dem Klima und vor allem dem afrikanischen und indianischen Einschlag der Bewohner verdankt São Paulo seine extreme Vitalität und Extrovertiertheit, und trotz seiner weithin berüchtigten Kriminalität kann man als Europäer über die »Großherzigkeit«[4] der Menschen nur staunen. Sie äußert sich in der Körperbetontheit der Brasilianer ebenso wie im völlig unbefangenen Umgang miteinander. »Es ist der Wunsch der Ureinwohner, die Eroberer zu berühren, den wir auf unterschiedliche Weise am Leben erhalten.«[5] Und so zeigt man nicht nur sich selbst gern, sondern auch das, was man hat und verkaufen will. Die einfachen, voll gestopften Läden in dem Viertel, in dem sich das Atelier befindet, stehen sperrangelweit offen und die Auslagen quellen bis auf den Gehweg, wo auch die Straßenhändler ihre Waren feilbieten.

Künstlerische Anfänge

Anfang der 1980er Jahre begann die Zusammenarbeit der Brüder, als Fernando sein Architekturstudium abgeschlossen und Humberto ein Studio in São Paulo bezogen hatte. Nach seiner Ausbildung als Jurist hatte Humberto sich Mitte

3 Fernando und Humberto Campana in einem Interview mit dem Designmuseum London, veröffentlicht auf der Website: http://www.designmuseum.org/design/fernando-humberto-campana.

4 Humberto Campana in einem Interview mit Vik Muniz: »Campana Brothers«, in: *Bomb*, Nr. 102, Winter 2008, S. 27.

5 Ebenda.

Artistic Beginnings

The brothers began their collaboration in the early 1980s, just after Fernando completed his architectural degree and Humberto had acquired a studio in São Paulo. After having been initially trained as a lawyer, Humberto decided in the mid-1970s to pursue the life of an artist and spent months walking the beaches of Bahia and collecting seashells. He glued them in ornamental patterns on elaborately shaped wooden frames and sold them with considerable success as mirror and picture frames.

What might sound like neo-hippie décor or a beachcomber's vacation project actually bears a strong connection to Brazilian culture. The use of shells as a decorative ornament was a prevalent motif during the Baroque and Rococo periods – styles that still exert a lingering influence in South America due to the diffusion of courtly and religious art from Spain and Portugal throughout the continent. By instituting elements of their native culture, the colonial rulers of the seventeenth and eighteenth centuries not only consolidated their imported power but also shaped the standards by which the new society was forming. Viewed in this light, the art of this period comprises the historical foundation of Brazilian high culture. On the other hand, shells are also integral to the traditions of Brazilian folk art – from their usage in indigenous cultures up to their application in modern-day artisanal crafts.

In this respect, the exuberant and symmetrical arrangement of shells on Humberto's frames embraces the sweeping contours of the Baroque, while the limitation to this single artistic technique is rooted in native tradition. The Brazilian landscape itself can also be viewed as a source of inspiration, for 'the country is so Baroque that one has the impression that the style was born here', as writes landscape architect Roberto Burle Marx, who together with Oscar Niemeyer long defined the official face of modern Brazil.[6] 'What relates Brazil's Modernist strategy to the Baroque spirit', notes David K. Underwood, 'is the ritual synthesis of opposites.'[7] With the Campanas, this synthesis is expressed both in the nature of their collaborative relationship and in the character of their joint designs.

When Humberto returned to São Paulo in 1979, he began weaving baskets, trays, and bowls and carving bamboo cutlery. They sold so well that four years later his brother decided to join the venture, initially in a supporting role and then increasingly with his own ideas. In 1983, they founded Campana Objetos, which consisted of just one workshop located in a nondescript commercial district of São Paulo. The modest-sized business not only covered the living expenses of the brothers and operational costs but also allowed Humberto to pursue additional training in a wide range of art and crafts courses, such as sculpture, goldsmithing, and pottery. The freedom the Campanas carved out for themselves on this basis enabled the experimentations that eventually led to the development of their joint furniture designs.

Uncomfortable Designs

In 1988 and 1989, Fernando and Humberto created their first pieces of furniture, which were christened As Desconfortáveis (The Uncomfortable Ones) by design historian Maria Helena

Humberto Campana at work on the terracotta sculpture Untitled, 1982.
Humberto Campana bei der Arbeit an der Terrakottaplastik Ohne Titel, 1982.

der 1970er Jahre für das Leben eines Künstlers entschieden und war monatelang die Strände von Bahia entlanggelaufen, um Muscheln zu sammeln. Er klebte sie zu Ornamenten aneinandergereiht auf üppig geformte Holzrahmen und verkaufte diese mit beachtlichem Erfolg als Spiegel- und Bilderrahmen.

Was nach Urlaubsbastelei und Hippieschmuck klingt, hat jedoch einen engen Bezug zur landestypischen Kultur: Dekorative Ornamente aus Muscheln sind ein geläufiges Motiv aus dem Barock und Rokoko – Stile, die über die höfische und sakrale Kunst Spaniens und Portugals einen bis heute spürbaren Einfluss in Südamerika haben. Mit ihrer heimatlichen Kultur definierten die Kolonialherren des 17. und 18. Jahrhunderts nicht nur ihre importierte Macht, sondern auch den Standard einer neu zu etablierenden Gesellschaft. So gesehen bildete die Kunst dieser Zeit das historische Fundament der brasilianischen Hochkultur. Andererseits gehören Muscheln auch zum festen Bestand der traditionellen brasilianischen Volkskunst – vom Gebrauch bei den indigenen Völkern bis zum heutigen Kunsthandwerk.

Die überbordende, symmetrische Anordnung der Muscheln auf Humbertos Rahmen greift die geschwungenen Formen des Barock auf, die Beschränkung auf dieses einzige gestalterische Medium steht hingegen in der Tradition der Naturvölker. Dabei ist auch die brasilianische Landschaft selbst Inspirationsquelle, denn: »Das Land ist so barock, dass man den Eindruck haben könnte, der Stil wäre hier entstanden«[6], schreibt der Landschaftsarchitekt Roberto Burle Marx, der zusammen mit Oscar Niemeyer lange Zeit das offizielle Gesicht des modernen Brasiliens prägte. Was Brasiliens Strategie des Modernismus mit dem barocken Geist verbinde, so heißt es bei David K. Underwood, »ist die rituelle Synthese von Gegensätzen«.[7] Bei den Campanas schlägt sich diese Ritualisierung sowohl in der Art ihrer Zusammenarbeit als auch in ihren gemeinsamen Entwürfen nieder. Als Humberto 1979 nach São Paulo zurückgekehrt war, begann er mit dem Flechten von Körben, Tabletts und Schalen und dem Schnitzen von Bambusbestecken, die er so gut verkaufen konnte, dass sich sein Bruder vier Jahre später zunächst als Unterstützung und dann zunehmend mit eigenen Vorstellungen der Unternehmung anschloss. Gemeinsam gründeten sie 1983 die Firma Campana Objetos, die nur aus einer Werkstatt in einem unscheinbaren Ladenviertel São Paulos bestand. Das kleine Unternehmen finanzierte nicht nur das Leben der Brüder und den laufenden Betrieb, sondern ermöglichte Humberto auch eine Fortbildung in den verschiedensten Kursen für Kunst und Handwerk, wie zum Beispiel Bildhauerei, Goldschmieden oder Töpfern. Der Freiraum, den die Campanas sich mit dieser Basis erarbeiteten, erlaubte ihnen die Experimente, die schließlich in der Entwicklung gemeinsamer Möbelentwürfe mündeten.

Unbequeme Entwürfe

In den Jahren 1988 und 1989 schufen Fernando und Humberto ihre ersten Möbel, die Maria Helena Estrada und die Galeristin Adriana Adam Desconfortáveis (Unbequeme) tauften. Der Größe und Form nach sind diese rostigen Stahlobjekte zwar als Stühle oder Sessel zu erkennen, aber zur Benutzung laden sie nicht ein; vielmehr wirken diese »Avantgarde-Möbel«, wie der Untertitel ihrer ersten Ausstellung sie nannte, als Plastiken – aggressiv verzerrte Symbole bürgerlicher Kultur.

6 Roberto Burle Marx, Arte & Paisagem: conferências escolhidas [Art & Landscape: Selected lectures] (São Paulo: Nobel, 1987), as quoted in David K. Underwood, 'Toward a Phenomenology of Brazil's Baroque Modernism', in Brazil: Body and Soul, ed. Edward J. Sullivan (New York: Guggenheim Museum Publications, 2001), p. 526.

7 Underwood, 'Toward a Phenomenology of Brazil's Baroque Modernism', p. 530.

6 Roberto Burle Marx: Arte & Paisagem: conferências escolhidas, São Paulo, Nobel, 1987, zit. nach David K. Underwood: »Toward a Phenomenology of Brazil's Baroque Modernism«; in: Edward J. Sullivan: Brazil: Body and Soul, Guggenheim Museum Publications, New York 2001, S. 526.

7 Underwood, a.a.O., S. 530 (Anm. 6).

Estrada and gallery owner Adriana Adam. As far as their size and shape are concerned, these rusted steel objects are no doubt recognizable as chairs or armchairs, however they are not particularly inviting when it comes to actual use. Rather, these 'avant-garde furniture pieces', as they were termed in the subtitle of their first exhibition, function as sculptures – aggressively distorted symbols of bourgeois culture.

At the time, Brazilian design was exclusively oriented towards the reception of commercially successful European works. The provocative socio-critical designs of the 1970s and 1980s, such as those by Archizoom, Stiletto, or Pentagon, were barely known to the public. In terms of artists, and as far as the Campanas' personal tastes are concerned, Humberto was interested in the works of Jackson Pollock, Alexander Calder, and Henry Moore, while Fernando admired the painters Jean-Michel Basquiat and A. R. Penck. Yet upon encountering the works of designer Danny Lane, in a 1988 exhibition of his work held at Adam's Nucleon 8 gallery in São Paulo, they were both sparked with an instant enthusiasm, recognizing in his furniture an approach similar to their own: 'The fact that [he] didn't care if people bought his chairs or found them comfortable was liberating', recounted Fernando when asked recently to describe Lane's influence.[8] One year later, Adam's gallery went on to exhibit the *Desconfortáveis* chairs, which were celebrated by the press as a sensation.

Though isolated within the Brazilian design landscape of the time, *As Desconfortáveis* had a clear connection to the art of the period. In 1983, for example, the seventeenth biennial for contemporary art in São Paulo featured works by A. R. Penck, Keith Haring, Jean-Michel Basquiat, Kenny Sharf, and Anish Kapoor, as well as a special exhibition dedicated to the Fluxus movement, represented by Nam June Paik and Wolf Vostell. Another exhibition at the biennial was devoted to Brazilian feather headdresses – a curatorial decision that sought not only to arouse appreciation in Native Indian art but to cause provocation within an art establishment that was predominately Western-oriented. Although Fernando worked at the biennial – among other capacities, as an assistant to photographer Pierre Keller, who nowadays, as head of the ECAL University of Art and Design, regularly invites the Campanas to Lausanne for workshops – it is difficult to say how consciously he and Humberto processed all the impressions they took in from the cultural scene of the time. Nevertheless, what is certain is that they are both blessed with a highly sensitive perception and have 'their guts in the right place', as Lélia Arruda, project coordinator in the Campanas' studio, puts it. Their oeuvre is firmly anchored in their early work and in the artistic and critical environment of the period, even though the appearance of their designs has changed considerably and their original subversive nature operates nowadays from a position of playful confidence and ease.

Prior to the *Desconfortáveis* series, the Campanas produced two other furniture pieces. These were triggered by a significant traumatic experience that Humberto underwent in 1988, when, in search of artistic reorientation, he travelled to Arizona to explore the Grand Canyon on a white-water rafting trip. Along the river, he noticed stones on which Native Indians had painted spiral motifs and later that night dreamt of being swallowed up by a spiral. The very next day, when the journey continued, his raft capsized and was dragged under in a whirlpool. Humberto just barely managed

The chairs *Negativo* by Humberto and *Positivo* by Fernando Campana, 1988. Die Stühle *Negativo* von Humberto und *Positivo* von Fernando Campana, 1988.

8 Lauris Morgan-Griffiths, 'Fraternity, Fun, and Furniture', *Financial Times*, 9 March 2007.

Das brasilianische Design dieser Zeit war ganz auf die Rezeption der kommerziell erfolgreichen, europäischen Gestaltung ausgerichtet. Von den provokanten, gesellschaftskritischen Entwürfen der 1970er und 1980er Jahre, von Archizoom, Stiletto oder Pentagon, war der Öffentlichkeit kaum etwas bekannt. Künstlerisch entdeckte Humberto damals Jackson Pollock, Alexander Calder und Henry Moore, während Fernando die Maler Jean-Michel Basquiat und A. R. Penck schätzte. Von Danny Lane aber, der 1988 in Adriana Adams Galerie Nucleon 8 in São Paulo seine Arbeiten zeigte, waren beide auf der Stelle begeistert, denn seine Möbel verfolgten einen ähnlichen Ansatz wie ihre eigenen: »Die Tatsache, dass es ihn nicht kümmerte, ob die Leute seine Stühle kauften oder sie bequem fanden, war befreiend«, so Fernando Campana über Lanes Einfluss.[8] Und so zeigte Adams Galerie schon ein Jahr später die *Desconfortáveis*, die von der Presse als Sensation gefeiert wurden.

In der brasilianischen Designlandschaft standen die *Desconfortáveis* damals isoliert, gleichwohl gibt es den bereits erwähnten Bezug zu Kunst und Design ihrer Zeit. So zeigte 1983 die 17. Biennale für zeitgenössische Kunst in São Paulo unter anderem Arbeiten von A. R. Penck, Keith Haring, Jean-Michel Basquiat, Kenny Sharf und Anish Kapoor. Der Fluxus-Bewegung um Nam June Paik und Wolf Vostell war eine Sonderschau gewidmet. Eine weitere Sonderausstellung der Biennale präsentierte brasilianischen Federschmuck, was als Wertschätzung der indianischen Kunst zu verstehen war, aber auch als Provokation des hauptsächlich an westlicher Kunstproduktion orientierten Establishments. Fernando arbeitete bei dieser Biennale unter anderem als Betreuer für den Fotografen Pierre Keller, der heute als Leiter der Designhochschule ECAL die Campanas regelmäßig zu Workshops nach Lausanne einlädt. Wie bewusst Fernando und Humberto Campana ihre Eindrücke aus der damaligen Kulturszene verarbeitet haben, lässt sich schwer sagen. Fest steht, dass sie mit einer hochsensiblen Wahrnehmung gesegnet sind und »ihre Eingeweide am richtigen Fleck« haben, wie Lélia Arruda, Projektleiterin im Atelier der Campanas, es ausdrückt. Ihr Œuvre ist im Frühwerk und im künstlerisch-kritischen Umfeld seiner Zeit fest verankert, auch wenn sich das Erscheinungsbild der Entwürfe stark verändert hat und das Subversive von damals heute aus einer spielerischen Souveränität heraus wirkt.

Der Auslöser für ihre ersten, der Serie der *Desconfortáveis* noch vorangehenden Möbel war bezeichnenderweise ein traumatisches Erlebnis: 1988 suchte Humberto nach einer künstlerischen Neuorientierung und reiste nach Arizona, um bei einer Wildwasserfahrt den Grand Canyon zu erkunden. Nachdem er entlang des Flusses immer wieder Steine bemerkt hatte, die von Indianern mit Spiralmotiven bemalt worden waren, träumte er nachts, dass eine Spirale ihn verschlingen würde. Bei der Weiterfahrt am nächsten Tag kenterte sein Boot, geriet in einen Strudel, und Humberto konnte sich nur mit knapper Not retten. Zurück in São Paulo verarbeitete er das Erlebnis in dem aus Stahlplatten und -stäben geschweißten Stuhl *Negativo*, aus dessen Rücken er eine Spirale schnitt. Sein Bruder reagierte darauf, indem er diese ausgeschnittene Spirale als Rückenlehne für einen eigenen Stuhl verwendete, den er *Positivo* nannte – womit er nicht nur das Spiel von Figur und Grund, sondern auch persönlich eine gegensätzliche, komplementäre Grundhaltung meinte. Die Geschichte mag wie eine jener symbolisch aufgeladenen Initialzündungen klingen, mit denen im Nachhinein so viele Künstlerviten begründet werden. Das damalige Ereignis setzte aber tatsächlich eine Dynamik in Gang, die bis heute präsent und unverbraucht ist und die Humberto als »zwei Flüsse, die ineinanderfließen und sich gegenseitig beruhigen« beschreibt.[9]

8 Lauris Morgan-Griffiths: »Fraternity, Fun and Furniture«, in: *Financial Times*, 9. März 2007.

9 Humberto Campana im Interview mit dem Autor, a.a.O. (Anm. 1).

to escape. Back in São Paulo, he worked through the experience by cutting a spiral out of the back of a chair made of welded steel plates and poles and naming the chair *Negativo.* His brother responded by using the cut-out spiral as a backrest for a chair of his own and christening it *Positivo* – by which he not only meant the interplay of figure and field but also a personal contrasting and complementary core stance. The story sounds like one of those typical, symbolically loaded initial sparks that provide the *ex post facto* rationale for innumerable artistic careers. In the Campanas' case, however, this seminal episode instigated a dynamic that remains present and undepleted to this very day and that Humberto describes as 'two rivers that calm one another and blend together.'[9]

The Working Process

While setting the direction for the brothers' collaborative work, the technique of using a found object, a discarded piece of waste, which Fernando employed for *Positivo,* typifies his personal attitude towards the design process. Even as a schoolboy he preferred to paste together his pictures from magazine clippings rather than to laboriously draw or paint them himself. His avowed affinity to Pop Art, with its veneration of the mundane and the reproduced, also fits in with this disposition.[10] Yet above all, *Positivo* and *Negativo* mark the beginning of the Campanas' career as designers, for although these first two chairs and the forty-some other objects of the *Desconfortáveis* series may emanate from artistic impulses, they expressly present themselves neither as art nor as handicrafts but as design. More precisely, they form the constitutive basis of the brothers' collaboration in the artistic design of articles intended for daily use – even if the *Desconfortáveis* themselves are described today by Fernando as 'functional sculptures': 'We probed the artistic potential of discomfort, the poetry of the distorted, the poetry of error.'[11]

Together, the Campanas have developed a personal signature of distinctive author-created design, whereby their dialogue-based work method engenders a quality that has been fundamental to their ability to create such a heterogeneous oeuvre with enduring success. Despite all the collaborative aspects of their work, it is important for Fernando and Humberto to preserve their individuality and even fortify one another through their differences, for 'working as a team affects the way the public sees us: not as one person, but as a brand.'[12] Humberto explains: 'Whereas I bring more of the techniques, the inspiration in its raw state, Fernando transforms that. He pushes me to rethink an idea.'[13] Those who have observed the two at work come away with the impression that they mutually 'enlighten' one other: Humberto thinks with his hands while Fernando works with his head; one articulates 'what the other has not yet become conscious of.'[14] But they both contribute creative ideas for new projects in equal measure. And when necessary, they are ready to correct each other: 'Whenever one of us is failing, the other arrives and either puts some energy into the process or says "No, your idea is stupid, let's drop it".'[15]

Dorival Pereira Barbosa at work on a *Sushi 4* armchair, 2008.
Dorival Pereira Barbosa bei der Arbeit an einem *Sushi 4*-Sessel, 2008.

The first *Favela* armchair, 1991.
Der erste *Favela*-Sessel, 1991.

9 Humberto Campana, interview by the author, May 2008.
10 'I was more influenced by Pop'; 'I am more of a Pop person'. Fernando Campana, interview by the author.
11 Fernando Campana, in Muniz, 'Campana Brothers', p. 24.
12 Humberto Campana, in Muniz, 'Campana Brothers', p. 25.
13 Humberto Campana, interview by the author.
14 Ibid.
15 Ibid.

Der Arbeitsprozess

Fernandos Verfahren beim *Positivo,* ein Fundstück, ein Abfallprodukt zu verwenden, ist wegweisend für das gemeinsame Werk und typisch für seine Einstellung zum Gestaltungsprozess: Schon als Schüler zog er es vor, seine Bilder aus ausgeschnittenen Drucksachen zu kleben, anstatt sie mühsam selber zu malen. Auch seine erklärte Affinität zur Pop-Art mit ihrer Aufwertung des Alltäglichen und Reproduzierten passt zu dieser Einstellung.[10] *Positivo* und *Negativo* markieren aber vor allem die Anfänge der Campanas als Designer, denn diese beiden ersten Stühle und an die vierzig weitere Objekte der *Desconfortáveis-Serie* mögen zwar künstlerischen Impulsen entspringen, aber sie firmieren ausdrücklich weder als Kunst noch als Kunsthandwerk, sondern als Design. Genauer gesagt begründeten sie die Komplizenschaft der Brüder im künstlerischen Gestalten von Gebrauchsgegenständen – auch wenn die *Desconfortáveis* heute von Fernando als »funktionale Skulpturen« bezeichnet werden. »Wir haben das künstlerische Potential des Unbequemen ausgelotet, die Poesie des Deformierten, des Defekts.«[11]

Zu zweit entwickelten die Campanas die persönliche Handschrift eines unverkennbaren Autorendesigns, wobei ihre dialogische Arbeitsweise eine Qualität birgt, die es ihnen überhaupt erst ermöglicht, mit anhaltendem Erfolg ein derart heterogenes Werk zu schaffen. Bei aller Gemeinschaftlichkeit in der Arbeit ist es Fernando und Humberto jedoch wichtig, ihre Individualität zu bewahren und sich in Eigenarten sogar zu bestärken, denn »als Team zu arbeiten, hat Einfluss darauf, wie die Öffentlichkeit uns wahrnimmt – nicht als eine Person, sondern als Marke«.[12] Humberto erklärt: »Ich bringe eher die Technik ein, die Inspiration für die Rohfassung, und Fernando transformiert das. Er sorgt dafür, dass ich eine Idee überdenke.«[13] Wer die beiden bei der Arbeit beobachtet, hat den Eindruck, sie »erleuchten« sich gegenseitig: Humberto denkt mit den Händen und Fernando arbeitet mit dem Kopf. Der eine formuliert, »was dem andern noch unbewusst ist«.[14] Aber beide bringen gleichermaßen schöpferische Ideen in neue Projekte ein. Und wenn nötig, korrigieren sie sich gegenseitig: »Wann immer einer von uns auf dem Holzweg ist, kommt der andere und steckt entweder noch Energie in den Prozess oder sagt: ›Nein, das war eine blöde Idee von dir, lass uns das abbrechen.‹«[15]

Noch heute werden in ihrem Atelier nahezu alle Produkte fast ohne Zeichnungen direkt in handgearbeiteten Modellen entwickelt, einschließlich jener Möbel, Leuchten und Accessoires, die von anderen Firmen seriell hergestellt werden. Einen wichtigen Anteil an der Umsetzung und Ausformulierung der Entwürfe hat seit 1993 der Autodidakt Dorival Pereira Barbosa, der als Produktionsleiter und Vorarbeiter des Ateliers fungiert und dessen ästhetische Sensibilität die Campanas besonders schätzen. Je nach anfallenden Arbeiten stehen ihm zwischen zwei und vier Arbeiter für das Flechten, Rollen, Kleben oder Schweißen zur Seite, während im Lager andere an Polstermöbeln nähen.

10 »Ich war eher vom Pop beeinflusst.« oder »Ich bin mehr ein Mensch des Pop.«, ebd.
11 Fernando Campana in einem Interview mit Vik Muniz, a.a.O., S. 24 (Anm. 4).
12 Humberto Campana in einem Interview mit Vik Muniz, a.a.O., S. 25 (Anm. 4).
13 Humberto Campana im Interview mit dem Autor, a.a.O. (Anm. 1).
14 Ebenda.
15 Ebenda.

Even today, nearly all the products that come out of the studio – which was re-christened as Campana Design in 2006/7 – are still directly developed in hand-built models with almost no preliminary drawings, including the furniture, lights, and accessories that are then serially manufactured by other companies. Since 1993, a good amount of the implementation and formulation of the designs has been handled by the self-taught Dorival Pereira Barbosa, who essentially serves as production manager and foreman of the studio and whose aesthetic sensitivity is especially valued by the Campanas. Depending on the particular design involved, between two and four additional workers assist him with the weaving, rolling, gluing, or welding, while others in the warehouse perform the sewing on upholstered furniture. Since 2002 and 2005, respectively, office manager Leo Kim and project coordinator Lélia Arruda have been among the closest and most trusted employees. The two polyglot friends act as intermediaries between the Campanas and their customers and are intensely involved in the planning of each project as well as in the creative process itself, aided by Diogo Matsui's drawings and research.

Views of the Environment

With nearly all of their designs, the Campanas' work begins with a sensory experience in which a certain material becomes charged with meaning. In most cases, this material also serves as a medium by which the brothers reflect on their environment. In 1990, for instance, they created the *Natureza Morta* (Still Life) partition screen, for which they used synthetic resin to affix – in a month-long process – lumps of charcoal onto a wooden box. To protect the delicate surface from being damaged – and to keep the charcoal from rubbing off when touched – they inserted velvet-trimmed openings on the sides of the box in order to enable the

The Marginal Tietê slum in Saõ Paulo, 1998.
Das Elendsviertel Marginal Tietê in Saõ Paulo, 1998.

screen's transportation. Since the earliest of times, screens have not only served as a mobile partitioning of spaces but have also functioned as picture carriers. Yet the massive dimensions of *Natureza Morta* and the use of black as the symbolic negative of an image simultaneously transform the screen into a monolithic sculpture. Furthermore, the appearance of the screen's sculptural material is so unexpected that on initial perception only its seemingly precious and fragile high-gloss facets are registered. The charcoal that we normally associate with soot-filled cities of centuries past is elevated to an artistic material and is thus able to refer to levels of meaning that lie beyond its utilitarian value: the shortage of resources, the pollution of the environment, the slash-and-burn clearance of primeval forests. Of course, from a designer's perspective, the Campanas' use of synthetic resin in the manufacturing of the screen might raise questions concerning the integrity of materials, yet the brothers could not care less about this contradiction; for them it was a matter of practicality and they simply used the material that was available to them at the time.

Rock formations in the Atacama Desert, Chile, photographed by Fernando Campana, 2006.
Felsformationen in der Wüste Atacama, Chile, fotografiert von Fernando Campana, 2006.

With the *Favela* armchair of 1991, the Campanas turned their attention to their social environment. They adapted the aesthetics of hammered-together shacks, which abound in the endlessly proliferating slums of Brazil, to an armchair and gave it the form of a throne – in honour and recognition of the autonomy and creativity of the favelas. In this regard, Brazilian artist Vik Muniz aptly refers to the *gambiarra*, a problem-solving strategy that typi-

Seit 2002 beziehungsweise 2005 gehören auch der Büroleiter Leo Kim und Projektleiterin Lélia Arruda zu den engsten Mitarbeitern des Ateliers, das 2006/07 in die Firma Campana Design überführt wurde. Die beiden polyglotten Freunde sind die Mittler zwischen den Campanas und ihren Kunden und beteiligen sich intensiv an der Planung wie auch am kreativen Prozess, den Diogo Matsui mit Zeichnungen und Materialrecherchen unterstützt.

Ansichten der Umwelt

Am Anfang der Arbeit steht für die Campanas bei fast allen Entwürfen eine sinnliche Erfahrung, die sich am Material auflädt, und meistens dient ihnen solch ein Material als Medium einer Reflexion über ihre Umwelt. So entstand 1990 der Wandschirm *Natureza Morta* (Stillleben oder Tote Natur), für den sie in monatelanger Arbeit Kohlebrocken mit Kunstharz auf einem Holzkasten befestigten. Um die empfindliche Oberfläche vor Schäden zu schützen und zu verhindern, dass die Kohle beim Berühren abfärbt, brachten sie seitlich mit Samt gefasste Öffnungen an, mithilfe derer das Objekt transportiert werden kann. Nun dienen Wandschirme seit jeher nicht nur der mobilen Unterteilung von Räumen, sondern auch als Bildträger. Die massive Stärke des *Natureza Morta* aber und das Schwarz als symbolisches Negativ eines Bildes verwandeln den Paravent zugleich in eine monolithische Skulptur. Dabei erscheint das bildnerische Material so unerwartet, dass man zunächst nur die wertvoll und fragil wirkenden glänzenden Facetten wahrnimmt. Die Kohle, mit der wir normalerweise die verrußten Städte der vergangenen Jahrhunderte assoziieren, wird hier zum künstlerischen Werkstoff geadelt und kann so auf Bedeutungsebenen verweisen, die jenseits ihres Gebrauchswerts liegen: die Knappheit der Ressourcen, die Verschmutzung der Umwelt und die Brandrodungen des Urwalds. Dass die Campanas Kunstharz zur Montage verwendeten, mag aus Sicht des Designers die Ehrlichkeit gegenüber dem Material in Frage stellen. Die Brüder scherten sich aber nicht um diesen Widerspruch – für diesen praktischen Teil der Arbeit benutzten sie einfach das Material, das gerade zur Verfügung stand.

Mit dem Sessel *Favela* (Elendsviertel) thematisierten die Campanas 1991 ihre soziale Umwelt. Die Ästhetik der zusammengehämmerten Bretterbuden in den endlos wuchernden Slums adaptierten sie für einen Sessel, dem sie die Form eines Throns gaben – als Würdigung der dort herrschenden Autonomie und Kreativität. In diesem Zusammenhang verweist der brasilianische Künstler Vik Muniz zu Recht auf die *gambiarra,* eine Problemlösungsstrategie, die typisch ist für den Erfindungsreichtum der Brasilianer: »*Gambiarra* bezieht sich auf kuriose Lösungen, unglaubliche Kombinationen, Reparaturen, die so grobschlächtig und offensichtlich sind, dass sie das vorhandene Problem eher sichtbar machen, als es zu beheben. Brasilianer rühmen sich damit, Flugzeuge mit Büroklammern zu reparieren, Fische mit rezeptpflichtigen Medikamenten zu ködern oder Spucke als Mörtel zu verwenden. Demzufolge sind selbst Städte, die Regierung und ganze Glaubenssysteme zu *gambiarras* geworden. Der Mangel an materieller und psychologischer Sicherheit wird nur durch den Einfallsreichtum der Überlebenskünstler dieses Volkes ersetzt, das für die Gegenwart lebt.«[16]

16 Muniz, a.a.O., S. 22 (Anm. 4).

fies Brazilian resourcefulness: 'Gambiarra refers to an unlikely mend, an unthinkable coupling, a solution so raw and transparent that it illustrates the problem at hand instead of eliminating it. Brazilians pride themselves on repairing airplanes with paperclips, catching fish with prescription drugs as bait, or using saliva as a building material. Consequently, cities, the government, and belief systems have become gambiarras themselves: the survivalist ingenuity of a people who live for the present alone compensates for the lack of material and psychological security.'[16]

In addition to targeted reception of literature, music, film, and other art forms produced in Brazil, the Campanas investigate their identity through numerous trips to culturally or geographically unique locations within their native country. During these travels, they discovered the raffia palm fibres that they used for the first time in the 2003 crystal chandelier *Prived Oca* (Own House), which they designed for Swarovski. *Oca* is the name given to the raffia-covered dome-shaped huts that are inhabited by Native Indians in certain regions of Brazil. In the brothers' chandelier of the same name, cascades of glittering crystals fall from the fringes like tentacles of a jellyfish, illuminated by interspersed chains of LEDs – a magnificent contrast that mixes cheap and precious, genuine and fake.

Invited the following year by the Cologne furniture fair to realize their *Ideal House* in one of its exhibition halls,[17] the brothers proposed to erect a dome-shaped structure, reaching from the ceiling down to the floor and completely covered with raffia, as 'a sort of meditation space'.[18] The motif was then employed a third time in their contribution to the exhibition *My Home*, held in 2007 at the Vitra Design Museum in Weil am Rhein. By extending the canopy covering the doorway of the museum's building (designed by Frank Gehry) with a raffia curtain that reached to the ground, the brothers devised a spectacular entrance for the exhibition, creating a distinct space that was adorned with LEDs that shone like stars. As in the past, the Campanas opted for poetry over finger wagging in drawing attention to the importance of original materials and traditional methods.

One of the Campanas' most recent furniture series, *Transplastics*, in which inexpensive mono-block chairs made of PVC are 'enmeshed' with wicker, provides a final example of their approach to the environment. The work conveys a sensitive yet sober appraisal of the contradictory world that surrounds them and offers a response that is both humorous and profound. While typical Brazilian wicker terrace furniture found itself displaced in the twentieth century by plastic substitutes, in this series nature and traditional artisanal handicrafts seem to re-conquer lost terrain.[19] With their adaptive reworking of the chair, the Campanas lend both an individuality and a material and aesthetic value to the anonymous mass-produced article; they liberate traditional handicrafts from a nostalgic, folkloric niche and give them a new, contemporary significance. Although the execution of a few dozen of their designs does not in itself ensure a revival of basketware and wickerwork, the example that these works give to designers, producers, craftspeople, and artisans (and not least to consumers) can certainly illuminate possible directions for local branches of trade.

16 Muniz, 'Campana Brothers', p. 22.
17 Along with the Campanas, French designers-brothers Ronan and Erwan Bouroullec were also invited to participate in the fair and realize an *Ideal House* of their own.
18 Fernando Campana, interview by Klaus Meyer, 'Humberto and Fernando Campana', *Design Report,* March 2004, p.32.
19 Françoise Foulon makes an analogous though more general appraisal of limited-edition design: 'As if design were freeing itself

Construction of the entrance to the *My Home* exhibition at Vitra Design Museum, 2007.
Bau des Eingangs zur Ausstellung *My Home* im Vitra Design Museum, 2007.

Zur Auseinandersetzung mit ihrer Identität gehören für die Campanas neben der gezielten Rezeption von Literatur, Musik, Film und anderen Kunstproduktionen, die in Brasilien entstehen, zahlreiche Reisen an kulturell oder geografisch interessante Orte ihrer Heimat. Die Raffia-Palmfaser, mit der sie erstmals 2003 im Kristalllüster *Prived Oca* (eigenes Haus) für Swarovski arbeiteten, haben sie im Rahmen solcher Recherchen gefunden. *Ocas* nennt man in Brasilien die kuppelförmigen Hütten der indianischen Ureinwohner, die in einigen Landstrichen mit Raffia gedeckt sind. Beim gleichnamigen Kronleuchter fallen aus den Fransen Kaskaden glitzernder Kristalle, wie Tentakel einer Qualle, die von dazwischen hängenden LEDs beleuchtet werden – ein herrlicher Kontrast, der Billiges und Kostbares, Echtes und Falsches verknüpft.

Als sie ein Jahr später von der Kölner Möbelmesse eingeladen wurden, in einer der Hallen ihr *Ideal House* zu realisieren,[17] schlugen sie für das Innere eine kuppelförmige, von der Decke bis zum Boden reichende, komplett mit Raffia bedeckte Konstruktion vor, »eine Art Meditationsraum«[18]. Ein drittes Mal verwendeten sie das Motiv dann in ihrem Beitrag zu der von Vitra initiierten Ausstellung *My Home,* die 2007 in Weil am Rhein stattfand. Hier verhalfen sie der Präsentation zu einem spektakulären Entree, indem sie den Baldachin über dem Eingang des Museumsbaus von Frank Gehry mit einem Vorhang aus Raffia bis hinunter auf den Boden verlängerten und so einen eigenen Raum schufen, in dem die LEDs wie Sterne leuchteten. Wie schon zuvor lenkten sie auch hier nicht mit erhobenem Zeigefinger, sondern mit Poesie die Aufmerksamkeit auf die Bedeutung von ursprünglichen Materialien und traditionellen Methoden.

Wenn die Campanas schließlich in einer ihrer jüngsten Möbelserien, den so

Members of the Kuikuro tribe in front of their *ocas* in Parque Nacional do Xingu, 1978.
Mitglieder vom Stamm der Kuikuro vor ihren *ocas* im Xingu-Nationalpark, 1978.

genannten *Transplastics,* billige Monoblock-Stühle aus PVC mit Korbgeflecht »umgarnen«, dann spricht daraus eine sensible, aber nüchterne Bestandsaufnahme ihrer widersprüchlichen Lebenswelt und eine ebenso humorvolle wie tiefsinnige Reaktion darauf. Während im 20. Jahrhundert Kunststoffmöbel die typisch brasilianischen Terrassenmöbel aus Korbgeflecht verdrängten, scheinen sich in dieser Serie die Natur und das traditionelle Handwerk verloren gegangenes Terrain zurückzuerobern.[19] Der anonymen Massenware verleihen die Campanas mit ihrer Bearbeitung Individualität und einen materiellen sowie ästhetischen Wert; sie holen das traditionelle Handwerk aus der spießigen Folkloreecke und geben ihm eine neue, zeitgemäße Bedeutung. Dabei bewirkt die Umsetzung von ein

17 Für dieselbe Möbelmesse 2004 realisierte auch das französische Designstudio und Brüderpaar Ronan und Erwan Bouroullec ein *Ideal House.*
18 Fernando Campana in einem Interview mit Klaus Meyer, »Humberto und Fernando Campana«, in: *Design Report,* März 2004, S. 32.
19 Zu einer analogen Einschätzung kommt auch eine allgemeine Betrachtung des Autorendesigns bei limitierten Editionen: »Als hätte es sich von der Massenproduktion befreit, als würde es angesichts der Invasion von Objekten, der Überproduktion und des übersteigerten Konsums nach einem neuen Lebenshauch suchen, so führt Design für limitierte Auflagen das Wissen um hohe Qualität wieder ein; ungefähr so wie die angewandte Kunst zu Beginn des 20. Jahrhunderts.«, Françoise Foulon in: Karolien van Cauwelaert (Hrsg.): *Design/Art Limited Editions,* Stichting Kunstboek, Oostkamp 2008; S. 119.

Between Design and Art

Design 'has to have a meaning,'[20] emphasizes Humberto, referring to the role of the object as bearer of emotion and significance, aside from its practical functionality. In design as in art, it is common to utilize the name of an object to indicate this meaning. The names of most Campana designs single out aspects that are plainly evident or that provide a link to initial associations. At first, these names may appear naive or random because they invoke simple and concrete aspects such as positive and negative, rock, nests, string, and the like. But then again that is precisely what the brothers aim to do: to show that the marvels and infinite possibilities of our world lie right in front of our noses and that all we need is to see and use them. Fernando and Humberto are 'deep about being superficial,'[21] writes Muniz. Underlying their directness, which is as disarming as their verbal spontaneity, is an extraordinarily sure-footed flair for both sense and sensuality.

Regarding the furniture and accessories that Fernando and Humberto design, it is evident that appearance and aura take precedence over classical functionality – lightness, ergonomics, or spatial efficiency are not what they are after. Nonetheless, the function and potential usefulness of their objects are necessary for the meaning and significance to become effective: as mere sculpture, a *Favela* armchair would affect a disinterested viewer differently from one who also contemplates using it. To the extent that the usability of an object is what distinguishes design from art, the Campanas ultimately appear to be designers who make use of artistic means in order to convey statements about feelings, identity, the environment – and, not least, about design. As shown by the history of art and design, however, it is very much undecided how far the aesthetic experience can be understood as a function of a work or to what extent a meaning that goes beyond the function can be considered part of its utility. The Campanas, as evinced by their oeuvre, play precisely on this ambivalence.

Accumulations

From a purely artistic and technical perspective, the work of the Campanas falls under the category of plastic art. More precisely, the forms of their objects are not extracted from raw materials in a subtractive process but are additively built up from them. The Campanas avail themselves of this technique as a means of expression that draws its power from unusual materials used in combination. This method has its roots in the seashells that Humberto accumulated together in his early mirrors. Likewise, one of the brothers' first collaborative pieces

from mass production, as if it were looking for a new breath of life in the context of the invasion of objects, overproduction and overconsumption, design in limited editions reintroduces high quality know-how in somewhat the same manner as the decorative arts in the beginning of the 20th century.' Françoise Foulon, in Karolien van Cauwelaert, ed., *Design/Art Limited Editions* (Oostkamp: Stichting Kunstboek, 2008), p. 119.
20 Morgan-Griffiths, 'Fraternity, Fun, and Furniture'.
21 Muniz, 'Campana Brothers', p. 22.

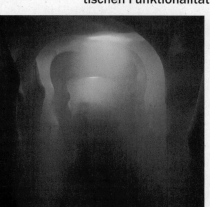

Installation for *Vogue*/Tactel Party, 2001.
Installation für die *Vogue/*Tactel-Party, 2001.

The *Geográfica* table, 1992.
Der Tisch *Geográfica,* 1992.

paar Dutzend ihrer Entwürfe an sich noch keine Wiederbelebung des Korbflechterhandwerks, aber das Beispiel, das diese Arbeiten Designern, Produzenten, Handwerkern und Kunsthandwerkern und nicht zuletzt den Konsumenten geben, kann lokalen Wirtschaftszweigen durchaus eine Richtung weisen.

Zwischen Design und Kunst

Design »muss eine Bedeutung haben«,[20] betont Humberto und meint damit die Rolle des Objekts als Gefühls- und Bedeutungsträger gegenüber seiner praktischen Funktionalität. Im Design wie in der Kunst ist es üblich, den Namen eines Objekts als Hinweis auf seine Bedeutung zu verwenden. Die Namen der meisten Campana-Entwürfe greifen Aspekte heraus, die offen zutage liegen oder an die sich die ersten Assoziationen knüpfen. Sie mögen zunächst naiv oder zufällig erscheinen, weil sie so Einfaches und Konkretes wie Positiv und Negativ, Felsen, Nester, Schnur und dergleichen benennen. Aber genau darum geht es den Brüdern: zu zeigen, dass das Wunderbare der Welt und ihre unendlichen Möglichkeiten direkt vor unserer Nase liegen und wir sie nur zu sehen und zu nutzen brauchen. Fernando und Humberto sind »tiefgründig in ihrer Oberflächlichkeit«[21], befindet Vik Muniz, und hinter ihrer Direktheit, die so entwaffnend ist wie ihre spontane Rede, verbirgt sich ein außerordentlich sicheres Gespür für Sinn und Sinnlichkeit.

Dass Aussehen und Ausstrahlung ihrer Entwürfe Vorrang haben vor jeder klassischen Funktionalität, ist in Anbetracht der Möbel und Accessoires, die Fernando und Humberto entwerfen, evident – auf Leichtigkeit, Ergonomie oder Platzersparnis kommt es ihnen nicht an. Dennoch bedarf es der Funktion, des möglichen Gebrauchs ihrer Objekte, um die Bedeutungen auch wirksam werden zu lassen: Als bloße Skulptur würde ein *Favela*-Sessel den reinen Betrachter anders berühren als denjenigen, der auch erwägt, Benutzer zu sein. Sofern die Nutzbarkeit eines Objekts das ist, was Design von Kunst unterscheidet, erscheinen die Campanas schließlich als Designer, die sich künstlerischer Mittel bedienen, um Aussagen zu treffen über Gefühle, Identität, Umwelt – und nicht zuletzt über Design. Inwieweit allerdings das ästhetische Erlebnis als Funktion eines Werkes verstanden werden kann beziehungsweise eine über die Funktion hinausgehende Bedeutung als Teil seines Nutzens, ist – wie Kunst- und Designgeschichte zeigen – keineswegs entschieden. Die Campanas, so lehrt der Blick auf ihr Gesamtwerk, spielen mit genau dieser Ambivalenz.

Akkumulationen

Betrachtet man nun das Werk der Campanas aus rein künstlerisch-technischer Perspektive, so läßt sich feststellen, dass es sich dabei um Plastiken handelt: die Formen der Gegenstände werden nicht im subtraktiven Vorgehen aus den Materialien herausgeholt, sondern additiv aus ihnen aufgebaut. Den Campanas dient das Verfahren als ein Ausdrucksmittel, das seine Kraft aus ungewöhnlichen Materialien und ihrer Kombination bezieht. Begonnen hat diese Methode mit den Akkumulationen in Humbertos Muschelspiegeln, und eine der ersten gemeinsamen Arbeiten der Brüder war ebenfalls eine Akkumulation: 1989 ein aus Blechabfällen zusammengeschweißter Stuhl *Ohne Titel,* der die folgenreiche Idee einführte, Möbel aus den Fragmenten industriellen

20 Zitiert nach Morgan-Griffiths (Anm. 8).
21 Muniz, a.a.O., S. 22 (Anm. 4).

also had the form of a cluster of objects – their 1989 untitled chair, which was welded together from scraps of sheet metal, thus introducing the idea of constructing furniture from fragments of semi-finished industrial products. The off-centre curved form of this chair and its high-gloss polished surfaces suggest the influence of Ron Arad's furniture sculptures, which had garnered international attention at the time. The distinct originality of the Campanas, however, lies in the fact that they built the chair from an assortment of wastes and scraps that they had accumulated. Questions of the material and its integrity, origin, naturalness, and significance had already presented themselves to Humberto while combing the beaches of Bahia for seashells; and they continued to occupy both of the brothers in São Paulo, where the endlessly sprawling city constitutes the natural environment and urban waste becomes raw material.

The *Casulo* cabinet, 1989.
Der Schrank *Casulo,* 1989.

The *Geográfica* table, which they created two years later, borrows its form directly from that of their aforementioned untitled chair. Its top is made of pieces of particle board that are held together with epoxy resin and is supported by three legs, which are likewise composed of wood particles. However, instead of the wholly free contours that characterize the chair, the table depicts a map of Brazil, portraying it as a clod of earth that is divided into numerous small districts. Thus, in contrast to Alvar Aalto's *Savoy* vases, which are symbolic of Finland's pure and harmonic landscape, the Campanas put forward a collage of set pieces in order to describe the urban sprawl and disintegration of Brazil. At the same time, however, a biographical interpretation presents itself as another way of reading the piece. Speaking of the 1991 *Favela* armchair, Humberto emphasizes 'how fragmented [his] life always is or was' and how he had attempted 'to manifest that idea in a kind of chair that is chaotic in its very construction.'[22] This disjointedness is no doubt expressed also in the *Geográfica* table and it recurs throughout his entire oeuvre, from some of his first terracotta sculptures of the early 1980s to the *Nazareth* centrepieces, made of porcelain, which the brothers created in 2008 for Bernardaud in Limoges.[23]

Jumbles and Knots

In 1989, directly following the *Desconfortáveis* series, the Campanas' *Casulo* (Cocoon or Seed Pod) cabinet launched their *Organicos* line, which continued through 1990. This series was characterized by pieces of metal intersected with fragments of wood that the brothers had found in nature.[24] *Casulo* itself was inspired by a work of graffiti depicting a ball surrounded by a whir of lines: the body of the cabinet is constructed from an irregular coarse steel mesh – a feature that has reappeared in a large number of the brothers' subsequent designs – while a forked branch, tacked onto the outer skin, serves as a handle for opening it.[25]

22 Humberto Campana, interview by the author.
23 These drastically 'disjointed' pieces are named in honour of Humberto's long-time friend, Brazilian artist Nazareth Pacheco.
24 Typical examples from this series are the *Costela* (Rib) and *Bola* (Beet) fruit dishes, which evoke motifs from nature that suggest ephemerality.
25 Similarly, in the *Liana* chair from the *Desconfortáveis* series, two individual wires entwine the dual supports of the backrest and thus merely suggest its form. In the *Peixe* (Fish) chair from this same series, an entire bundle of wires is employed. This more clearly defines the back and gives it the contours of a fish fin, to which the title alludes.

Halbzeugs aufzubauen. Die exzentrisch gekrümmte Form dieses Objekts und seine hochglänzend polierten Oberflächen legen nahe, dass es unter dem Eindruck jener Möbelplastiken entstand, mit denen Ron Arad damals international Furore machte. Die den Campanas eigene Originalität zeigte sich jedoch darin, dass sie den Stuhl aus einer Anhäufung von Abfällen bauten. Die Fragen an das Material, nach seiner Integrität, seinem Ursprung, seiner Natürlichkeit und seiner Bedeutung hatten sich Humberto in Bahia beim Muschelnsammeln gestellt, und sie stellten sich den Brüdern ebenso in São Paulo, wo die endlos wuchernde Stadt zur natürlichen Umgebung und der urbane Abfall zum Rohmaterial wird.

Der Tisch *Geográfica,* der zwei Jahr später entstand, lehnt sich formal unmittelbar an diesen Stuhl an. Statt einer völlig freien Form ergeben hier die mit Epoxydharz zusammengehaltenen Pressspanstückchen ein Abbild der brasilianischen Landkarte als eine in viele kleine Distrikte unterteilte Erdscholle, die auf drei ebenso bruchstückhaften Beinen steht. Was in Alvar Aaltos *Savoy*-Vasen noch als Symbol einer reinen, harmonischen Landschaft Finnlands erscheint, wird bei den Campanas zu einer Collage aus Versatzstücken, die die Zersiedelung und Zerstörung Brasiliens beschreibt. Doch auch eine biografische Lesart bietet sich an: In einem Interview betonte Humberto, wie fragmentiert sein Leben ist und schon immer war und dass er schon mit dem *Favela* versucht hatte, »diese Idee in einer Art von Sessel zu manifestieren, der in seiner Konstruktion zutiefst chaotisch ist«.[22] Diese Zerrissenheit zeigt sich bereits Anfang der 1980er Jahre in mehreren frühen Terrakotta-Plastiken sowie zwanzig Jahre später in den Porzellan-Fruchtschalen *Nazareth,* die 2008 für Bernardaud in Limoges entstanden.[23]

Haufen und Knäuel

Direkt im Anschluss an die *Desconfortáveis* entstand 1989 das Schrankmöbel *Casulo* (Kokon oder Samenkapsel), das die bis 1990 verfolgte *Organicos*-Serie begründete, in der die Campanas Teile aus Metall mit gefundenen Holzstücken aus der Natur kreuzten.[24] Inspiriert von einem Graffiti, das einen von Linien umschwirrten Ball zeigte, verwendeten sie für den Korpus des *Casulo* ein unregelmäßiges, grobmaschiges Stahlgeflecht, wie es auch bei späteren Entwürfen immer wieder zum Einsatz kam. Eine Astgabel, die an die Außenhaut geheftet ist, dient als Griff zum Öffnen des Schranks.[25]

Aus dem Prinzip gingen 1990 drei weitere Möbelstücke hervor: zunächst der Kleiderständer *Alvo* (Zielscheibe), dessen Name auf die Form der Zielscheibe verweist und gleichsam dazu auffordert, seine Kleidung auf den Ständer zu werfen.[26] Als zweite Konsequenz aus dem *Casulo* entstand 1990 wie ein Knäuel unregelmäßig gebogener Armiereisen der Sessel *Bob,* den Humberto

22 Humberto Campana im Interview mit dem Autor, a.a.O. (Anm. 1).
23 Die drastisch »zerrissenen« Schalen sind nach Humbertos langjähriger Künstlerfreundin Nazareth Pacheco benannt.
24 Typisch für diese Serie sind etwa die Fruchtschalen *Costela* (Rippe) und *Bola* (Rübe), weil sie Motive aus der Natur zeigen, die Vergänglichkeit suggerieren.
25 Im Stuhl *Liana* (Liane) der *Desconfortáveis* sind es noch zwei einzelne Drähte, die sich um die beiden Streben einer Rückenlehne schlingen, die damit nur angedeutet wird. Im Stuhl *Peixe* (Fisch) dieser Serie ist es ein ganzes Bündel von Drähten, das die Lehne klarer definiert und dabei eine Fischflosse formt, auf die auch der Titel verweist.
26 Dieser Kleiderständer leitet sich zugleich aus der minimalistischen Raumfigur der *Grelha*-Plastik von 1987 her. Im Laufe der 1980er Jahre hatte Humberto seine Arbeit mehr und mehr auf abstrakte Raumstudien verlegt. So entstand u.a. die Plastik *Grelha* (Gitter, Grill) aus geschweißtem Armierstahl, die auf den ersten Blick wie das filigrane Gebilde einer Raumplastik wirkt, auf den zweiten Blick aber das Gerippe eines Stuhls erkennen lässt.

In 1990, the Campanas applied the principle of the Casulo to three further pieces of furniture. First came the *Alvo* (Target) clothes stand, whose name effectively calls on users to fling their clothes at it.[26] Following it were the *Bob* armchair – a knot of irregularly bent steel wires that Humberto welded for his friend Robert Wasilewski – and the *Fios* (String) table, a variation of which was created three years later by employing a finer, smoother structure. *Bob* and *Fios* come across like syntheses of drawings by Giacometti and the wire figures of a Cocteau or a Calder. They became forerunners to numerous objects that seem to materialize in a state of constant vibration.[27]

During the ensuing years, the brothers produced two variations on this theme: jumbles and knots, or straight lines and twisted lines, which both play on the illusion of a random and alterable configuration. The knots of twisted lines can be interpreted as symbols of the chaos of nature, while the jumbles of straight lines can be viewed as derivatives of urban disarray. The titles of the objects seem to substantiate these connotations. From the idea of the knot, the Campanas developed the *Ninhos* (Nests) series of small aluminium wire baskets as well as the *Novelo* (Clew) sofa and other seating furniture. This group can also be said to include the transparent *Anemone* armchair, whose shape came to Humberto in a dream,[28] and the *Corallo* wire mesh armchair, both of which were designed for Edra. Three-dimensional jumbles form the *Escultura* (Sculpture) screen of 1993. Further examples are the *Batuque* (Drummer) vases, the *Blow Up* fruit dish, the *Pedra* furniture line, and an explosion-like installation that the brothers mounted in the narrow stairwell of the Arte e Arquitectura Building in São Paulo in 2007. In 1995, a two-dimensional version of the theme appeared in the *Zig Zag* screen – a chrome-plated steel frame, densely woven with purple PVC cords and set on edge atop stilts.[29]

In 2007, the Campanas utilized the entire thematic spectrum of jumbles and knots for the set and costumes they designed for the production of a ballet inspired by Ovid's *Metamorphoses,* their chaotic structures offering a fruitful motif aptly suited for the depiction of continual transformation. In close collaboration with choreographer Frédéric Flamand, whom they had gotten to know in São Paulo in 1983, and his company of dancers from the Ballet National de Marseille, they used a lim-

Foyer of the Arte e Arquitectura Building in São Paulo with a view of the stairwell with the installation *Blow Up* of 2007.
Foyer des Arte e Arquitectura Building in São Paulo mit Blick in das Treppenhaus mit der Installation *Blow Up* von 2007.

Scene from rehearsals of the ballet *Métamorphoses* by the Ballet National de Marseille, photographed by Fernando Campana, 2007. Szene aus den Proben zum Ballett *Métamorphoses* des Ballet National de Marseille, fotografiert von Fernando Campana, 2007.

für seinen Freund Robert Wasilewski schweißte, sowie der Tisch *Fios* (Schnur), von dem drei Jahre später eine Variante mit geglätteter, feinerer Struktur geschaffen wurde. *Bob* und *Fios* wirken wie Synthesen aus den Zeichnungen Giacomettis und den Drahtfiguren eines Cocteau oder Calder und wurden zu Vorläufern zahlreicher Objekte, die sich in ständiger Vibration zu materialisieren scheinen.[27]

In der Folge ergaben sich zwei Varianten des Themas: Haufen und Knäuel beziehungsweise gerade und ungerade Linien, die beide mit der Illusion einer zufälligen und veränderbaren Anordnung spielen. Die Knäuel aus geschwungenen Linien lesen sich wie Symbole für das Chaos der Natur, die Haufen aus Geraden als Derivate eines urbanen Chaos. Die Titel der Objekte scheinen diese Konnotationen zu belegen. Aus der Idee des Knäuels entwickelten die Campanas die *Ninhos* (Nester) genannte Serie kleiner Aluminiumdrahtkörbe, das Sofa *Novelo* (Knäuel) und weitere Sitzmöbel. Zu dieser Gruppe kann man auch den durchsichtigen *Anemone*-Sessel zählen, dessen Gestalt Humberto in einem Traum erschienen war,[28] und den Drahtgeflechtsessel *Corallo* – beide für Edra.

Dreidimensionale Anhäufungen von Geraden bildeten 1993 den Wandschirm *Escultura* (Skulptur), die *Batuque* (Trommler)-Vasen, die Fruchtschale *Blow Up* (Explosion) aus Stahlstäben, die *Pedra* (Fels)-Möbelserie sowie eine explosionsförmige Installation im beengten Treppenhaus des Arte e Arquitectura Building in São Paulo. Als zweidimensionales Gewebe taucht das Thema zuerst 1995 im Wandschirm *Zig Zag* auf, ein verchromtes Stahlgerüst eines hochkant auf Stelzen gestellten Kastens, der mit violetten PVC-Schnüren dicht umwoben ist.[29]

Die gesamte Bandbreite der Topoi Netz und Knäuel nutzten die Campanas 2007 für das Bühnenbild und die Ausstattung eines Balletts nach Ovids *Metamorphosen,* denn die ungeordneten Strukturen bieten ein adäquates und ergiebiges Motiv zur Darstellung ständiger Verwandlung. In enger Zusammenarbeit mit dem Choreografen Frédéric Flamand, den sie bereits 1983 in São Paulo kennen gelernt hatten, und seinen Tänzerinnen und Tänzern vom Ballet National de Marseille entwarfen sie die Requisiten und Kostüme, die mit wenigen, aber vielseitig einsetzbaren Elementen auskommen und in ihrer Konzentration und Expressivität an die Arbeiten Isamu Noguchis für Martha Graham erinnern. Knäuel, Netze und Haufen sind die Akkumulationen, die die Campanas am häufigsten variiert haben. Die ungewöhnlichsten, von einem »Rohmaterial« am

---

26 The stand takes its form also from the minimalist spatial figure of Humberto's *Grelha* (Grille) sculpture of 1987. During the 1980s, Humberto increasingly turned to abstract spatial compositions in his work. *Grelha* is but one example of this tendency of his. Made of welded sheathed steel, it initially appears to be the filigree form of a sculpture but upon closer inspection can be recognized as the frame of a chair.

27 In 1985, the Austrian group B.R.A.N.D constructed the *2.85* sofa exclusively from entangled loops of metal. However, it seems unlikely that *Casulo* or *Bob* were derived from this sofa, not only because of the scant publicity that it received but primarily because of the stringent manner in which Campana designs are developed.

28 The idea for the armchair came 'like a gift from heaven. It looks exactly as I had dreamt it. The next day I found a long section of tubing in our studio and began to assemble the chair with my bare hands.' Humberto Campana, interview by Taissa Buescu, 'Humberto & Fernando', *Elle Décor,* June 2006, p.242.

29 The screen served as the basis for Edra's 2001 circular screen of the same name. The idea has since been employed by the Campanas, in different colour variants, for a number of interiors and installations.

27 Bereits 1985 hatte die österreichische Gruppe B.R.A.N.D das Sofa *2.85* ebenfalls ausschließlich aus verwickelten Metallschlaufen gebaut. Eine Herleitung des *Casulo* oder des *Bob* aus diesem Möbel ist jedoch unwahrscheinlich; nicht nur weil das *2.85*-Sofa kaum publiziert wurde, sondern vor allem weil die Entwicklung der Campana-Entwürfe so stringent verläuft.

28 Die Idee zu dem Sessel kam Humberto Campana »wie ein Geschenk des Himmels. So wie er ist, habe ich ihn geträumt. Am nächsten Tag fand ich ein langes Stück Rohr in unserem Atelier und begann ihn mit bloßer Hand zusammenzubauen.« Humberto Campana in einem Interview mit Taissa Buescu: »Humberto & Fernando«, in: *Elle Décor,* Juni 2006, Jahrgang 7, Nr. 6, S. 242.

29 2001 diente der Wandschirm als Grundlage für Edras runden *Zig Zag*-Wandschirm. Die Idee haben die Brüder seither in verschiedenen Farbvarianten für etliche Interieurs und Installationen eingesetzt.

ited number of highly versatile elements for their designs, thus achieving a concentration and expressiveness reminiscent of Isamu Noguchi's works for Martha Graham.

Throughout the years, jumbles and knots are the accumulation motifs that the Campanas have subjected to the most frequent variation. The most unusual of these, and also the one furthest removed from 'raw material', appears in the armchairs made of stuffed toys, which first came out in 2002 and are a further development of the bundled-up fabric rolls of the brothers' *Sushi* furniture line. The inspiration for the *Banquete* (Feast) armchair – and the variations of it that were designed for Moss, Target, Disney, and other clients – comes from the kitschy stuffed animals available en masse in toy shops, carnivals, and coin-operated arcade games. 'Our background is clearly the countryside. We have always accepted and loved the kitsch part of that!'[30] confesses Fernando. The 'Banquete' section of the Campanas' award-winning website, which was designed by the Brazilian postproduction studio F/Nazca,[31] describes precisely this naive, imaginative relationship to everyday culture. In 2003, the brothers developed another variation of the armchair – *Multidão* (Crowd) – for which they utilized a particular type of rag doll made in a northern province of Brazil. 'Using cheap, readily available material in such abundance, they create the illusion of luxury', wrote Sophie McKinlay that very year.[32]

Objets Trouvés

When the Campanas used multiple layers of ordinary bubble wrap as the upholstery for their 1995 *Plastico Bolha* (Bubble Wrap) easy chair, the MoMA staff was not entirely prepared for such a contrivance. While unpacking the piece for the museum's 1998 exhibition *Projects 66,* which was devoted to the Campana brothers and Ingo Maurer as the great poets of contemporary design, one of the employees came close to destroying the chair because he assumed the real artwork lay underneath all the plastic.

The mistake, however, is forgivable. Placing familiar materials and motifs in an unexpected context and reinterpreting them as materials for new objects is a deliberate strategy of Fernando and Humberto. It frequently involves allowing the materials to 'mature' and then placing them in new combinations and associations. When they come upon mass-produced commodities – such as wire, aluminium or steel rods, PVC cords and tubes – in the building supplies and hardware stores of São Paulo, they usually do not yet have an idea for their application but rather a sheer fascination with one or more of their features: their surface, their pliability, their transparency, their lustre, their structure, or the cultural meanings associated with them. In order to establish a purposeful connection with a certain material, the Campanas, in most cases, need to first become accustomed to its properties and connotations, to feel it with their own hands, try it out and let it rest; the idea for its appropriate use will come sooner or later – or never – but under no circumstances is it anything planned. As Humberto explains, the inspiration 'comes suddenly [...] without any intention. Whenever I have purposely looked for inspiration, I have gone completely wrong.'[33] Only through this

Improvised washing facility in Jalapão, photographed by Humberto Campana, 2004.
Improvisierte Waschgelegenheit in Jalapão, fotografiert von Humberto Campana, 2004.

weitesten entfernten Anhäufungen aber sind die ab 2002 entstandenen Sessel aus Stoffspielzeug – eine Weiterentwicklung der gebündelten Stoffrollen ihrer *Sushi*-Möbel. Die Anregung zu den *Banquete* (Gelage) genannten Sesseln und verschiedenen Varianten davon für Moss, Target, Disney und andere Kunden sind kitschige Plüschtiere, wie sie massenhaft in Spielwarenläden, auf Jahrmärkten und in Glücksspielautomaten angeboten werden. »Wir kommen eindeutig vom Lande, und den dazugehörigen Kitsch haben wir immer akzeptiert und geliebt!«[30], bekennt Fernando. Das Kapitel »Banquete« auf der wunderbaren, von F/Nazca gestalteten Website der Campanas[31] beschreibt genau dieses naive, phantasievolle Verhältnis zur Alltagskultur. 2003 entwarfen sie als Variation den Sessel *Multidão* (Menschenmenge), für den sie eine bestimmte Sorte von Stoffpuppen aus einer nördlich gelegenen Provinz verwenden. »Mit dem Einsatz billigen, leicht verfügbaren Materials in so einem Überfluss erzeugen sie die Illusion von Luxus«, schrieb 2004 Sophie McKinlay.[32]

Objets Trouvés

Als die Campanas 1995 zur Polsterung ihres Sessels *Plastico Bolha* (Luftpolsterfolie) mehrere Lagen ordinärer Luftpolsterfolie verwendet hatten, war man im Museum of Modern Art auf diesen Kunstgriff nicht vorbereitet: Beim Auspacken des Möbels für die Ausstellung *Projects 66,* die das MoMA 1998 den Campanas und Ingo Maurer als den großen Poeten des Designs widmete, hätte ein Mitarbeiter des Museums den Sessel fast zerstört, weil er das eigentliche Kunstwerk unter all dem Plastik vermutet hatte.

Das Versehen ist entschuldbar, denn den Motiven und Materialien einen für das Auge des Betrachters unerwarteten Kontext zu geben und sie als Werkstoffe für neue Gegenstände umzuinterpretieren, hat für Fernando und Humberto Campana Methode. Für sie selbst sind es aber meist vertraute Materialien und Motive, die sie »reifen« lassen und in neue Zusammenhänge stellen. Wenn sie Draht, Aluminium- oder Stahlstäbe, PVC-Schnüre und -Schläuche als Massenware in den Geschäften São Paulos entdecken, gibt es meist noch keine Idee für eine Anwendung, sondern vor allem Faszination: für die Oberfläche, die Biegsamkeit, die Transparenz, den Glanz, die Struktur oder die Bedeutung. Um die Verbindung zu einem bestimmten Gebrauchsgegenstand herzustellen, müssen sich die Brüder in den meisten Fällen an diese Eigenschaften und Konnotationen erst gewöhnen, das Material immer wieder in der Hand wiegen, ausprobieren und ruhen lassen. Die Idee für den passenden Einsatz kommt früher oder später – oder nie, aber keinesfalls geplant: Die Inspiration »kommt plötzlich [...] unbeabsichtigt. Wann immer ich bewusst nach Inspiration gesucht habe, lag ich vollkommen falsch.«[33] Erst über diesen Aneignungsprozess kann das ganze grafische oder bildhauerische Potential eines Rohstoffs entdeckt werden. So werden selbst die sperrigsten Materialien formbar und können mit den konstruktiven und funktionalen Anforderungen in Einklang gebracht werden.

Die unter einer Straßenbrücke oder an einer Häuserecke unvermittelt entstehenden Lebensräume der Armen in São Paulo, die Improvisation, mit der sie den Mangel an Ressourcen kompensieren, um zu einer Behausung, zu

30 Fernando Campana, interview by the author.

31 See www.campanas.com.br. The website, which includes music by André Abujamra, was designed under the direction of Ana Carolina Ramos. It received multiple awards at the Cannes Film Festival.

32 Sophie McKinlay, pamphlet published in conjunction with the exhibition *Zest for Life: Fernando and Humberto Campana,* Design Museum London, 2004.

33 Humberto Campana, interview by the author.

30 Fernando Campana im Interview mit dem Autor, a.a.O. (Anm. 1).

31 Siehe www.campanas.com.br. Die Website mit der Musik von André Abujamra wurde gestaltet unter der Leitung von Ana Carolina Ramos und wurde beim Filmfestival von Cannes mehrfach ausgezeichnet.

32 Sophie McKinlay: Pamphlet zur Ausstellung *Zest For Life – Fernando und Humberto Campana;* Design Museum London 2004.

33 Humberto Campana im Interview mit dem Autor, a.a.O. (Anm. 1).

process of appropriation can the full graphic or sculptural potential of a raw material be discovered. In this manner, even the bulkiest of materials can become malleable and be brought into harmony with structural and functional requirements.

The living spaces of the poor, which suddenly materialize beneath an overpass or at a street corner in São Paulo, and the improvisation with which they compensate for their lack of resources in order to attain a dwelling place, furnishings, or living equipment provide the Campanas with continual examples of the charm and personality of ephemeral stopgap solutions. In their works, they refer to this 'beauty of materials that are often ignored by common bystanders, so as to subvert their point of view. ... Living in São Paulo pressed us to exercise the transformation of chaos into beauty. It takes effort and careful looking for the city to reveal itself as interesting, vibrant, and poetic.'[34]

Good examples of this are the *Jenette* chair and the *Tatoo* table. *Tatoo* obtains its appeal from the identical industrially manufactured drain strainers that the brothers used in order to create an ornamentally perforated table top whose shadow projects a patterned carpet onto the floor beneath. As for *Jenette,* it was inspired by the bristles of street brooms, which seemed to be both stiff and flexible enough to accommodate the function of a comfortable backrest; even so, it did not satisfy the necessary safety requirements and for Edra's version a metal plate was hidden in the tuft to provide additional support. Once again, the emphasis in these designs is not on their functionality but on the images. With their objects, the Campanas sketch portraits of the surrounding environment that are distinguished by their ability to transcend the local context and refer to collages of reality as a fundamental encapsulation of our times. This language and the message it conveys are universal; in the brothers' own words, good design is 'a testimony to our times'[35] and their objects tell stories from the neighbourhood on the other side of the globe. Cristina Morozzi thus describes their works as 'epic, like all narratives from the Southern Hemisphere. In the North, by contrast, stories take the form of news because an event is always one of a thousand other possibilities and the necessities of survival do not give each and every thing a definitive, almost sacred value.'[36]

Fernando and Humberto pursue their 'amorphous, imprecise ideas'[37] in an intuitive, experimental process that begins with the exploration of the streets and shops of their city, of nature (to which they regularly retreat), or of their own studio, which has accumulated a considerable stock of completed and semi-completed objects. It often happens that they prematurely abandon a project and put it aside until much later when they hit on a compelling idea for its further development. This continuous involvement with materials and object studies also explains the great consistency of their terminology: 'Sometimes, when I'm in the studio – and there is a heap of materials over there – a bright idea comes along all of a sudden. From then on begins a kind of flirtation with a material that stands up in front of me asking, What can I be transformed into?'[38]

This was how the *Vermelha* armchair came about in 1993. 'The idea emerged when we bought a large bundle of rope from a street stall and brought it back to the studio. When we placed it on a table, we observed it deconstructing before our eyes. At that moment we both looked at each other and almost simultaneously remarked: "This is the chair we want to build. It is a representation of Brazil in its beautiful chaos and deconstructiveness."'[39]

Mobiliar oder Gerätschaften zu kommen, liefert den Campanas ständig Beispiele für den Charme und die Persönlichkeit ephemerer Notlösungen. Auf diese Art der »Schönheit von Materialien, die von den Passanten meist ignoriert wird«, verweisen sie in ihren Arbeiten, »um herkömmliche Betrachtungsweisen zu unterlaufen. [...] Das Leben in São Paulo hat uns zur Transformation von Chaos in Schönheit gezwungen. Man muss sich schon anstrengen und ein aufmerksames Auge haben, um die Stadt als interessant, pulsierend und poetisch wahrzunehmen.«[34]

Gute Beispiele dafür sind der Stuhl *Jenette* und der Tisch *Tatoo.* Der *Tatoo* bezieht seinen Reiz aus einer Addition identischer, industriell gefertigter Abflusssiebe zu einer ornamental durchbrochenen Tischplatte, deren Schattenwurf einen gemusterten Teppich unter den Tisch projiziert. Für den *Jenette* entdeckten sie die Borsten von Straßenbesen, die sowohl steif als auch flexibel genug erschienen, um der Funktion einer bequemen Rückenlehne zu entsprechen. Der erforderlichen Sicherheit entsprach dies allerdings so wenig, dass für Edras Version eine Metallplatte in dem Büschel versteckt wurde, die beim Anlehnen Halt bietet. Noch einmal: Nicht die Funktionen, sondern die Bilder stehen im Vordergrund dieser Entwürfe. Mit ihren Objekten zeichnen die Campanas Porträts ihrer Lebenswelt, deren besondere Kunst darin besteht, dass sie über den lokalen Kontext hinaus auf die Collagen der Wirklichkeit als grundsätzliche Verfasstheit unserer Zeit verweisen. Diese Sprache und Botschaft sind universell. Gutes Design ist, wie sie selbst sagen, »ein Zeugnis unserer Zeit«[35], und ihre Gegenstände erzählen Geschichten aus der Nachbarschaft vom anderen Ende der Welt. So beschreibt Cristina Morozzi die Arbeiten als »episch, wie alle Erzählungen aus der südlichen Hemisphäre. Im Norden hingegen heißt das Erzählen Berichten, weil ein Ereignis immer eines von tausend anderen Möglichkeiten ist und die Notwendigkeit des Überlebens nicht allem und jedem einen definitiven, fast heiligen Wert gibt.«[36]

Fernando und Humberto folgen ihren »amorphen, unpräzisen Ideen«[37] in einem intuitiven, experimentellen Prozess, der mit Entdeckungen in den Straßen und Läden ihrer Stadt beginnt, in der Natur, in die sie sich regelmäßig zurückziehen, oder im eigenen Studio, wo sich ein großer Fundus fertiger und halbfertiger Objekte angesammelt hat. Häufig kommt es vor, dass sie Projekte frühzeitig abbrechen, um erst viel später darauf zurückzugreifen, wenn sie die zündende Idee für deren Weiterentwicklung haben. Diese ständige Präsenz von Materialien und Objektstudien erklärt auch die große Konsistenz ihrer Terminologie: »Manchmal, wenn ich im Atelier bin – und dort gibt es eine Menge von Baustoffen –, kommt mir plötzlich ein genialer Einfall. Das ist dann wie ein Flirt mit einem Material, das mich anschaut und fragt: ›In was könnte ich verwandelt werden?‹«[38]

So entstand 1993 auch der *Vermelha*-Sessel: »Die Idee kam uns, als wir bei einem Straßenverkäufer ein großes Bündel Seil gekauft und ins Atelier geholt hatten. Als wir es auf den Tisch legten, beobachteten wir, wie es vor unseren Augen auseinander fiel. In dem Moment schauten wir uns an und sagten fast gleichzeitig: ›Das ist genau der Stuhl, den wir bauen wollen – wie Brasilien, in seiner Schönheit aus Chaos und Verfall.‹«[39]

Ihr erster Anlauf, den Stuhl zu realisieren, war 1992/93 der *3 em 1* (Drei in Einem). Zwar taten sie ihr Möglichstes, »die Dekonstruktion in dem Stuhl zu wiederholen«, und untersuchten aufmerksam »den Aufbau dieser Unordnung in den Seilen«[40], die sie um einige Gewindestangen als Rückenlehne drapierten. Doch der Rest des Stuhls wollte einfach nicht dazu passen, weil hier in der Tat drei verschiedene Gestaltungselemente in einem Objekt vereint wurden, nämlich Seile, Holzscheiben und gewickelter Draht. Es musste also

34 Fernando Campana, in Muniz, 'Campana Brothers', p. 38.

35 Fernando and Humberto Campana, interview by the author.

36 Cristina Morozzi, 'Il saper fare come spirito del luogo' [Know-how as the spirit of a place], in *Campanas,* ed. Maria Helena Estrada (São Paulo: Bookmark, 2003), p. 48.

37 Fernando Campana, interview by the author.

38 Humberto Campana, interview by the author.

39 Fernando and Humberto Campana, interview, Design Museum London.

34 Fernando Campana in Muniz, a.a.O., S. 38 (Anm. 4).

35 Humberto und Fernando Campana im Interview mit dem Autor, a.a.O. (Anm. 1).

36 Cristina Morozzi: »Il saper fare come spirito del luogo«, in: *Campanas,* hrsg. von Maria Helena Estrada, Bookmark, São Paulo 2003, S. 48.

37 Fernando Campana im Interview mit dem Autor, a.a.O. (Anm. 1).

38 Humberto Campana im Interview mit dem Autor, a.a.O. (Anm. 1).

39 Fernando und Humberto Campana in einem Interview mit dem Designmuseum London, veröffentlicht auf der Website: http://www.designmuseum.org/design/fernando-humberto-campana.

40 Humberto Campana im Interview mit dem Autor, a.a.O. (Anm. 1).

Their first attempt to realize the chair was the *3 em 1* (Three in One) of 1992/93. They did their utmost 'to replicate this deconstruction in the chair' and were 'very careful to study the structure of the mess of ropes'[40] that they draped around several threaded metal rods to form the backrest. Yet the remainder of the chair simply did not want to fall in line because, as indicated by its name, three different design elements were united here in one object, wooden discs and wrapped wire being the two other ingredients thrown in the mix alongside the ropes. A clearer structure was needed and this was initially provided by the model of the famous *Grand Confort* club chair by Le Corbusier. Based on its form, an aluminium frame was constructed, which the Campanas then wrapped with rope until the result was a reasonably comfortable seat. They called it *Azul* (Blue), after the colour of the rope, and followed the same formula shortly thereafter with another chair: *Verde* (Green). Yet it was not until the *Vermelha* (Red) armchair that they managed not only to combine the chaos of rope loops with the frame alluded to in *3 em 1* but also to form a coherent overall image.[41] Many years later, the contiguously arrayed discs of *3 em 1* reappeared as ornamental upholstery in the *Harumaki* and *Sushi* furniture pieces. 'We work in a trial and error process,' explains Fernando, 'whereby errors often indicate new directions.'[42]

The *Fitas* coffee table, 1993.
Der Couchtisch *Fitas*, 1993.

Paper Pieces

Fernando and Humberto assimilate themselves to the city in which they live and this includes, not in the least, a self-organizing recycling of waste: people set out on the street what they think others might still be able to use and in next to no time someone has come along and collected it.[43] The cardboard sheets that are used by the homeless as insulation mats, seat pads, or primitive dwelling places gave them the idea of utilizing the material's transparency, which only becomes evident when looking directly at the narrow-cut edges of the sheets. From 1993 to 1995, they developed a whole line of lamps and screens based on cardboard and entitled *Papel* (paper). These pieces persuasively combine the appeal of the material's texture with the connotation of waste. The principle was soon extended to tables and seating furniture, applying a synthetic resin to stiffen and stabilize the cardboard. With these objects there is also an inversion of the relationship between packing and packed, for when en route to collectors and exhibitions, the valuable furniture pieces always travel in solid wood crates.

In one of the workshops that the Campanas regularly conduct together with the Vitra Design Museum at the Domaine de Boisbuchet, they attempted to further develop the aforementioned *Ideal House* that they had designed for the 2004 Cologne furniture fair by making a complete house made of cardboard. The idea was inspired not in the least by a conference pavilion made of cardboard tubes that Japanese architect Shigeru Ban had erected on the workshop grounds. However, no suitable technical solution could be found for the house and, after numerous experimental models and drawings, the brothers decided to turn their attention to utensils and furniture and ended up concentrating on the devel-

40 Humberto Campana, interview by the author.

41 The pivotal solution for the structure reputedly came from an unassuming object created years earlier: the *Bola* fruit dish, with its three roots as feet and its upwardly curving arms that hold the fruit.

42 Fernando Campana, interview by the author.

43 'São Paulo has a spontaneous recycling system, which we often use in order to get rid of our waste by simply putting it in front of the studio.' Fernando Campana, interview by the author.

eine klare Struktur her, die zunächst das Vorbild des berühmten Clubsessels *Grand Confort* von Le Corbusier lieferte. Nach dessen Form wurde ein Aluminiumgestell gebaut, das die Campanas so oft mit Seil umwickelten, bis ein einigermaßen bequemer Sitz entstanden war. Ihn nannten sie *Azul* (Blau), nach der Farbe des Seils, und demselben Schema folgte kurz darauf ein Stuhl: *Verde* (Grün). Erst mit dem Sessel *Vermelha* (Rot) gelang es jedoch, das Chaos der Schlaufen nicht nur mit dem im *3 em 1* angedeuteten Gestell, sondern auch zu einem schlüssigen Gesamtbild zu verbinden.[41] Viel später tauchten die dicht aneinander gesetzten Scheiben des *3 em 1* dann als ornamentale Polster in den *Harumaki*- und *Sushi*-Möbeln wieder auf. »Wir arbeiten nach der Versuch-und-Irrtum-Methode«, so Fernando, »wobei die Irrtümer uns oft neue Richtungen weisen.«[42]

Arbeiten aus Papier

Fernando und Humberto eignen sich die Stadt, in der sie leben, als ihre natürliche Umwelt an, und dazu gehört nicht zuletzt ein sich selbst organisierendes Recycling von Abfällen: Jeder stellt das an die Straße, was ihm für Andere noch brauchbar erscheint, und binnen kürzester Zeit wird es aufgesammelt.[43] Ein Stapel Pappe, wie er von Obdachlosen als Isoliermatte, Sitzunterlage oder für primitive Behausungen verwendet wird, brachte sie auf die Idee, die Transparenz zu nutzen, die man erst bemerkt, wenn man direkt auf die schmalen Schnittkanten der Pappen blickt. Von 1993 bis 1995 entwickelten sie daraus mit *Papel* (Papier) eine ganze Serie von Leuchten und Paravents, die den Reiz der Textur mit der Konnotation des Abfalls überzeugend kombinieren. Das Prinzip wurde bald auf Tische und Sitzmöbel ausgeweitet, wobei Kunstharz den Karton versteift und stabilisiert. Mit diesen Objekten kehrte sich schließlich auch das Verhältnis von Verpackung und Verpacktem um, denn zu Sammlern und Ausstellungen reisen die wertvollen Möbel stets in soliden Holzkisten.

Bei einem der Workshops, die die Campanas zusammen mit dem Vitra Design Museum regelmäßig auf der Domaine de Boisbuchet durchführen, entstand im Anschluss an ihr *Ideal House* für die Kölner Möbelmesse die Idee eines kompletten Hauses aus Pappe. Angeregt wurde der Gedanke nicht zuletzt durch einen Konferenzpavillon aus Papprohren, den der japanische Architekt Shigeru Ban auf dem Workshopgelände errichtet hatte. Für das Haus fand sich keine geeignete technische Lösung und so konzentrierten sich die Brüder nach etlichen experimentellen Modellen und Zeichnungen schließlich auf die Entwicklung eines Hockers, der aus mehreren, wie Eierkartons ineinander gesteckten Lagen Pappmaché besteht. Zusammen mit dem Vitra Design Museum und einem Verpackungshersteller versuchen die Campanas hier ihr erstes skulpturales Möbel zu entwickeln, das vollständig aus einem recycelten und recycelbaren Material besteht und zugleich rein industriell hergestellt und somit preiswert sein soll.

Kunsthandwerk und Serienproduktion

Tatsächlich entwerfen die Campanas nicht nur für aufwändige, handwerkliche Fertigungen, sondern bemühen sich auch um die Verknüpfung ihres künstlerischen Ansatzes mit der industriellen Produktion. Das beweist eine Gruppe

41 Wobei die entscheidende Lösung für die Struktur vermutlich ein Jahre früher entstandenes, unscheinbares Objekt lieferte: die Fruchtschale *Bola* (Rübe) mit ihren drei Wurzeln als Füßen und den nach oben gebogenen Stielen zum Auffangen der Früchte.

42 In einem Interview mit dem Autor a.a.O. (Anm. 1).

43 »Sao Paulo besitzt ein spontanes Recycling-System, das wir selbst häufig benutzen, um unseren Abfall loszuwerden, indem wir ihn einfach vors Atelier stellen.«, Fernando Campana in einem Interview mit dem Autor a.a.O. (Anm. 1).

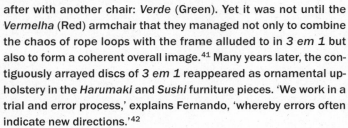

opment of a stool made of multiple layers of papier mâché, nested like egg cartons. Together with the Vitra Design Museum and a packaging manufacturer, they are currently attempting to develop their first sculptural furniture piece composed entirely of this material, which is both recycled and recyclable and, at the same time, industrially manufactured and thus inexpensive.

Handicrafts and Mass Production

The Campanas do not limit themselves to designs intended for elaborate manually performed fabrication but also strive to link their artistic approach with industrial production. This is demonstrated by a group of furniture pieces, lamps, and office accessories, which were produced primarily between 1997 and 2001 and are characterized by flexed synthetic or metal planes. A number of these more 'rationally' designed objects were originally developed for mass production, even if they ultimately remained limited to smaller editions: the *Cone* armchair produced by Edra, the *Jequitiba* lamp (named after a species of tree) and the *Labirinto* (Labyrinth) shelf designed for two Brazilian companies, and the *Inflável* (Inflatable) side table developed for the MoMA in New York. At first glance, these objects are barely recognizable as Campana designs, for the clear geometric forms that take shape in smooth industrial materials seem uncharacteristically cold compared to the rest of the brothers' œuvre. They evince a seemingly abrupt emergence of a formal relationship with the functionalist industrial design that has dominated the curriculum of Brazil's design schools since 1964, following the model set by the Ulm School of Design.[44] Yet the affinity between the brothers' designs and the buildings of Oscar Niemeyer or the *Spatial Reliefs* of the constructivist sculptor Hélio Oiticia also suggests an artistic inspiration. Thus, it should not come as any surprise that while Fernando and Humberto present their work as dealing with imperfection,[45] they also claim that their utmost objective is structural perfection:[46] 'We really want to make objects very perfect, very minimalistic, and we never achieve that situation.'[47]

This dual commitment to artistic fragmentation and functionalist perfection reveals that this group of objects is not set apart from the rest of the oeuvre as radically as it might first appear. They are long preceded by a series of complex terracotta sculptures that Humberto created in the early 1980s from a juxtaposition of tapered boards. The *Desconfortáveis* series of 1989 also featured a number of chairs with clear, more or less geometric forms; while the *Fitas* (Strips) coffee table of 1993, with its stringing together of riveted aluminium strips, constitutes a link between the recurring theme of material densification and that of the flexed surface. In addition, there are a number of objects in the brothers' oeuvre that combine the basic form of a simple flexed plane made of synthetic material with the motif of the objet trouvé. In fact, some of the pieces in question are key works that introduced highly innovative

Favela armchair, a mural and, to the left, a small garden designed by Fernando and Humberto Campana for the JWT agency in São Paulo. *Favela*-Sessel, ein Wandbild und links eine kleine Gartenanlage von Fernando und Humberto Campana für die Agentur JWT in São Paulo.

von Möbeln, Leuchten und Büroaccessoires aus gebogenen Kunststoff- oder Metallflächen, die hauptsächlich zwischen 1997 und 2001 entstand. Einige dieser eher rational konstruierten Gegenstände wurden tatsächlich zur Serienreife entwickelt, selbst wenn es am Ende nur bei kleineren Auflagen blieb: der Sessel *Cone* (Trichter), den Edra produziert, die Leuchte *Jequitiba* (benannt nach einer Baumart) und das Regal *Labirinto* (Labyrinth) für zwei brasilianische Firmen sowie der für das New Yorker MoMA entwickelte Beistelltisch *Inflável* (Aufblasbar). Als Campana-Entwürfe sind diese Objekte zunächst kaum zu erkennen, denn die klaren geometrischen Formen aus glatten Industriematerialien wirken im Kontrast zum übrigen Werk merkwürdig kalt. Scheinbar unvermittelt taucht hier eine formale Beziehung zum funktionalistischen Industriedesign auf, wie es in Brasilien erst ab 1964 nach dem Vorbild der Hochschule für Gestaltung Ulm gelehrt wurde.[44] Die Verwandtschaft der Entwürfe mit Bauten Oscar Niemeyers oder den *Spatial Reliefs* des konstruktivistischen Bildhauers Hélio Oiticia legt jedoch auch eine künstlerische Inspiration nahe. So verwundert es nicht, dass Fernando und Humberto zwar einerseits betonen, dass ihre Arbeit »von der Unvollkommenheit« handele,[45] doch andererseits sagen, dass es ihnen in erster Linie um konstruktive Perfektion gehe.[46] »Wir wollen Objekte wirklich ganz perfekt machen, ganz minimalistisch, und diesen Zustand erreichen wir nie.«[47]

Das doppelte Bekenntnis sowohl zu künstlerischer Fragmentierung als auch zum Streben nach funktionalistischer Perfektion hebt diese Gruppe von Objekten jedoch nicht so radikal vom übrigen Werk ab, wie es zunächst den Anschein hat. Ihnen weit voraus ging eine Reihe von Terrakottaplastiken, die Humberto Anfang der 1980er Jahre als komplexe Gebilde aus gegeneinander gesetzten, spitz auslaufenden Flächen formte. 1989 entstanden dann in der Reihe der *Desconfortáveis* auch einige Stühle mit klaren, mehr oder minder geometrischen Flächen. Der Couchtisch *Fitas* (Bänder) verknüpfte 1993 in der Aneinanderreihung genieteter Aluminiumstreifen das immer wiederkehrende Thema der Materialverdichtung mit dem der gebogenen Fläche. Zudem gibt es einige Objekte, die die schlichte Form einer einfachen, gebogenen Kunststofffläche mit dem Sujet des Objet Trouvé kombinieren. Tatsächlich handelt es sich dabei um Schlüsselwerke, die innovative und erfolgreiche Ideen einführten. Das erste von ihnen besteht aus einem Stück Antirutschmatte, das über ein schlichtes Drahtgestell gebogen ist – die Leuchte *Estela* (Stele) von 1996, die ein Jahr später in das Programm des italienischen Herstellers Oluce aufgenommen wurde. Das gummiartige Ethylenvinylacetat (EVA), das die Campanas hier erstmals verwendeten, ist an sich ein befremdliches, haptisch unangenehmes Material. Fernando und Humberto aber nutzen nicht nur die funktionalen Qualitäten der Matte, ihre Transparenz, Wärme-

44 In 1964, the Escola Superior de Desenho Industrial was founded in Rio de Janeiro as South America's first academy of design, featuring a curriculum based on that of the Ulm School of Design. A number of the instructors in Rio de Janeiro had also come from Ulm.

45 'Our work is about imperfection.' Humberto Campana, interview in *Campane di Campanas,* a film directed by Thais Stoklos, 2005.

46 'The most important thing that we always wanted in our work [is] perfection—perfection in terms of structure.' Fernando Campana, interview by the author.

47 Humberto Campana, video interview, *Dezeen,* 3 Nov. 2008, http://www.dezeen.com/2008/11/03/campana-brothers-video-interview-1/.

44 1964 wurde in Rio de Janeiro Südamerikas erste Designhochschule, die Escola Superior de Desenho Industrial gegründet, deren Lehrplan auf dem der Hochschule für Gestaltung Ulm aufbaute. Auch etliche Lehrer waren von Ulm nach Rio de Janeiro gekommen.

45 »Our work is about the imperfection.« Humberto Campana im Film *Campane di Campanas* von Thais Stoklos, 2005.

46 »The most important thing that we always wanted in our work [is] the perfection – perfection in terms of the structure.« Fernando Campana in einem Interview mit dem Autor, a.a.O. (Anm. 1).

47 Humberto Campana in einem Video-Interview, *Dezeen,* 3. Nov. 2008, http://www.dezeen.com/2008/11/03/campana-brothers-video-interview-1/.

and successful ideas. The first of these – the *Estela* (Stele) lamp of 1996, which was taken up the following year by Italian manufacturer Oluce – consists of a piece of anti-slip matting that is folded over a simple wire frame. The rubber-like ethylene vinyl acetate (EVA) of the mat, used here by the Campanas for the first time, is itself a rather off-putting and haptically unpleasant material; yet Fernando and Humberto not only make use of its functional qualities – its transparency, heat resistance, and pliability – but also bring a shine to the cheap and the ugly in the truest sense of the word, thus realizing the lesson they have been taught by their environment: 'The beauty of São Paulo is in its ugliness, and this ugliness forces you to find beauty.'[48] Later they utilized rolls and bundles of EVA for the upholstery of their *Sushi* furniture line, in which this versatile material sparks a veritable firework of colours and forms.

Installation for the *Projeto ABC* exhibition in 1991 at the Pinacoteca do Estado in São Paulo. Installation für die Ausstellung *Projeto ABC,* 1991 in der Pinacoteca do Estado in São Paulo.

When the Campanas develop their products in collaboration with a company, they often work with motifs that they have already explored in one-off pieces and limited editions. The two *Batuque* vases for Cappellini, a series of necklaces, earrings, and rings for H. Stern, the line of recyclable plastic shoes and bags for Brazilian fashion label Grendene, the vases, bowls, and other accessories for Alessi, the *Drosera* 'wall pockets' for Vitra (named after a genus of carnivorous plants), and a growing number of furniture pieces for Edra – all of these are important examples of the process by which they employ, in varying degrees of apparency, motifs that have already become trademarks of their experimental and limited-edition work. But while some of these industrial products are thoroughly convincing, others are recognizable – and in some cases even blatantly – as adaptations of the tried and tested model. The most successful seem to be those that are manufactured by hand – which once again attests to their sculptural origin – yet even these can end up a mere backdrop. Such was the case when, in the design of their *Ideal House* for the Cologne fair, the Campanas re-translated the criss-cross pastiche of the superimposed wooden slats of the *Favela* armchair back into a shack, as a metaphor for a dwelling place that everyone can build for themselves. However, the strongest works emerge when Fernando and Humberto approach a theme free from any concerns as to practical utility. In this regard, the wall reliefs for the Moss Gallery in New York and for the foyer of the JWT advertising agency in São Paulo, which embrace the South American tradition of murals, and the stage design for a production of Sergei Prokofiev's musical fable *Peter and the Wolf* are some examples from a long series of purely artistic works that border the design career of the Campanas.

Relationships: Massimo Morozzi, Nazareth Pacheco, Andrea Branzi

Throughout the Campanas' career, there are a number of individuals who have not only left enduring marks on their oeuvre but have also influenced the direction it was to take at certain points along the way. Of special significance to their work is their relationship with the Italian furniture manufacturer Edra and its art director Massimo Morozzi. Morozzi is credited with having been the first to discover the international market potential of the brothers' ideas; while their *Vermelha* and *Favela* armchairs, which are manufactured by Edra, have become their 'calling cards' in contacts with

48 Humberto Campana, interview by author.

beständigkeit und Biegsamkeit. Sie bringen auch das Billige und Hässliche im wahrsten Sinne des Wortes zum Leuchten – ganz so, wie ihre Umgebung es sie gelehrt hat: »São Paulos Schönheit liegt in seiner Hässlichkeit, und die Hässlichkeit zwingt dich, Schönheit zu finden.«[48] Später verwendeten sie das EVA in Rollen und Bündeln für die Polsterung ihrer so genannten *Sushi*-Möbel, bei denen dieses vielseitige Material ein wahres Feuerwerk an Farben und Formen entfacht.

Wenn die Campanas ihre Produkte in Kooperation mit einer Firma entwickeln, dann arbeiten sie oft mit Motiven, die sie in Unikaten und Kleinserien bereits erprobt haben. Das gilt für die zwei Vasen *Batuque* (Trommler) für Cappellini, eine Serie von Colliers, Ohrringen und Ringen für den brasilianischen Juwelier H. Stern, für eine Serie recycelbarer Plastikschuhe und -taschen der brasilianischen Firma Grendene, für Vasen, Schalen und andere Accessoires von Alessi, die »Wandtaschen« *Drosera* (benannt nach einer Gattung fleischfressender Pflanzen) für Vitra und eine wachsende Zahl von Möbeln für Edra, um die Wichtigsten zu nennen.

Mehr oder weniger offensichtlich werden hier Motive verwendet, die in Experimenten, Einzelstücken und Kleinserien zu Markenzeichen geworden sind. Während manche der Ergebnisse unverhohlene, mitunter plumpe Adaptionen der bewährten Muster bleiben, sind andere durchaus überzeugend. Am gelungensten erscheinen diejenigen, die in Handarbeit hergestellt sind, was einmal mehr ihren skulpturalen Ursprung bestätigt. Allerdings können auch diese zur bloßen Kulisse geraten, wie beim Entwurf ihres *Ideal House* für die Kölner Messe, für den die Campanas das Prinzip der quer übereinander liegenden Bretter des *Favela*-Sessels zurückübersetzten in eine Bretterbude als Metapher für eine Behausung, die sich jeder selbst bauen kann. Die stärksten Arbeiten entstehen dort, wo Fernando und Humberto völlig frei vom Gedanken an den praktischen Nutzen mit einem Thema umgehen: Wandreliefs für die New Yorker Galerie Moss und für das Foyer der Werbeagentur JWT in São Paulo, die die südamerikanische Tradition der *murales* aufgreifen, und Figuren für das Bühnenbild zu Sergei Prokofiews musikalischem Märchen *Peter und der Wolf* sind Beispiele aus der langen Reihe rein künstlerischer Werke, die die designerische Laufbahn der Campanas säumen.

Beziehungen – Massimo Morozzi, Nazareth Pacheco, Andrea Branzi

Es gibt im Leben der Campanas Personen, die im Werk nicht nur nachhaltige Spuren hinterlassen haben, sondern an gewissen Punkten auch dessen Richtung beeinflussten. Eine besondere Bedeutung hat ihre Beziehung zum italienischen Möbelhersteller Edra und dessen Art Director Massimo Morozzi. Ihm kommt das Verdienst zu, als erster in den Möbelideen der Brüder das Potential für den internationalen Markt entdeckt zu haben. Die Sessel *Vermelha* und *Favela* aus der Edra-Produktion wurden zu ihren »Visitenkarten« bei allen weiteren Firmen. Zusammen mit Morozzi entwickelten sie den *Vermelha*-Sessel, ihr erstes serienreifes »Polster«-Möbel, und auch ihre ersten konventionell gepolsterten Möbel: 2002 das Sofa *Boa* und ab 2005 die *Historia Naturalis* genannte Gruppe mit den Sofas *Kaiman Jacarè* (benannt nach dem Brillenkaiman) und *Aster Papposus* (benannt nach einer Seesternart).[49]

48 Humberto Campana im Interview, a.a.O. (Anm. 1).
49 Der Titel der Gruppe nimmt auf die 1648 erschienene *Historia Naturalis Brasiliae* Bezug – ein in seinen detaillierten Beschreibungen und Illustrationen einzigartiges Zeugnis über die Naturgeschichte Brasiliens.

other companies. Together with Morozzi they developed the *Vermelha* armchair – their first furniture piece intended for serial production – as well as the *Boa* sofa of 2002 and the *Historia Naturalis* group, which was begun in 2005 with the *Kaiman Jacarè* (named after the spectacled caiman) and *Aster Papposus* (named after a species of starfish) sofas.[49]

With these sofas, the Campanas did not proceed from found materials as they usually do but followed the impressions they had gleaned from Brazil's animal kingdom. The studio in São Paulo then rendered these impressions in small fabric models, which served as the basis for their serial production by Edra. Thus, although running counter to Fernando and Humberto's usual work method, the success of these seating and lounging landscapes is primarily due to the free plastic design Morozzi allowed them to pursue as well as the joint intuitive probing of the theme.[50] The design of the *Boa* sofa, with which the series was launched, makes a formal reference to two important early works of the brothers: the *Bob* armchair and their first museum exhibition, entitled *Projeto ABC,* which was held in 1991 at the Pinacoteca do Estado in São Paulo. The museum had originally invited artist Nazareth Pacheco, a friend of Humberto's, to create new works for a solo exhibition. At the sculptor's recommendation, the Campanas were added to the show and given a room of their own in which they exhibited four of their works. As could be expected, it being one of the most important museums in Brazil, Fernando and Humberto provided a programmatic exhibition as well as a reference to their fundamental artistic impulses. Above all, however, their installation presented itself as an incredibly powerful and autonomous work. Unfortunately, only photos remain of the piece, depicting a surreal three-dimensional still life made of four objects. The first is a large aluminium cone, resembling a cornucopia or a quiver, which rests on the floor in the middle of the room, a wriggle of dark velvet-covered worms protruding from it. Positioned nearby are four wooden piles, encircled at half-height by a kind of snake upholstered in purple velvet. Only the third object resembles – albeit remotely – a piece of furniture: a beanbag covered with purple velvet, which is nevertheless too big to sit on and comes across more as an amorphous mass. Finally, a monumental bone, covered in light blue velvet, leans against the front wall and is the only clearly recognizable motif, seemingly citing Claes Oldenburg's oversized *Softenings* while simultaneously acting as a portentous reference to Andrade's *Cannibal Manifesto.*

The biomorphous forms that the Campanas explored in this exhibition subsequently re-emerged in the furniture they designed for Edra: the snake reappeared as the *Boa* sofa, while the bone and beanbag can be viewed as forerunners to the idea of enlargement that comes into play not only in *Boa* but in *Kaiman Jacarè* and *Aster Papposus* as well. In a similar fashion, the motif of knotted branches evolved into the first model of the *Vermelha* armchair, developed for a 1993 gallery exhibition in São Paulo. Half a decade later, Edra came out with its serial version.

The fact that Morozzi recognized the outstanding creative talent of the Campanas is probably not in the least due to the keen eye he developed as founding member of the design group Archizoom. After all, there is an affinity between the works of the Campanas and those of Andrea Branzi, who had established Archizoom in 1966, and which becomes immediately apparent upon comparing

Collezione Sugheri, designed by Andrea Branzi for the Galleria Clio Calvi e Rudy Volpi in 2007 and produced by Cirva Massilia.
Collezione Sugheri, 2007 von Andrea Branzi für die Galleria Clio Calvi e Rudy Volpi entworfen, produziert von Cirva Massilia.

Hierfür gingen sie nicht von vorgefundenen Materialien aus, sondern folgten Eindrücken aus der brasilianischen Tierwelt, die das Studio in São Paulo in kleine Stoffmodelle als Grundlage für Edras Serienproduktion übertrug. Dass dieses Verfahren entgegen Fernandos und Humbertos üblicher Arbeitsweise so erfolgreich war, ist zum einen der freien plastischen Gestaltung zu verdanken, die Morozzi ihnen für diese Sitz-Liege-Landschaften ermöglichte, und zum anderen dem gemeinsamen, intuitiven Herantasten an das Thema.[50] Mit dem Sofa *Boa* bezog sich diese Gestaltung auf zwei wichtige Frühwerke: auf den Sessel *Bob* und auf die erste Museumsausstellung der Campanas 1991 unter dem Titel *Projeto ABC* in der Pinacoteca do Estado in São Paulo. Das Museum hatte ursprünglich Humbertos künstlerische Weggefährtin Nazareth Pacheco eingeladen, neue Werke für eine Einzelausstellung zu schaffen. Auf die Empfehlung der Bildhauerin hin kamen die Campanas mit vier Arbeiten hinzu, denen ein eigener Raum gewidmet wurde. Es mag zu erwarten gewesen sein, dass Fernando und Humberto in diesem Werk für eines der wichtigsten Museen Brasiliens etwas Programmatisches abliefern würden, das zugleich Bezug auf ihre grundlegenden künstlerischen Impulse nahm. Vor allem aber präsentierte sich ihre Installation als ungeheuer kraftvolle, unabhängige Arbeit. Leider existieren heute nur noch Fotos, die ein dreidimensionales, surreales Stillleben zeigen: Auf dem Boden liegt in der Mitte des Raums wie ein Füllhorn oder Köcher ein großer Aluminiumkegel, aus dem mit dunklem Samt bezogene Würmer ragen. In der Nähe stehen vier Holzpfähle, die auf halber Höhe von einer Art Schlange aus violettem Samtpolster umwunden sind. Das dritte Objekt erinnert zumindest entfernt an ein Möbel: ein mit violettem Samt bezogener Sitzsack, der zum Sitzen jedoch zu groß ist und eher als amorphe Masse wirkt. An der Stirnwand schließlich lehnt als einziges eindeutiges Motiv monumental vergrößert ein Knochen aus hellblauem Samtpolster, der Claes Oldenburgs überdimensionierte *Softenings* zu zitieren scheint und zugleich wie ein Menetekel auf Andrades' *Kannibalistisches Manifest* verweist.

Die biomorphen Formen, zu denen die Campanas in dieser Ausstellung fanden, tauchten später in Möbeln für Edra wieder auf: Das Motiv des Knäuels im Geäst verarbeiteten sie 1993 für eine Galerieausstellung in São Paulo zum ersten Modell des *Vermelha*-Sessels, den Edra fünf Jahre später in ein Serienprodukt übersetzte. Die Schlange erscheint Jahre später wieder als *Boa*-Sofa, und Knochen und »Sitzsack« lieferten die Idee der Vergrößerung, die bei *Boa, Kaiman Jacarè* und *Aster Papposus* zum Tragen kommt.

Dass der Architekt und Designer Morozzi die herausragende gestalterische Begabung der Campanas erkannte, ist wohl nicht zuletzt seinem Blick zu verdanken, den er als Gründungsmitglied der Gruppe Archizoom geschult hat. Immerhin existiert zwischen den Arbeiten der Campanas und denen Andrea Branzis, der 1966 der Initiator von Archizoom war, eine Verwandtschaft, die unmittelbar einleuchtet, wenn man Branzis *Animali Domestici* (Haustiere) einigen Geschöpfen der Campanas gegenüberstellt – etwa der Fruchtschale *Jabuticaba* (benannt nach einer tropischen Baumart) oder dem Stuhl *Taquaral* (Bambushain). Bei Branzi wie bei den Campanas entstehen Individualität und Vitalität aus einer Spannung zwischen künstlichen und organischen Elementen, zwischen Objet Trouvé und Konstruktion. Schon eine 1989 entstan-

49   The title of the group refers to the *Historia Naturalis Brasiliae,* a unique document of the natural history of Brazil, which was published in 1648 and includes detailed descriptions and illustrations.

50   See Morozzi's own account in 'Design under the Signs of Chaos and Order: The Campana Brothers and Their Collaboration with Edra', in this catalogue.

50   Vergleiche Morozzis Bericht »Design im Zeichen von Chaos und Ordnung« im vorliegenden Katalog.

Branzi's *Animali Domestici* (Domestic Animals) to a number of the Campanas' designs that take after wildlife: the *Jabuticaba* (named after a tropical tree species) fruit dish, for example, or the *Taquaral* (Bamboo Grove) chair. With both Branzi and the Campanas, individuality and vitality result from a tension between artificial and organic elements, between objet trouvé and construction. A 1989 series of solid wood seats with thick rubber beams as backrests is acknowledged by Humberto as having been inspired by Branzi. This piece later evolved into the first work in which the Campanas integrated finished products into their design: the *Martelo* (Hammer) chair, in which they replaced the original rubber beams with rubber mallets – an important precursor to their material discoveries of the ensuing years. To date, Fernando and Humberto have never met Branzi, but, time and again, when they encounter his works, they are struck by the similarities. Such was the case in 2000 when they collaborated with Venini on an edition of glass objects interlaced with branches that was commissioned by the Moss Gallery in New York and shortly thereafter saw a very similar design in an exhibition of Branzi's at the Fondation Cartier in Paris: 'Sometimes I think our works overlap each other,' says Humberto.[51]

A *congado* dance in Olímpia in the state of São Paulo.
Tanz eines *congado* in Olímpia im Bundesstaat São Paulo.

Sushi and Harumaki:
The Formation of New Materials

In their unexpected combinations of materials, the Campanas essentially follow the principle of collage. Originally from the realm of folk art, this technique was rediscovered by Cubism, enhanced by Surrealism, and then taken as a point of departure for Pop Art. To this day it remains the most frequently applied stylistic means for expressing rupture and fragmentation. What distinguishes the brothers' recurring series of works primarily focusing on Japanese topoi, however, is that they conceptually go a step further and combine fragments into a single substance.

This series of works, which began in 2002 with the brothers' *Sushi* line, has its origins a year earlier when Fernando and Humberto were invited to outfit Oscar Niemeyer's OCA Pavilion in São Paulo for a party that fashion magazine *Vogue* was putting on together with Tactel in order to promote the latter's eponymous line of nylon fabric. Valued for its haptic qualities, the Campanas used the fabric as covering for the partitions they designed as well as for two types of stools, which introduced new terminologies into their work. For the first type of stool, they covered variously sized wooden blocks with the material, underneath which they distributed small irregularly shaped pads that made the surface appear blotched with hive-like welts. In 2007, they took up this idea once again for the *Dado Couro* (Leather Cube) stool: this time they covered a wooden core with soft leather, under which coconut fibres were used to give the appearance of a similar blister-like rash. The second type of stool designed for the *Vogue* party was a round pouffe, whose upholstery consisted of long, tightly bundled nylon strips of various colours. This stool was directly translated into the 2002 *Sushi* armchair, which the Campanas designed for Edra and which consists of tufts of various types of woven textiles, felt, and EVA stretched over a polyurethane core. Similar bundles of textiles and synthetic mats were later used to create the *Sushi* fruit dish, the *Vitória Régia* stool (named after a water lily found in the Amazon), the *Sushi 3* chair and *Sushi 4* armchair, and the *Buriti* vase (which takes its name from a type of palm tree).

Rolled bundles of mixed fabrics – this time cut into discs – form the thin, colourfully patterned upholstery of the *Sushi 2* chair of

51 Humberto Campana, interview by the author.

dene Serie massiver Holzsitze mit dicken Gummibalken als Rückenlehnen war, so bestätigt Humberto, von Andrea Branzi inspiriert. Daraus entstand auch der erste Entwurf, in den die Campanas fertige Gegenstände integrierten: der Stuhl *Martelo* (Hammer), bei dem sie die Gummibalken durch Gummihämmer ersetzten – eine echte Initialzündung für ihre Materialfindungen der folgenden Jahre. Fernando und Humberto haben Branzi bis heute nie getroffen, aber wenn sie seinen Werken begegnen, fallen ihnen die Gemeinsamkeiten immer wieder auf. So etwa 2000, als sie mit Venini eine Edition von Glasobjekten mit Ästen für die New Yorker Galerie Moss anfertigten und kurz darauf einen ganz ähnlichen Entwurf in einer Ausstellung Branzis in der Pariser Fondation Cartier sahen: »Manchmal denke ich, unsere Werke überschneiden sich.«[51]

Sushi und Harumaki: die Entstehung neuer Materialien

In den abrupten Kombinationen von Materialien verfahren die Campanas nach dem Prinzip der Collage. Ursprünglich aus der Volkskunst stammend wurde diese Technik vom Kubismus wiederentdeckt, vom Surrealismus etabliert und dann zu einem Ausgangspunkt der Pop-Art. Bis heute ist sie das häufigste Stilmittel, um Entzweiung und Fragmentierung zu vermitteln. In den 2002 mit den so genannten *Sushis* beginnenden und vorwiegend auf japanische Topoi verweisenden Werkserien gehen die Campanas konzeptionell allerdings einen Schritt weiter und setzen die Fragmente zu einem einzigen Werkstoff zusammen.

Ihren Ursprung hatte die Serie *Sushi* schon im Jahr 2001, als Fernando und Humberto eingeladen waren, Oscar Niemeyers OCA Pavillon in São Paulo für

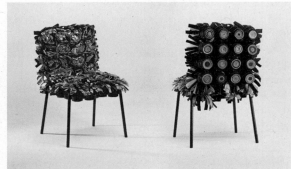

The *Sushi 3* chair, 2002.
Der Stuhl *Sushi 3*, 2002.

ein Fest einzurichten, das das Modemagazin *Vogue* zusammen mit der Firma Tactel veranstaltete, um für deren gleichnamigen Nylonstoff zu werben. Die Campanas nutzten das wegen seiner haptischen Qualitäten geschätzte Textil für die Bespannung von Raumteilern sowie für zwei Arten von Sitzhockern, mit denen sie neue Terminologien in ihr Werk einführten. Für die eine Sorte Hocker bespannten sie unterschiedlich große Quader mit dem Stoff und verteilten darunter unregelmäßige kleine Polster, so dass sich die Oberfläche wie mit Quaddeln übersät wölbte. 2007 griffen sie diese Idee für ihren Sitzhocker *Dado Couro* (Lederwürfel) wieder auf; diesmal bespannten sie einen Holzkern mit weichem Leder, unter dem sich aus Kokosfasern ein ähnlicher blasenartiger Ausschlag bildete. Die anderen Hocker für die *Vogue*-Party waren runde Puffs, deren Polsterung aus langen, dicht gebüschelten, verschiedenfarbigen Streifen des Nylons bestand. Die direkte Übersetzung der *Vogue*-Hocker in ein Produkt erfolgte 2002 für Edra mit dem Sessel *Sushi*, der aus Büscheln verschiedener Textilgewebe, Filz und EVA über einem Polyurethankern besteht. Aus solchen gebündelten Textilien und Kunststoffmatten gingen später die Fruchtschale *Sushi* hervor, der nach einer Amazonas-Seerose benannte Hocker *Vitória Régia,* der Stuhl *Sushi 3,* der Polstersessel *Sushi 4* und die nach einer Palmenart benannte Vase *Buriti*.

51 Humberto Campana im Interview mit dem Autor, a.a.O. (Anm. 1).

2002, the *Sonia Diniz* easy chair of 2003 (named after a well-known Brazilian design dealer), and the *Harumaki* chair of 2004/5. Here the Campanas returned to the motif of contiguously arrayed discs that they had employed earlier in their *3 em 1* chair. The mix of colours emphasizes the variety of the materials; and since only their cut edges remain visible, it is as if they had been placed under a magnifying glass, thus resembling the computer-generated images that are used to explain fractal geometry and chaos theory. The series culminated in the *Tokyo Garden* centrepiece, which Humberto produced in 2005 for the Japanese magazine *Casa Brutus*. The magazine had invited various designers to create their ideal garden and Humberto used a colourful rolled synthetic fabric to construct a miniature one atop seven long-stemmed wine glasses. The water-filled glasses form miniature pools with small sprigs of dill floating on the surface. Standing on its glass pedestals, the object presents itself as a near-perfect encapsulation of Japanese aesthetics: controlled and staged nature, the rock garden with pebbles raked in wave patterns, the animation of artificial universes.

Computerized image of a cluster of Mandelbrot sets (named after Benoît Mandelbrot) as an illustration of chaos theory.
Computergrafische Darstellung einer Mandelbrot-Menge (nach Benoît Mandelbrot) zur Illustration der Chaostheorie.

Antibodies:
Back to Nature, with Plastic

While the *Sushis* and *Harumakis* can be read as a mix of materials, frozen in the process of being stirred and yet to be transformed into a homogeneous substance, the wicker-and-plastic objects of the *Transplastics* series, produced since 2005, appear as unsuccessful hybrids or androgynous beings that have been spawned through transplantations. Humberto describes the series as originating 'in a vision we imagined: what if one day the earth was covered in plastic? Plants would have to adapt to this plastic soil.'[52] In fact, the wickerwork of these furniture pieces, lamps, and accessory items sprawls like living tissue over plastic chairs, water canisters, or rubber tyres. However, in *Trans...chair* – an armchair created in late 2007 for an exhibition at the Cooper-Hewitt National Design Museum in New York – this relationship is turned on its head. Here, the wicker chair seems to have been out-and-out invaded by plastic wares that have forced brightly coloured blossoms out of their 'host'. The first public presentation of the still incomplete series was held at the Albion Gallery in London during the summer of 2007. The exhibition featured several pieces of furniture, such as the *TransRock* seating landscape and the *Una Famiglia* three-seater, as well as a number of light fixtures. In most of them, the wicker seems to emanate directly from the shape of the mass-produced plastic objects it envelops and then to detach itself from them, acquiring a life of its own. The highlight of the exhibition was a number of lamps in which the wickerwork seems to have digested the plastic object. Here the natural fibre develops in entirely irregular shapes so as to form, with the support of underlying wire frames, an island accompanied by a few floating clouds and two meteorites. The incorporated and processed plastic protrudes from their surfaces as white luminous globes, reminiscent of the strange mushrooms that pop up out of the ground in Hergé's *The Adventures of Tintin* story 'The Shooting Star'. These lamps – so-called even though it is uncertain whether the function of lighting ever played a role in their figuration – appear to be allegories

The *Trans...chair* for the Cooper-Hewitt National Design Museum in New York, 2007.
Der *Trans...chair* für das Cooper-Hewitt National Design Museum in New York, 2007.

Ein ebenfalls gerollter Stoffmix, allerdings in flache Scheiben geschnitten, bildet die dünnen, bunt gemusterten Polsterungen beim Stuhl *Sushi 2* aus dem Jahr 2002, beim Sessel *Sonia Diniz* aus dem Jahr 2003 (benannt nach einer bekannten brasilianischen Designhändlerin) und dem *Harumaki*-Stuhl von 2004/05. Hier greifen die Campanas auf das Motiv der aneinandergereihten Scheiben zurück, das sie schon im *3 em 1* verwendet hatten. Verschiedene Farben betonen die Unterschiedlichkeit der Materialien, und da nur deren Schnittkanten sichtbar bleiben, erscheinen sie wie unter einem Vergrößerungsglas, wobei sie an jene computergenerierten Bilder erinnern, die fraktale Geometrie und Chaostheorie erklären. Ihren Abschluss fand die Serie in dem Tafelaufsatz *Tokyo Garden,* der 2005 für das japanische Magazin *Casa Brutus* entstand, das verschiedene Designer eingeladen hatte, ihren idealen Garten zu entwerfen. Humberto legte aus buntem, gerolltem Kunststoffmaterial einen Miniaturgarten auf sieben hochstieligen Weingläsern an. Die mit Wasser gefüllten Gläser bilden Teiche, in denen kleine Dillzweige schwimmen. Auf seinen gläsernen Sockeln präsentiert sich das Objekt als Skulptur – eine geradezu perfekte Übertragung der japanischen Ästhetik mit ihrer kontrollierten und inszenierten Natur, den wellenförmig geharkten Steingärten und der Animation künstlicher Welten.

Antikörper: mit Plastik zurück zur Natur

Während man aus den *Sushis* und *Harumakis* noch das unvollendete »Verrühren« unterschiedlicher Materialien zu einem homogenen Werkstoff lesen kann, wirken die seit 2005 entstehenden *Transplastics* aus Korbgeflecht und Plastik wie verunglückte Hybriden oder zwitterhafte Wesen, die aus Transplantationen erwachsen sind. Den Ursprung der *Transplastics* erklärt Humberto als eine »Phantasie, in der wir uns vorstellten: Wie wäre es, wenn die Erde eines Tages mit Plastik bedeckt wäre? Die Pflanzen würden sich diesem Kunststoffboden anpassen müssen.«[52] Tatsächlich wuchert das Korbgeflecht dieser Möbel, Leuchten und Accessoires wie lebendes Gewebe über Kunststoffstühle, Wasserkanister oder Gummireifen. In dem Ende 2007 entstandenen *Trans...chair,* den sie anlässlich einer Ausstellung für das Cooper-Hewitt National Design Museum in New York anfertigten, kehrt sich dieses Verhältnis jedoch um. Hier scheint eine Invasion von Plastikwaren den Korbsessel regelrecht befallen zu haben, um aus dem »Wirtskörper« bunte Blüten zu treiben.

Die erste öffentliche Präsentation der damals noch unvollständigen Serie in einer Ausstellung der Londoner Galerie Albion von Juni bis August 2007 zeigte mehrere Möbel wie die Sitzlandschaft *TransRock* und den Dreisitzer *Una Famiglia* sowie eine Reihe unterschiedlicher Leuchten. Bei den meisten der gezeigten Objekte setzt das Korbgeflecht die Formen der Plastikartikel zunächst fort, um sich dann aber von ihnen zu lösen und ein Eigenleben zu entfalten. Den Höhepunkt der Serie bildete eine Reihe von Leuchten, in denen das Korbgeflecht den Kunststoff bereits verdaut zu haben scheint. Hier findet die Naturfaser zu völliger Unregelmäßigkeit zurück und nimmt, von darunter liegenden Drahtgestellen gehalten, die Gestalt einer Insel mit ein paar schwebenden Wolken und Meteoriten an. Aus ihnen quillt das einverleibte und verarbeitete Plastik in Gestalt weißer, kugeliger Leuchtkörper,

52 Muniz, a.a.O., S. 28 (Anm. 4).

52 Humerto Campana, in Muniz, 'Campana Brothers', p. 28.

of the four elements: water, earth, fire, and air. Thus, after their twenty-year odyssey through the seas of design, the Campanas once again dropped anchor in the territory of art and, in the process, arrived back at their beginnings: 'It has taken me twenty years to mature this idea and to take back on this material that appealed to me in my first steps as a designer', Humberto has said, speaking of the wicker that features throughout the *Transplastics* series.[53]

Already in 1997, with their *Mixed Series,* the Campanas had begun articulating their conceptual combinations of organic and inorganic, natural and industrial, warm and cold materials. One of the first results of their work with this kind of mixed media was the *Animado* (Animated) rug in which they combined a cow hide with synthetic turf. In the *Shark* armchair of the same series, designed in 2000, a bent polycarbonate board forms the seat and backrest and is edged with a border of woven cane that connects it to a stainless steel frame. This piece not only merges the clean lines of Brazilian modernism with the sensuality of traditional handicrafts but also constitutes a link between Humberto's early wicker objects and the brothers' recent *Transplastics* series.

In their most recent installations the Campanas dispense altogether with the contrast between natural and artificial materials. In a group of three seating islands entitled *Diamantina,* which the brothers produced for the 2008 Design Miami show in which they were presented with the Designer of the Year award, the wickerwork seems to break open in numerous places, like the blossoms of a cactus, with luminous violet-hued amethysts adorning the spiky fringes. Diamantina, a small town in the Brazilian highlands, which has been an important diamond-mining site since the seventeenth century and was added in 1999 to UNESCO's World Heritage List due to its rich Baroque architecture, is representative of Brazil's hidden and often endangered treasures. Thus, alluding to Jules Verne's famous novel, Fernando describes the *Diamantina* installation as 'our own journey to the centre of the earth',[54] which in fact is a journey that began already in 1990 with the *Natureza Morta* screen that was made of charcoal.

Today, wickerwork provides the brothers with a nearly unlimited playing field for plastic design and with even more freedom than the upholstery of the *Historia Naturalis* series. After the wires, tubes, pieces of wood, layers of paper, and clusters of stuffed animals and dolls, the Campanas have found their way to a material that always retains – even in freely formed objects – the connotation of furniture while allowing – vis-à-vis the relationship between form and function – the transcendence of any and all boundaries separating design from fine art.

A tree root in the Amazon rainforest in the state of Pará, photographed by Fernando Campana, 2005.
Eine Baumwurzel im Amazonas-Urwald im Bundesstaat Pará, fotografiert von Fernando Campana, 2005.

One of the three *Diamantina* seating units for Design Miami, shortly before completion, 2008.
Eine der drei *Diamantina*-Sitzinseln für Design Miami, kurz vor der Fertigstellung, 2008.

die an jene seltsamen Pilze erinnern, die in Hergés »Tim und Struppi«-Geschichte *Der Geheimnisvolle Stern* überall aus dem Boden schießen. Diese Leuchten, sofern die Funktion der Beleuchtung überhaupt noch eine Rolle spielt, scheinen wie Allegorien der Elemente Wasser, Erde, Feuer und Luft.

Nach ihrer langen Odyssee durch das Design werfen die Campanas hier ein weiteres Mal Anker als Künstler und sind zugleich wieder bei ihren Anfängen angelangt: »Es hat zwanzig Jahre gebraucht, um diese Idee zur Reife zu bringen und zu diesem Material, das mich [schon] bei meinen ersten Schritten als Designer ansprach, zurückzukehren.«[53] Ihre konzeptionellen Verknüpfungen von organischen und anorganischen, natürlichen und industriellen oder warmen und kalten Materialien hatten die Campanas bereits in der ab 1997 verfolgten *Mixed Series* (Gemischte Serie) artikuliert. Eines der ersten Ergebnisse ihrer Arbeit mit dieser Form von Mixed Media war der Teppich *Animado* (Belebt), in dem sie Kuhfell und Kunstrasen miteinander konfrontierten. Beim Sessel *Shark* (Hai), den sie 2000 für dieselbe Serie entwarfen, säumt eine Borte aus Binsengeflecht die geknickte Polycarbonatfläche für Sitz und Rückenlehne und verbindet diese mit einem Edelstahlgestell, wodurch Flexibilität und Komfort angedeutet werden. Das Objekt schlägt sowohl die Brücke zum brasilianischen Modernismus als auch zu Humbertos Flechthandwerk aus seinen kunsthandwerklichen Anfängen und den *Transplastics* aus der jüngsten Zeit.

Für ihre letzten, Ende 2008 entstandenen Installationen verzichteten die Campanas ganz auf den Kontrast mit künstlichen Materialien. In der aus drei Sitzinseln bestehenden Gruppe *Diamantina,* die die Campanas für eine Präsentation auf der Messe Design Miami anlässlich ihrer Auszeichnung als »Designer of the Year« fertigten, scheint das Korbgeflecht wie Blüten eines Kaktus an mehreren Stellen aufzubrechen. Die stachelig abstehenden Korbfransen fassen violett leuchtende Amethyste ein. Diamantina, eine Kleinstadt im brasilianischen Bergland, die seit dem 17. Jahrhundert ein bedeutender Fundort von Diamanten ist und wegen ihrer reichen barocken Sakralarchitektur seit einigen Jahren zum Unesco-Weltkulturerbe gehört, steht stellvertretend für die verborgenen und oft gefährdeten Kostbarkeiten Brasiliens. In Anspielung auf Jules Vernes Roman beschreibt Fernando die *Diamantina*-Installation als »unsere Reise zum Mittelpunkt der Erde«.[54] Doch begonnen hatte diese Reise eigentlich schon 1990 mit dem aus Kohle gefertigten Wandschirm *Natureza Morta.*

Heute bietet das Korbgeflecht den Brüdern ein nahezu unbeschränktes Spielfeld plastischer Gestaltung – freier noch als die Polster der *Historia Naturalis.* Nach den Drähten, Schläuchen, Holzstücken, Papierlagen und Plüschtier- oder Puppenhaufen haben die Campanas hier zu einem Material gefunden, das auch in noch so frei geformten Objekten stets die Konnotation des Möbels behält, im Hinblick auf Form und Funktion aber erlaubt, jede Grenze zur bildenden Kunst zu überschreiten.

53 Humberto Campana, interview in press release for the exhibition *Transplastic,* Albion Gallery, London 2007.
54 Fernando Campana, interview by the author.

53 Humberto Campana, in: Pressemitteilung der Albion Gallery zur Ausstellung *Transplastic,* London, 2007.
54 Fernando Campana im Interview mit dem Autor, a.a.O. (Anm. 1).

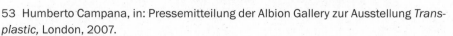

study for the *Kaiman Jacarè* sofa
Studie für das Sofa *Kaiman Jacarè*
model Modell
2006
16×70×43 cm (variable variabel)

textile figure Stofffigur
Mandacaru Curupira
(Little Forest Spirit Cactus
Kleiner Waldgeist-Kaktus)
prototype for Prototyp für:
Alessi spa, Omegna Crusinallo
2006
41×25×25 cm (variable variabel)

fruit bowl Fruchtschale
Costela (Rib Rippe)
one-off piece Unikat
1990
22×54×22 cm

sofa Sofa
Kaiman Jacarè
serial model Serienmodell:
Edra spa, Perignano
2006
100 × 700 × 500 cm (variable variabel)

wastebasket Papierkorb
Untitled Ohne Titel
study Studie
2008
52×38×36 cm

screen Wandschirm
Amarelo (Yellow Gelb) (detail Detail)
one-off piece Unikat
2006
225 × 160 × 30 cm (variable variabel)

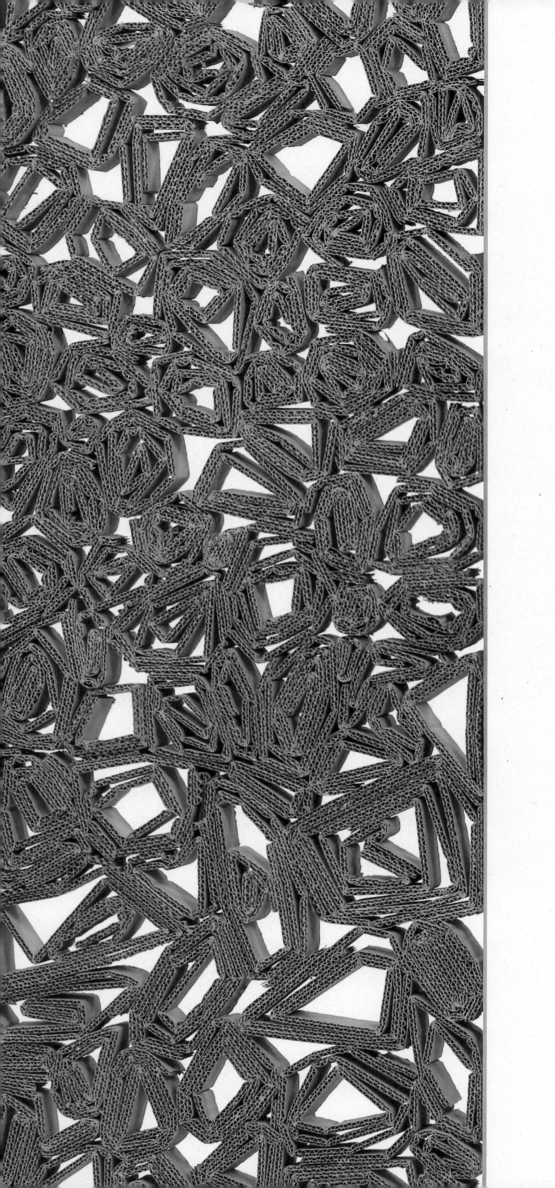

panel Tafel (detail Detail)　　　chair Stuhl
Papel II (Paper II Papier II)　Untitled Ohne Titel
one-off piece Unikat　　　　　study Studie
2001　　　　　　　　　　　　　2006
180×50×5 cm　　　　　　　　87×76×32 cm

sculpture Plastik
Untitled Ohne Titel
1982
80×40×40 cm

**Leben unter dem Halbmond –
Die Wohnkulturen der
arabischen Welt**

Paperback
Format 33 x 24 cm
Seiten / pages 320
mehr als 430 meist farbige
Abbildungen / over 430
mainly color illustrations
Hrsg. / Editor: Alexander
von Vegesack, Mateo Kries

ISBN 978-3-931936-44-0
Art. Nr. 20010401
(Deutscher / German Text)

**Living under the Crescent
Moon – Domestic Culture
in the Arab World**
ISBN 978-3-931936-41-9
Art. Nr. 20010402
(Englischer / English Text)

**Vivir bajo la Media Luna –
Las culturas domésticas del
mundo árabe**
ISBN 978-3-931936-45-7
Art. Nr. 20010404
(Spanischer / Spanish Text)

**100 Masterpieces aus der Sammlung
des Vitra Design Museums**

Paperpack
Format 30 x 23 cm
Seiten / pages 270
350 Abbildungen/illustrations
Hrsg. / Editor: Alexander von Vegesack,
Mathias Schwartz-Clauss, Peter Dunas

ISBN 978-3-9804070-2-1
Art. Nr. 20010001
(Deutscher / German Text)

**100 Masterpieces from the
Vitra Design Museum Collection**
ISBN 978-3-9804070-3-8
Art. Nr. 20010002
(Englischer / English Text)

**100 chefs-d'œuvre de la
Vitra Design Museum**
ISBN 978-3-9804070-4-5
Art. Nr. 20010003
(Französischer / French Text)

**100 Obras maestras de la
Colección del Vitra Design Museum**
ISBN 978-3-931936-63-1
Art. Nr. 20010004
(Spanischer / Spanish Text)

Verner Panton – Das Gesamtwerk

Hardcover
Format 29,5 x 23 cm
Seiten / pages 384
650 Abbildungen / illustrations
Inkl. / Includes CD-ROM
Hrsg. / Editor: Alexander
von Vegesack, Mathias Remmele

ISBN 978-3-931936-22-8
Art. Nr. 20016301
(Deutscher / German Text)

Verner Panton – Das Gesamtwerk

Paperback
Format 29,5 x 23 cm
Seiten / pages 384
650 Abbildungen / illustrations
Hrsg. / Editor: Alexander
von Vegesack, Mathias Remmele

ISBN 978-3-931936-21-1
Art. Nr. 20016101
(Deutscher / German Text)

Verner Panton – Complete Works
ISBN 978-3-931936-23-5
Art. Nr. 20016102
(Englischer / English Text)

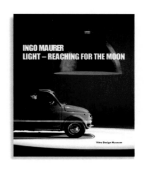

**Ingo Maurer
Light – Reaching for the Moon**

Paperback
Format 27 x 21cm
Seiten / pages 176
ca. 100 farbige Abbildungen /
colour illustrations
Herausgeber / Editor:
Alexander von Vegesack,
Jochen Eisenbrand

ISBN 978-3-931936-43-3
Art. Nr. 20010509
(Deutscher und Englischer /
German and English Text)

ISBN 978-3-931936-62-4
Art. Nr. 20010504
(Spanischer und Englischer /
Spanish and English Text)

**Marcel Breuer –
Design und Architektur**

Hardcover
Format 25,5 x 24,5 cm
Seiten / pages 320
ca. 300 Abb. / illus.
Hrsg. / Editor: Alexander
von Vegesack, Mathias Remmele

ISBN 978-3-931936-46-4
Art. Nr. 20010301
(Deutscher / German Text)

**Marcel Breuer –
Design and Architecture**
ISBN 978-3-931936-42-6
Art. Nr. 20010302
(Englischer / English Text)

Automobility – Was uns bewegt

Paperback
Format 29 x 20 cm
Seiten / pages 384
600 Abbildungen / illustrations
Hrsg. / Editor: Alexander
von Vegesack, Mateo Kries

ISBN 978-3-931936-17-4
Art. Nr. 20015601
(Deutscher / German Text)

**OPEN HOUSE – Architektur und
Technologie für intelligentes Wohnen**

Paperback
Format 22,7 x 28,7 cm
Seiten / pages 268
ca. 300 Abbildungen / pictures
Hrsg. / Editor: Alexander von
Vegesack, Jochen Eisenbrand

ISBN 978-3-931936-65-5
Art. Nr. 20008201
(Deutscher / German Text)

**OPEN HOUSE. Architecture and
Technology for intelligent Living**
ISBN 978-3-931936-66-2
Art. Nr. 20008202
(Englischer / English Text)

**Thonet
Stahlrohr-Möbel**

Reprint
Format 21 x 15 cm
84 Karten in einer Mappe /
84 cards in folder
70 Abbildungen / illustrations
Herausgeber / Editor:
Alexander von Vegesack

ISBN 978-3-9802539-3-2
Art. Nr. 20000101
(Deutscher und Englischer /
German and English Text)

www.design-museum.com

Vitra Design Museum, Charles-Eames-Str. 1, D-79576 Weil am Rhein, Tel. +49 (0)7621-702 3718, Fax +49 (0)7621-702 4718, verlag@design-museum.com

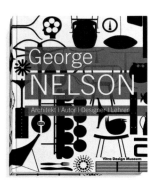

**George NELSON //
Architekt, Autor, Designer,
Lehrer**

Hardcover
Format 23,5 x 28 cm
Seiten / pages 352
300 Abbildungen,
überwiegend farbig
300 pictures,
Herausgeber / Editor:
Alexander von Vegesack,
Jochen Eisenbrand

ISBN 978-3-931936-81-5
Art. Nr. 20052301
(Deutscher / German Text)

**George NELSON //
Architect, Writer, Designer,
Teacher**
ISBN 978-3-931936-82-2
Art. Nr. 20052302
(Englischer / English Text)

**Le Corbusier –
The Art of Architecture**

Hardcover
Format 22 x 31 cm
Seiten / pages 398
500 Abb., davon 233 farbige
und 267 Duplex-Abbildungen /
500 pictures (233 color and
267 duplex-illustrations)
Herausgeber / Editor:
Alexander von Vegesack,
Stanislaus von Moos,
Arthur Rüegg, Mateo Kries

ISBN 978-3-931936-71-6
Art. Nr. 20012101
(Deutscher / German Text)

**Le Corbusier –
The Art of Architecture**
ISBN 978-3-931936-72-3
Art. Nr. 20012102
(Englischer / English Text)

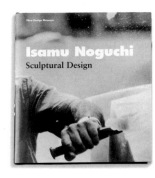

**Isamu Noguchi –
Sculptural Design**

Hardcover
Format 28,5 x 25 cm
Seiten/pages 320
155 Abb. davon 80 farbige
und 75 S/W-Abbildungen /
155 pictures (80 color and
75 b/w-illustrations)
Herausgeber / Editor:
Alexander von Vegesack,
Jochen Eisenbrand,
Katharina V. Posch

ISBN 978-3-931936-33-4
Art. Nr. 20017001
(Deutscher / German Text)

ISBN 978-3-931936-38-9
Art. Nr. 20017003
(Französischer / French Text)

**Jean Prouvé – Die Poetik des
technischen Gegenstandes**

Hardcover
Format 28 x 23 cm
Seiten / pages 393
895 Abb. davon 240 farbige
und 655 Duplex-Abbildungen /
895 pictures (240 color and
655 duplex-illustrations)
Herausgegeber / Editor:
Alexander von Vegesack
Mitherausgeber / Co-editor:
Bruno Reichlin
Konzept / conzept:
Catherine Dumont d'Ayot

ISBN 978-3-931936-53-2
Art. Nr. 20018501
(Deutscher / German Text)

**Jean Prouvé – The Poetics
of the Technical Objects**
ISBN 978-3-931936-54-9
Art. Nr. 20018502
(Englischer / English Text)

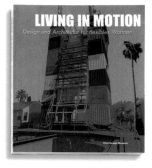

**Living in motion –
Design und Architekur
für flexibles Wohnen**

Paperback
Format 28 x 24 cm
Seiten / pages 288
mehr als 500 meist farbige
Abbildungen / over 500
mainly color illustrations
Herausgeber / Editor:
Alexander von Vegesack,
Mathias Schwartz-Clauss

ISBN 978-3-931936-34-1
Art. Nr. 20017901
(Deutscher / German Text)

**Living in Motion –
Design and Architecture
for flexible Dwelling**
ISBN 978-3-931936-35-8
Art. Nr. 20017902
(Englischer / English Text)

**Le Corbusier –
Studie über die Deutsche
Kunstgewerbebewegung**

Hardcover
Format 16,5 x 20 cm
Seiten / pages 224
116 Abb. (16 Farbtafeln und
100 Duplex-Abbildungen)
116 pictures (16 color and
100 duplex-illustrations)
Herausgeber / Editor:
Mateo Kries,
Alexander von Vegesack

ISBN 978-3-931936-28-0
Art. Nr. 20018601
(Deutscher / German Text)

**Le Corbusier –
A Study of the Decorative Art
Movement in Germany**
ISBN 978-3-931936-29-7
Art. Nr. 20018602
(Englischer / English Text)

**Grow your own house –
Simón Vélez und die
Bambusarchitektur /
Grow your own house –
Simón Vélez and the bamboo
architecture**

Paperback
Format 29 x 24 cm
Seiten / pages 265
300 Abbildungen / illustrations
Herausgeber / Editor:
Alexander von Vegesack,
Mateo Kries

ISBN 978-3-931936-25-9
Art. Nr. 20016509
(Deutscher und Englischer /
German and English Text)

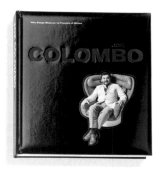

**Joe Colombo –
Die Erfindung der Zukunft**

Hardcover
Format 28 x 24 cm
Seiten / pages 304
515 Abbildungen / illustrations
Hrsg. / Editor: Alexander
von Vegesack, Mateo Kries

ISBN 978-3-931936-57-0
Art. Nr. 20018401
(Deutscher / German Text)

**Joe Colombo –
Inventing the Future**
ISBN 978-3-931936-58-7
Art. Nr. 20018402
(Englischer / English Text)

**Joe Colombo –
L'invention du futur**
ISBN 978-3-931936-73-0
Art. Nr. 20018403
(Französischer / French Text)

Vitra Design Museum Publications

Alle Publikationen des Vitra Design Museums erhalten Sie in ausgewählten Buchhandlungen oder direkt unter www.design-museum.com
All publications are available for purchase from our exclusive distributors, or ordered directly at www.design-museum.com

table centrepiece Tafelaufsatz
Nazareth (Bronze)
limited edition of 10 copies
Limitierte Auflage von 10 Exemplaren
Bernardaud, Paris
2008
19×36×42 cm

side table Beistelltisch
Inflável (Inflatable Aufblasbar)
one-off piece Unikat
1995
48×43×43 cm

side table Beistelltisch
Inflável (Inflatable Aufblasbar)
small series Kleinserie:
Museum of Modern Art, New York
1998
8×43×43 cm

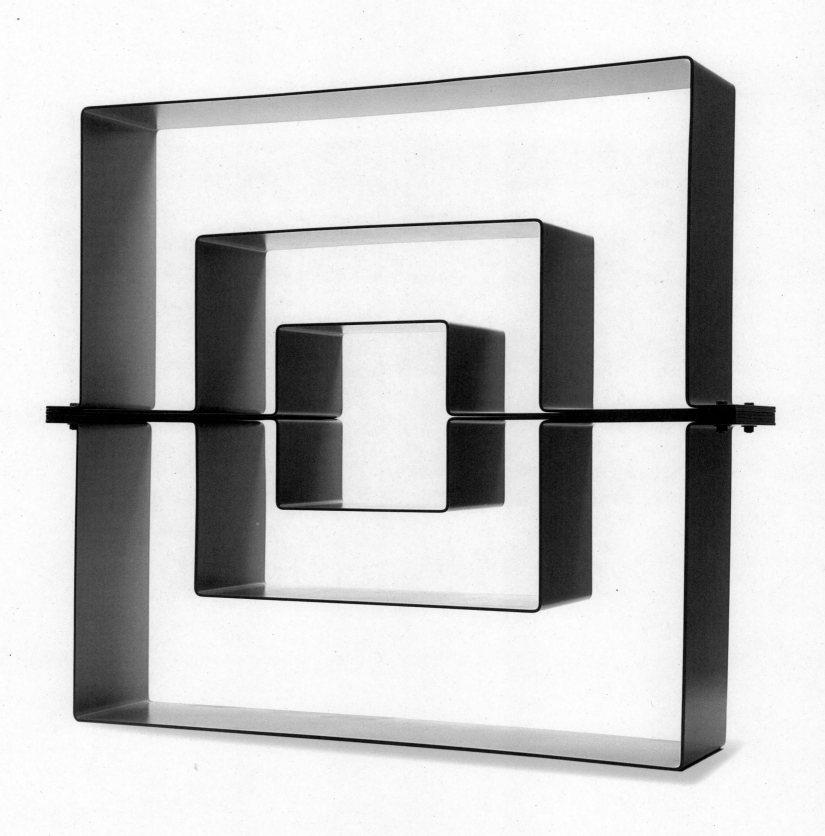

storage rack Regal
Labirinto (Labyrinth)
prototype Prototyp
1997
140×140×30 cm

armchair Armsessel
Vermelha (Red Rot)
serial model Serienmodell:
Edra spa, Perignano
1993
80×80×60 cm

Massimo Morozzi

Design Under the Signs of Chaos and Order. The Campana Brothers and Their Collaboration with Edra

Design im Zeichen von Chaos und Ordnung. Die Brüder Campana und ihre Zusammenarbeit mit Edra

Ordem y Progresso

Two things caught my eye when I first visited Brazil twenty-five years ago: the striking presence of its modernist architecture and the cold rationality of its design. The first descends from Le Corbusier's work in Brazil, later developed by the school of Lúcio Costa and Oscar Niemeyer. The second stems from the fact that the first generation of Latin-American designers was trained at the Ulm School of Design.

Seeing modern architecture in a tropical atmosphere, surrounded by palm and banana trees, made a strong impression on me. I was also struck by how closely Brazilian designers' work resembled that of the Germans. As if Dieter Rams and the white Braun universe had landed in the tropics. Unbelievable! Until then, my image of Brazil consisted of beaches, forests, samba, and carnival. One should not forget, however, that the words *Ordem y Progresso* (Order and Progress) are inscribed on the Brazilian flag, and that design has always played a major social role in the country.

In recent years, I have had the opportunity to present the work I have done with Fernando and Humberto Campana to Brazilian design schools and each time have had to deal with the complaint that the chairs they design are not very ergonomic! To this I answer by pointing out a classical design-school theme: the bus stop. There are some amazing ones in Brazil, especially in Curitiba, and they are no less 'rationally crazy' than any of the brothers' designs.

Edra

The story of Edra begins about twenty years ago. Valerio Mazzei and I set out to put together a catalogue of innovative furniture, based on the work of a group of designers of various backgrounds, ranging from Francesco Binfaré, Masanori Umeda, and Alessandro Mendini through Mario Cananzi and Roberto Semprini, a pair of young designers who had been trained at the Domus Academy in Milan, to Zaha Hadid, whose ambitious design for three sofas and a table we produced in the early 1990s.

Edra is located in Tuscany, in the province of Pisa, not far from the sea. The smell of the Mediterranean lingers in the air. The surrounding hills feature some of Italy's most beautiful landscapes and, since the Renaissance, have been home to its most astounding villas – then belonging to the Florentine nobility and now owned by British, Dutch, and German intellectuals, politicians, and businessmen. The cuisine is perfect in its simplicity and the wines are among the world's best. As far as industry is concerned, one should mention that the Vespa – a cult product of Italian design – was created by Piaggio just 10 kilometres away from Edra, in Pontedera. Although it was not the only consideration, having a landmark such as Piaggio

Massimo Morozzi shows Fernando and Humberto Campana the production area at Edra, 2002.
Massimo Morozzi zeigt Fernando und Humberto Campana die Produktion bei Edra, 2002.

within easy reach was of major importance to Edra. Also important was the proximity of Santa Croce sull'Arno's tanning facilities, which serve the entire Tuscan leather-goods industry, and of the Prato textile district. All of these circumstances have proven to be of great advantage in our work with the Campana brothers.

Fernando and Humberto

I first came into contact with Fernando and Humberto Campana in 1997, ten years after Edra was founded. I was leafing through Mel Byars's book *50 Chairs* (one of those numerous chair catalogues that are published on a regular basis) and came across a photograph of an armchair made with knotted rope and entitled *Azul*. The caption explained that it was a prototype made a few years earlier by two Brazilian brothers who lived and worked in São Paulo. I was very much impressed and extremely curious. I had never

Ordem y Progresso

Als ich vor 25 Jahren zum ersten Mal nach Brasilien kam, sprangen mir zwei Dinge ins Auge: die starke Präsenz der modernistischen Architektur und die kühle Rationalität des Designs. Erstere fußt auf dem Wirken Le Corbusiers in Brasilien und wurde dann von der Schule von Lúcio Costa und Oscar Niemeyer weiterentwickelt. Das rationalistische Design seinerseits lässt sich darauf zurückführen, dass die erste Generation lateinamerikanischer Designer an der Ulmer Hochschule für Gestaltung ausgebildet wurde.

Der Anblick moderner Architektur in diesem tropischen Klima inmitten von Palmen und Bananenstauden hat mir sehr imponiert. Nicht minder beeindruckend war es festzustellen, wie sehr die Arbeit der brasilianischen Designer derjenigen ihrer deutschen Kollegen ähnelte. Gerade so, als wären Dieter Rams und das weiße Universum des Max Braun in die Tropen verpflanzt worden. Ich traute meinen Augen nicht! Bis zu dieser Reise war auch meine Vorstellung von Brasilien eher mit Stränden, Wäldern, Samba und Karneval verbunden. Doch man sollte nicht vergessen: Auf der brasilianischen Fahne steht »Ordem y Progresso« geschrieben, Ordnung und Fortschritt, und schon immer hat Design eine wichtige soziale Rolle gespielt.

In den vergangenen Jahren hatte ich mehrfach die Gelegenheit, meine gemeinsamen Arbeiten mit Fernando und Humberto Campana an brasilianischen Designschulen zu präsentieren. Jedes Mal hörte ich Beschwerden, dass die von ihnen entworfenen Stühle nicht besonders ergonomisch seien! Als Entgegnung verweise ich auf ein anderes klassisches Designschul-Thema, und zwar die Bushaltestelle. Es gibt unglaubliche davon in Brasilien, vor allem in Curitiba – die sind nicht weniger vernünftig oder verrückt als irgendein Entwurf von Fernando und Humberto Campana.

Edra

Vor ungefähr zwanzig Jahren nahm die Geschichte von Edra ihren Anfang. Valerio Mazzei und ich begannen ein ganzes Sortiment an Möbeln, die in vielerlei Hinsicht innovativ waren, in Zusammenarbeit mit Designern unterschiedlicher Herkunft auf die Beine zu stellen, angefangen bei Francesco Binfaré, Masanori Umeda und Alessandro Mendini über zwei Jungdesigner namens Mario Cananzi und Roberto Semprini, die ihre Ausbildung an der Domus Academy in Mailand gemacht hatten, bis hin zu Zaha Hadid, mit der wir bereits in den 1990er Jahren sehr anspruchsvolles Mobiliar, drei Sofas und einen Tisch, herausbrachten.

Das Familienunternehmen Edra hat seinen Sitz in der Toskana in der Provinz Pisa unweit der Küste. Ein Duft von Mittelmeer schwebt hier in der Luft. Die Landschaften, Orte und Villen auf den umliegenden Hügeln gehören zu den schönsten, die Italien zu bieten hat. Die Renaissance-Villen, einst Eigentum des Florentiner Adels, sind heute im Besitz von Intellektuellen, Politikern und Unternehmern aus England, Holland und Deutschland. Die toskanische Küche ist in ihrer Einfachheit vollkommen, der Wein zählt zu den besten weltweit. Vom unternehmerischen Standpunkt gesehen ist es nicht unwichtig zu erwähnen, dass bei Piaggio in Pontedera, zehn Kilometer von Edra entfernt, die Vespa als eines der Kultobjekte des italienischen Designs geboren wurde. Auch wenn das nicht der einzige Grund war – die unmittelbare Nachbarschaft zu einer Landmarke wie Piaggio war für Edra extrem wichtig, genauso wie die Nähe zu den Gerbereien von Santa Croce sull'Arno (die die gesamte Lederwarenindustrie der Toskana versorgen) und zu den Textilfabriken von Prato. Alle diese Umstände haben sich in unserer Zusammenarbeit mit den Campana-Brüdern als äußerst vorteilhaft erwiesen.

heard of them before and had never seen anything like it. I managed to get a telephone number from friends and spoke to one of the brothers for the first time. On the other end of the line was Fernando and he, in turn, had never heard of Edra. Some time afterwards he told me that, initially, he thought it was a joke. I told him that we wanted to try making the armchair and that we needed some drawings and whatever else was required for producing a prototype. Two or three weeks later, we received a videotape showing a person knotting hundreds of metres of rope onto a metal frame. No drawing could illustrate the procedure. A few weeks passed and the first prototype of the *Vermelha* armchair was ready. Shortly after, Fernando and Humberto visited us in Tuscany and, thus, the first of an incredible array of objects, produced over a period of ten years, was launched.[1]
Many of the pieces that we have since manufactured were conceived and prototyped four, five, seven, even eight years earlier, but no one had shown any interest. They had remained unique pieces in the home of some collector friend or other, and, as they later admitted to me, the brothers had already thought of giving up.

The *Azul* armchair, 1993.
Der Sessel *Azul,* 1993.

Giuseppe: One Man, One Armchair

When we first made the *Vermelha*, we used 250 metres of rope per chair. Today we use 450. For the past ten years, the same person has been making the armchair: a wonderful craftsman named Giuseppe. He is the only person who can do it and he is constantly perfecting it. The initial 250 metres of rope have gradually risen to 450 in order to improve the quality of the seat. (Today, when I see the original, I find it awful.) Giuseppe takes pride in his work, as do all craftsmen who are constantly refining their ware. He has become a virtuoso at knotting rope and reminds me of the great lute makers of Cremona. It takes approximately four days to make a *Vermelha*. Each year we use, in the production of the *Cotton String* series, approximately eighty kilometres of rope, specially produced by fully-automated and extremely rapid machines in order to make the armchairs as comfortable as possible. At the end of the production process, there is only one man that checks it all, manually. When I think about it, I must admit that it is quite overwhelming: over the past ten years, we have sold just as many *Vermelha* armchairs as Giuseppe can make.

Giuseppe loops the upholstery for the *Vermelha* armchair.
Giuseppe beim Knüpfen des Polsters für den Sessel *Vermelha.*

1 The pieces designed by Fernando and Humberto Campana for Edra are, in chronological order: 1998: *Cotton String* series: *Vermelha* (armchair), *Azul* (armchair), *Verde* (chair); *Cone* (armchair). 2001: *Papel* (armchair, sofa, coffee table, and screen; limited edition); *Anemone* (armchair); *Zig Zag* (stool, bar stool, and screen). 2002: *Boa* (sofa); *Sushi* (armchair). 2003: *Favela* (armchair). 2004: *Corallo* (armchair). 2005: *Jenette* (chair). 2006: *Brasília* (table); *Kaiman Jacarè* (sofa); *Aster Papposus* (freestanding sofa). 2007: *Leatherworks* (chair and armchair). 2008: *Aguapè* (armchair); *Furworks* (armchair; limited edition).

Fernando und Humberto

Zehn Jahre nach der Gründung von Edra, also 1997, nahm ich zum ersten Mal von Fernando und Humberto Campana Notiz. Ich blätterte ein Buch von Mel Byars mit dem Titel *50 Chairs* durch; es war einer dieser Kataloge über Stühle, die in regelmäßigen Abständen veröffentlicht werden. Mein Blick fiel auf das Foto eines Sessels aus verknotetem Seil mit dem Namen *Azul*. In der Bildunterschrift stand, dass es sich um einen Prototyp handelte, den die Brasilianer Campana, die in São Paulo leben und arbeiten, einige Jahre zuvor entworfen hatten. Ich war sehr beeindruckt, und mich packte die Neugier. Der Name Campana war mir noch nicht untergekommen, und so etwas wie diesen Stuhl hatte ich nie zuvor gesehen. Über Freunde bekamen wir eine Telefonnummer heraus, und dann sprach ich zum ersten Mal mit einem der Campana-Brüder. Am anderen Ende der Leitung war Fernando, der seinerseits noch nie etwas von Edra gehört hatte. Einige Zeit später erzählte er mir, dass er meinen Anruf zunächst für einen Scherz gehalten habe. Ich sagte, dass wir versuchen wollten, den Stuhl *Azul* zu produzieren, und dass wir dafür die Zeichnungen und alles, was sonst noch für die Entwicklung eines Prototyps notwendig sei, bräuchten. Zwei oder drei Wochen später hatten wir eine Videokassette in der Post, die jemanden zeigte, der hunderte Meter Seil auf einem metallenen Webstuhl verknotete. Keine noch so detaillierte Zeichnung hätte dieses Verfahren sinnvoll wiedergeben können. Ein paar Wochen später stand der Prototyp des Sessels *Vermelha* fertig da. Kurze Zeit darauf kamen die Campanas zu uns in die Toskana, und die Geschichte dieser unglaublichen Galerie von Objekten, die wir in den nächsten zehn Jahren gemeinsam realisieren sollten, nahm ihren Anfang.[1] Vieles von dem, was wir produziert haben, hatten die Campanas vier, fünf, sieben, ja acht Jahre zuvor entworfen und Prototypen davon angefertigt, ohne dass sie jemanden interessiert hätten. Die Einzelstücke standen bei irgendwelchen Sammlerfreunden in der Wohnung herum und die Brüder spielten sogar mit dem Gedanken, ganz aufzuhören, wie sie mir später verrieten.

Giuseppe: ein Mann, ein Sessel

Für die ersten *Vermelha,* die wir produzierten, verwendeten wir pro Sessel 250 Meter Seil, heute sind es 450 Meter. Der Mann, der sie anfertigt, ist derselbe wie vor zehn Jahren. Er heißt Giuseppe und ist ein begnadeter Handwerker, der Einzige, der dazu imstande ist und der das Verfahren ständig verbessert. Aus den anfänglichen 250 Metern sind sukzessive 450 Meter geworden, weil sich dadurch die Qualität des Sessels verbessern ließ. (Wenn ich mir heute das Original ansehe, finde ich es scheußlich.) Für Giuseppe ist es eine Sache der Handwerkerehre, seine Arbeit immer weiter zu vervollkommnen. Inzwischen ist er ein Virtuose der »Seil-Locken« und wenn ich ihn sehe, muss ich an die berühmten Lautenbauer von Cremona denken. Für einen *Vermelha* sind rund vier Tage Arbeit nötig. Für die Produktion der Serie *Cotton String* verbrauchen wir jährlich rund 80 Kilometer Spezialseil (um die Sessel komfortabler zu machen), das mit extrem schnellen, vollautomatischen Maschinen hergestellt wird. Am Ende der Produktionskette steht ein einzelner Mann, der alles mit den eigenen Händen bewerkstelligt. Wenn ich darüber nachdenke, erscheint es mir geradezu überwältigend. Seit zehn Jahren verkaufen wir jährlich so viele *Vermelha,* wie Giuseppe anfertigen kann.

1 Folgende Objekte wurden von Fernando und Humberto Campana entworfen und von Edra produziert (in chronologischer Reihenfolge): 1998: Serie *Cotton String: Vermelha,* Sessel; *Azul,* Sessel, *Verde,* Stuhl; *Cone,* Sessel; 2001: *Papel,* Sessel, Sofa, Couchtisch und Paravent (limitierte Auflage); *Anemone,* Sessel; *Zig Zag,* Hocker, Barhocker, Paravent; 2002: *Boa,* Sofa; *Sushi,* Sessel; 2003: *Favela,* Sessel; 2004: *Corallo,* Sessel; 2005: *Jenette,* Stuhl; 2006: *Brasília,* Tisch; *Kaiman Jacarè,* Sofa; *Aster Papposus,* frei stehendes Sofa; 2007: *Leatherworks,* Stuhl und Sessel; 2008: *Aguapè,* Sessel; *Furworks,* Sessel (limitierte Auflage).

Abstraction and Immanence

Vermelha and *Cotton String* marked the beginning of the partnership between Edra and the Campana brothers. There could be no better combination. Edra comes with its Tuscan production history whereby craftsmen of longstanding traditions join forces with the latest industrial technologies in order to create high-quality products. Just think of the leather-goods sector, in which visceral and 'impure' tanneries have established memorable names, synonymous with elegance, such as Gucci, Prada, and Ferragamo. For their part, the Campana brothers practise a creative process in which conceptual thought and manual skill are employed simultaneously. Whether the material is traditional or not, it is considered from an unconventional angle and manipulated with childlike innocence in order to produce wondrous 'beings'. Each object comes as a surprise, as if pulled out of a magician's hat.

Edra has found itself perfectly at ease with this process. After ten years, we know each other so well that, sometimes, all it takes is a few words over the telephone or a trivial conversation over dinner to set hands into motion, be they ours or theirs. The prototypes are usually developed in-house by Edra, based on sketches or models received from the brothers, as well as plenty of telephone calls. Each time, special methods and techniques, which have never before been used, need to be developed. I remember one case – that of the *Boa* sofa – that we simply could not resolve. *Boa* consists of three tubes of velvet, each forty metres long and twenty-five centimetres in diameter, filled with padding and knotted together. After numerous attempts, we at Edra could not find a way of filling these tubes evenly. So, we called Fernando and Humberto, gave them the necessary materials, and said, 'Now you try!' Within a couple of days they had done it. Today, *Boa* – a softly enveloping spatial diagram – is produced via the 'muscular' efforts of four people. It is a performance fit for the theatre. Maximum abstraction and maximum immanence in one.

Crocodiles and Other Fabulous Creatures

Fernando, Humberto, and I have planned a trip to the Pantanal several times. The Pantanal is a large wetland region in the centre of Brazil. Supposedly, it is a paradigm of nature, one of the last surviving gardens of Eden. In truth, though, I think it is an infernal place, full of flies and mosquitoes, twenty-metre-long anacondas and hungry caimans. That is why we have never made the trip and in our conversations the word 'Pantanal' has become synonymous with a chaotic and primitive state of nature.

We did go to the seaside in Angra dos Reis. This is a region located to the west of Rio and dotted with so many islands that you never see the open sea. It is like being on the shores of a lake. The rain forest runs all the way down to the beach, so that the water is of a dark green colour, resembling crude oil. And to add to it all, the heat and humidity are suffocating. The whole place evokes an image of prehistoric times and you expect to see a dinosaur appear at any moment. The roundish humps of the islands look like large animals, at once horrible and placid.

Around the same time, I happened to go to Valparaiso in Chile for a conference. When I was there, my hosts took me to see the sea lions lolling about on the rocks of Vigna del Mar, on the edge of the ocean. These huge animals spend their

Abstraktion und Immanenz

Mit *Vermelha* und *Cotton String* beginnt die Zusammenarbeit zwischen Edra und den Campanas. Die beiden Akteure ergänzen sich auf kongeniale Weise. Edra steht in der Nachfolge einer erfolgreichen toskanischen Industriegeschichte, in der ein traditionsreiches Handwerk und die innovativsten Produktionsverfahren auf das Beste zusammenwirken und hochwertige Erzeugnisse hervorbringen. Man denke nur an die Herstellung von Lederwaren, die auf der organischen und »unreinen«, weil sinnlichen Handarbeit der Gerbereien beruht. Auf dieser Basis konnten sich elegante Marken wie Gucci, Prada und Ferragamo etablieren. Die Campana-Brüder ihrerseits praktizieren einen kreativen Prozess, bei dem Konzeption und manuelle Fertigung Hand in Hand gehen. Jedes Material, sei es herkömmlich oder innovativ, wird aus einer unkonventionellen Perspektive betrachtet und zugleich von ihnen selbst gleichsam mit kindlicher Unschuld bearbeitet. Wundersame »Wesen« entstehen daraus. Jedes Mal sind sie eine Überraschung, als hätte ein Zauberer sie aus dem Hut gezogen.

Edra kommt mit dieser Vorgehensweise der Campanas bestens zurecht. Nach zehn Jahren ist das Einvernehmen so gut, dass manchmal kurze Andeutungen am Telefon oder ein Gespräch im Restaurant über Gott und die Welt reichen, damit sie sich und wir uns an die Arbeit machen. In der Regel werden die Prototypen bei Edra aus zugeschickten Skizzen oder Modellen, vor allem aber nach unzähligen Telefonaten mit den Brüdern entwickelt. In jedem Fall müssen spezielle Methoden und Techniken, die es vorher noch nie gegeben hat, ausgearbeitet werden.

Um das zu illustrieren, möchte ich einen Fall schildern, bei dem wir mit unserem Latein am Ende waren. Es ging um das Sofa *Boa*: Es besteht aus drei jeweils 40 Meter langen Schläuchen mit Samtbezug – das sind also insgesamt 120 Meter Stoff –, die gefüllt und miteinander verknotet sind. Wir bekamen das einfach nicht hin (versuchen Sie sich vorzustellen, wie man einen 40 Meter langen Samtschlauch mit einem Durchmesser von 25 Zentimetern gleichmäßig füllen soll) und riefen also Fernando und Humberto an, schickten ihnen das nötige Material und baten sie, es ihrerseits zu probieren. Innerhalb weniger Tage hatten sie zuwege gebracht, was uns nicht gelingen wollte. Heute wird das Sofa *Boa*, ein raumgreifendes Diagramm von betörender Weichheit, mit der Muskelkraft von vier Männern hergestellt. Die Fertigung ist eine tolle Theaterperformance – höchste Abstraktion und höchste Immanenz in einem.

Krokodile und andere Fabelwesen

Fernando, Humberto und ich haben uns mehrmals vorgenommen, in den Pantanal zu reisen. Der Pantanal ist ein großes Feuchtgebiet im Herzen Brasiliens. Es ist das Paradigma der Natur schlechthin, eines der letzten Paradiese, die es auf der Welt noch gibt. In Wirklichkeit denke ich, dass es eine sumpfige Hölle ist, in der es von Fliegen und Stechmücken, zwanzig Meter langen Anakondas und hungrigen Kaimanen nur so wimmelt. Grund genug, warum wir diese Reise nie unternommen haben. Inzwischen steht das Wort Pantanal in unseren Gesprächen für einen urzeitlichen, magmaartigen Naturzustand.

Stattdessen sind wir ans Meer nach Angra dos Reis gefahren, eine Gegend westlich von Rio mit so vielen Inselchen, dass man das offene Meer nie sieht und sich auf einem Binnensee wähnt. Der Regenwald reicht bis an die

Advertising photo for *Kaiman Jacarè*.
Werbefoto für *Kaiman Jacarè*.

Küste heran, von daher ist das Wasser dunkelgrün, ja fast petrolfarben. Zudem herrscht eine erstickende Hitze und Feuchtigkeit – eine Landschaft wie aus der Frühgeschichte der Erde, wo Du förmlich darauf wartest, jeden Augenblick einen Dinosaurier aus dem Dickicht auftauchen zu sehen. Die rundlichen Rücken der Inselchen sind eigentlich große, furchterregende

days heaped one on top of the other, basking in the sunshine and emitting a nauseous smell.

Caimans resting in the Pantanal mud, placid dinosaurs in the ancestral waters of Angra dos Reis, sea lions sunbathing at Vigna del Mar – all terrifying and slightly disgusting images that nevertheless transmit a sense of comfort and total psychophysical well-being. I have no doubt whatsoever that these monsters live in a state of perfect bliss.

That is when *Historia Naturalis* began to take shape. That is where the large creature-sofas, *Kaiman Jacarè* and *Aster Papposus,* originated. Intended to accommodate the bodies of people, they combine relaxation with sheer disgust. Bodies and antibodies.

A few days ago, I received a postcard from Humberto with a picture of an anaconda that had just swallowed a whole calf. A hideous bulge protruded from its body. It was horrible. I may never get to see the Pantanal, but it continues to be a constant and inescapable presence in my life.

Mineralogy

Brasília is a magical city. According to legend, the location of Brazil's new federal capital, built in the 1950s, was prophesied in the second half of the nineteenth century by an Italian priest who had never been to Brazil. More importantly, however, the city's subsoil contains the country's largest deposit of semiprecious stones. This has generated the belief that the place is charged with a special energy. Communities of North American post-hippies have settled in the area in semispherical houses, said to be particularly well suited to absorbing the beneficial effects of this energy. This alone was enough to attract the Campana brothers' attention. Thus, we have visited Brasília together several times in order to try and learn its secret. These visits have led to the creation of the *Brasília* table, which is made up of a large number of coloured methacrylate mirror shards (it was simply impossible to use stones). The result is a concretion similar to those found in Brasília's mineral deposits. It is a 'mineral' table, made more of light than of matter. The luminous energy emanating from it is projected onto the ceiling with a kaleidoscopic effect. I think it is beautiful.

Brotas

Brotas is a small town in the state of São Paulo, approximately 200 kilometres northwest of the city that bears the state's name and serves as its capital. It used to lie at the centre of a major coffee-producing region. Now, however, the coffee that made the state's fortune, and that of many Italo-Brazilians, is no longer cultivated there, because of African competition, and the crops have been converted, mainly to citrus fruits. The Brotas countryside is lush and abounds with watercourses, rapids, and waterfalls, along which Humberto learnt to raft.

Brotas is the birthplace of the Campana brothers. Their mother Celia, their nanny Alice, and their aging Boxer dog Banzè still live there. Celia is a small, slender, and sprightly woman, until recently a heavy smoker. Alice is a dark-skinned lady, who took a plane for the first time in her life to attend the opening of the brothers' first exhibition in Brazil, held in 2003 in the central bank building in Brasília. The event moved her to tears.

The *Aster Papposus* free-standing sofa, designed for Edra in 2006.
Das frei stehende Sofa *Aster Papposus,* entworfen 2006 für Edra.

aber friedliche Tiere. Ungefähr zur selben Zeit führte man mich anlässlich einer Konferenz in Valparaíso (Chile) zu den Seelöwen auf den Felsinseln von Viña del Mar. Es sind riesige, übel riechende Tiere, die den lieben langen Tag in Haufen übereinander liegen und sich sonnen.

Kaimane, die reglos in den Sümpfen des Pantanal dösen, »versteinerte« Dinosaurier in den Urgewässern von Angra dos Reis, Seelöwen, die sich an der Sonne von Viña del Mar wärmen. Furchteinflößende Bilder sind das, auch ein bisschen Ekel erregend, und trotzdem vermitteln sie etwas sehr Behagliches, ein absolutes seelisches und körperliches Wohlbefinden. Es besteht kein Zweifel, dass diese Ungeheuer in einem Zustand vollkommener Glückseligkeit leben. Genau hier nimmt die *Historia Naturalis* ihren Anfang. Hier entstehen die großen Sofa-Wesen *Kaiman Jacarè* und *Aster Papposus,* die Menschenkörper umfangen sollen. Vollkommene Entspannung und absoluter Widerwille zugleich. Körper und Antikörper. Vor einigen Tagen bekam ich von Humberto eine Postkarte zugeschickt: Das Foto zeigt eine Anakonda, die gerade ein ganzes Kalb verschlungen hat. Der Körper weist eine grausige Wölbung auf. Ekelhaft. Wahrscheinlich werde ich den Pantanal nie sehen, aber in meinem Leben ist er stets präsent, beharrlich und unumgänglich.

Gesteinskunde

Brasília ist eine magische Stadt. Es heißt, das Areal, auf dem in den 1950er Jahren die neue Bundeshauptstadt Brasiliens errichtet wurde, sei Ende des 19. Jahrhunderts für diese Zwecke von einem italienischen Priester geweissagt worden, der Brasilien nie betreten hatte. Im Untergrund befindet sich die größte Halbedelstein-Lagerstätte des Landes. Das hat zu der Überzeugung geführt, dass dieser Ort mit einer ganz besonderen Energie aufgeladen ist. Im Umland leben nordamerikanische Hippies der zweiten Generation in halbrunden Häusern, weil diese Form angeblich am besten geeignet ist, die positive Wirkung der Energie aufzunehmen. Gründe genug also, um das Interesse der Campana-Brüder zu wecken. So waren wir mehrere Male zusammen in Brasília, um zu versuchen, das Geheimnis zu lüften. Daraus ist der Tisch *Brasília* entstanden, der, weil man den Stein unmöglich als solchen verwenden kann, aus unzähligen Splittern gefärbten, lichtreflektierenden Metakryls zusammengesetzt ist. Das Ergebnis ist eine schieferartige Konkretion, wie sie gelegentlich bei Gesteinsablagerungen zu beobachten ist. *Brasília* ist ein mineralischer Tisch, der mehr aus Licht als aus Materie besteht. Die Lichtenergie, die er ausstrahlt, wird an die Decke geworfen und erzeugt einen Kaleidoskopeffekt. In meinen Augen wunderschön.

Brotas

Fernando and Humberto Campana on a 2002 visit to the Cathedral of Brasília, photographed by Massimo Morozzi.
Fernando und Humberto Campana 2002 beim Besuch der Kathedrale von Brasília, fotografiert von Massimo Morozzi.

Brotas ist eine Kleinstadt circa 200 Kilometer nordwestlich von São Paulo, der Hauptstadt des gleichnamigen Bundesstaates. Eine Zeitlang lag sie im Zentrum eines Kaffeeanbaugebietes. Kaffee hat den Bundesstaat São Paulo und so manchen Italobrasilianer reich gemacht, aber wegen der afrikanischen Konkurrenz wird er heutzutage nicht mehr hier produziert; die Landwirtschaft wurde überwiegend auf Gemüseanbau umgestellt. Das Land um Brotas ist sehr grün und reich an Wasserläufen mit Stromschnellen und Wasserfällen, wo Humberto Raftingfahren gelernt hat.

Fernando and Humberto are very fond of Brotas as they are of their mother and their nanny. They visit Brotas regularly on weekends, unless they are exhibiting or lecturing somewhere around the world or preoccupied by the development of a project. They own a plot of land there, with a grove. In the middle of it, they have built a wooden observation tower where they go at night with friends to observe the stars.

A few years ago, they took me to Brotas to meet Celia and Alice. I returned the gesture by taking them to see my mother in Florence. On the day of the visit, we were in Barcelona for a lecture at the Associació de Disseny Industrial del Foment de les Arts Decoratives (ADIFAD) and I went shopping in the old Boqueria market on the Rambla for Catalan delicacies. We ate them that evening in the Florentine hills and my mother was just as delighted as I believe Celia is when she sees her children.

Jenette, Harlem, New York

Jenette Kahn lives in a small townhouse in Harlem, with her partner – an artist and craftsman – and four beloved cats, two striped and two spotted, with pointed ears and long legs. She was a high-ranking executive in the comic book division of Time Warner and is an original art collector. In 1998 she commissioned the Campana brothers to design her dining room and they, in turn, added yet another hybrid creature to our story: the *Jenette* chair. Originally with a wooden seat and a back made of hundreds of PVC bristles, I admit that initially I did not like it.

Eventually, in 2005, I had the chance to look at the chair from a different angle. I was thinking of making a series of totally monochromatic objects with the intention of radically dematerialising them (a practice that at the time was gaining ground also in other sectors – cars and Apple computers, for example). Thus, the Edra *Jenette* was born, made of rigid structural polyurethane moulded on a metallic core and a manually assembled backrest of approximately 900 flexible PVC bristles. It was a success.

On 20 May 2007, the day of Fernando's birthday, we were all invited to dinner at Jenette's house in Harlem. We sat in the original *Jenette* chairs, which were draped with white furs and dotted with Swarovski crystals. At the end of the meal, we were served *Jenette*-shaped biscuits, the work of a trusted confectioner, which were covered with white, green, red, yellow, and blue sugar – the colours in which our monochrome chair is distributed.

Apocalypse and Resurrection

Three years ago, the house next door to the Campana brothers' studio in São Paulo exploded due to a gas leak. The studio was not spared. The roof collapsed and everything was buried beneath the rubble. Luckily, the explosion happened during the night and there were no victims – apart, it seems, from about twenty cats that lived on the roof. Photographs show the studio in an apocalyptic state: roofless, filled with debris and dust, some of our prototypes sticking out from under the wreckage. In all my forty-five years in design, I could never have imagined such a disaster.

I think that Fernando and Humberto's creativity was born out of and developed through the state of permanent catastrophe that is Brazil. If they had lived in a world that functions in some orderly fashion, they would not have been constantly forced to improvise new strategies and to alter and adapt to their needs the scraps, refuse, and discarded bits of reality that seem to be amassed in the countries of the Southern Hemisphere. Humberto has often said to me, 'We were told from a very young age that ours was the country of the future. We have never seen that future.' The destruction of

Brotas ist die Geburtsstadt der Campana-Brüder. Hier leben die Mutter Celia, der uralte Hund Banzé, ein Boxer, und das Kindermädchen Alice. Celia ist eine

The Brotas train station, ca. 1999.
Der Bahnhof von Brotas, ca. 1999.

kleine, dünne, energische Frau, die bis vor kurzem noch Kette rauchte. Alice ist dunkelhäutig; zur Eröffnung der ersten den Campana-Brüdern in Brasilien gewidmeten Ausstellung 2003 in der Zentralbank von Brasília stieg sie zum ersten Mal in ihrem Leben in einen Flieger und war zu Tränen gerührt. Fernando und Humberto hängen sehr an ihrer Mutter, ihrem Kindermädchen, dem Boxerrüden und ihrer Heimatstadt. Wenn sie nicht gerade wegen einer Ausstellung, einer Konferenz oder der Betreuung ihrer Projekte irgendwo in der Welt unterwegs sind, fahren sie am Wochenende nach Brotas. Dort gehört ihnen ein Grundstück mit einem Wald, wo sie mittendrin einen Beobachtungsturm aus Holz errichtet haben. Nachts fahren sie mit Freunden dorthin, um sich die Sterne anzusehen.

Sie haben mich vor ein paar Jahren nach Brotas mitgenommen, und um mich zu revanchieren, habe ich sie dann meinerseits nach Florenz zu meiner Mutter eingeladen. Wir fuhren gemeinsam von Barcelona aus, wo wir an einer Konferenz der Associació de Disseny Industrial del Foment de les Arts Decoratives (ADIFAD) teilgenommen hatten, nach Florenz. Unmittelbar vor der Abfahrt bin ich auf die Ramblas zum alten Boqueria-Markt gegangen und habe katalanische Delikatessen besorgt, die wir dann am Abend vor der Kulisse der Florentiner Hügellandschaft in Gesellschaft meiner Mutter verspeist haben. Ich bin sicher, dass meine Mutter sehr glücklich war, so wie Celia sehr froh ist, wenn sie ihre Söhne sehen kann.

Jenette, Harlem, New York

In ihrer Villa auf Manhattan in Harlem lebt Jenette Kahn, zusammen mit ihrem Lebensgefährten, einem Kunsthandwerker, und vier innig geliebten Katzen, zwei getigerten und zwei gefleckten, mit spitzen Ohren und langen Beinen. Jenette Kahn hatte einen verantwortungsvollen Posten bei Time Warner im Comicbereich und ist außerdem eine originelle Kunstsammlerin. 1998 beauftragte sie die Campana-Brüder mit der Einrichtung des Esszimmers ihrer Villa. So entstand der Stuhl *Jenette* –ein weiteres »hybrides Wesen« unserer Geschichte: ursprünglich versehen mit einem Holzsitz und einer Lehne aus hunderten dünnen PVC-Stäben. Ich hatte den Stuhl früher einmal gesehen, aber zugegebenermaßen hatte er mir nicht gefallen. Schließlich konnte ich ihn 2005 in einen neuen Zusammenhang stellen. Mir schwebte eine Serie vollkommen monochromer Objekte vor, um sie radikal zu entmaterialisieren (im Übrigen ein Phänomen, das zu jener Zeit auch in anderen Bereichen wie bei Autos oder bei den Apple-Computern zu beobachten war). So entstand der *Jenette* von Edra, ein industriell gefertigter Stuhl aus formgepresstem steifem Strukturpolyurethan mit Metallkern und mit einer von Hand zusammengesetzten Rückenlehne aus 900 flexiblen feinen Rundstäben aus steifem PVC.

Am 20. Mai 2007 wurden wir alle anlässlich des Geburtstags von Fernando Campana zum Abendessen in die Harlemer Stadtvilla eingeladen und nahmen auf den original *Jenette*-Stühlen Platz, die rundum mit weißen Fellteilen bezogen waren, in denen Swarovski-Kristalle blitzten. Zum Ausklang wurde Gebäck in *Jenette*-Form serviert, das der Konditor des Vertrauens mit weißem, grünem, rotem, gelbem und blauem Zuckerguss, genau in den Farben unserer »monochromen« Stühle, überzogen hatte.

Apokalypse und Auferstehung

Vor drei Jahren flog das Haus neben dem Studio der Campanas in São Paulo wegen eines Lecks in der Gasleitung in die Luft. Das Campana-Studio blieb nicht verschont: Das Dach stürzte ein und alles wurde unter Trümmern begra-

their studio forced the brothers to start all over again with what they found lying around, weighing it up and trying to reassemble it into something useful. Such is the strategy of the favela.

Favela

Summer 2002. We are in Paris, discussing some new projects yet unable to reach anything conclusive. I say to myself: We need a strong stimulus here. So, one day, I take the brothers to Paris's Chinatown, in the thirteenth arrondissement, and we spend a few hours in the Tang brothers' Chinese supermarket. It is an orgy of goods, fragrances, and food, far removed from anything we are used to. They are enthusiastic and I have the notion that there will be a strong reaction. Then we go home – I to Milan, they to São Paulo – and I wait. Nothing happens. In early September I decide to go to São Paulo and resolve matters. While we are chatting in their studio, I see, lying on the table, a copy of *Tropical Modern* – a catalogue which I already know quite well. I start leafing through it and happen to see a photograph of the *Favela* armchair, a unique piece the brothers had made many years earlier for a collector friend. It hits me like a thunderbolt. What! How could we have overlooked something so remarkable? I decide then and there that we must turn it into a product. And so we do.

Favela is the only Edra product designed by the Campana brothers that is made outside Italy. It is manufactured in southern Brazil, in a joiner's shop owned by Germans, who are numerous and active in the area. It is yet another hybrid, as is inevitable in this story. The most Brazilian of products created with strictly Teutonic workmanship.

Nothing illustrates the Campana design strategy as well as *Favela*. After all, a favela is a self-built zero-cost habitat. Although it is usually found in conditions of extreme squalor, it is equally a place of intense creativity. Its inhabitants comb the city collecting scraps of all kinds with which they assemble their own private space. That is exactly how Kurt Schwitters used to produce his art in Berlin. The Campana brothers design their objects using the same process, adopting the same strategy. That is how we made *Favela*. It may have abject origins, but we immediately saw it as an impressive piece, a sort of barbarian throne. When it was presented at the 2003 Salone Internazionale del Mobile in Milan, I made a large round table, called it *Camelot*, and arranged twelve of the armchairs around it – for King Arthur and his knights.

In keeping with Oscar Niemeyer's project, the presidential offices in Brasília are furnished with the best design furniture of the 1950s, including that of Charles and Ray Eames. I believe the *Favela* could fit in quite well. This is, and will probably remain, nothing but an aspiration of mine. Nevertheless, the armchair itself fills me with great satisfaction and pride.

Glocal

There is a feature of the Campana brothers' work that strikes me as most impressive and, within today's design scene, as completely unique. It is their ability to be both totally local and totally global at the same time. Their work stems from and is fostered by the Brazilian context; yet it has no ethnic content, as unfortunately is too often the case. Ethnic localism is lethal; it can produce great loves but also burning disappointments. How many times have we bought a rug in an Eastern bazaar only to arrive home with our precious purchase and be embarrassed by it? It is different with the Campana brothers. The Brazilian catastrophe they describe be-

The studio in São Paulo after the explosion of a gas tank in the neighbourhood, 2005.
Das Atelier in São Paulo nach der Explosion eines Gastanks in der Nachbarschaft, 2005.

ben. Zum Glück geschah dies nachts und es waren keine Opfer zu beklagen, außer vermutlich zwei Dutzend Katzen, die auf dem Dach gehaust hatten. Aufnahmen zeigen das Studio wie nach der Apokalypse unter freiem Himmel, unter einer dicken Staubschicht und voller Trümmer, aus denen einige unserer Prototypen ragen. In all den Jahren, in denen ich im Designbereich tätig bin – 45 sind es, um genau zu sein –, habe ich mir so etwas nie vorstellen können. Ich denke, dass Fernandos und Humbertos Kreativität aus einer Situation der permanenten Katastrophe, wie sie in Brasilien herrscht, entsteht und sich entwickelt. Würden sie in einer anderen, gut funktionierenden, geordneten Welt leben (zumindest dem Anschein nach), wären sie nicht gezwungen, ständig neue Strategien zu erfinden. Sie müssten keine Abfälle, Unrat, Wirklichkeitsfetzen, die sich immer stärker auf die Länder des Südens zu konzentrieren scheinen, ummodeln und an die eigenen Bedürfnisse anpassen. Mehr als einmal hat mir Humberto gesagt: »Seit ich klein bin, wurde uns immer gesagt, wir seien das Land der Zukunft. Diese Zukunft haben wir nie gesehen.« So fängt man immer wieder von vorne an, sammelt ein, was nach der Katastrophe übrig geblieben ist, wägt ab und versucht die Reste zu etwas Brauchbarem zusammenzufügen. Das ist die Strategie der Favelas.

Favela

Sommer 2002. Wir sind in Paris, wo wir über neue Projekte reden. Doch es kommt nichts Konkretes dabei heraus. Ich sage mir: Wir brauchen einen starken Stimulus. Und so führe ich die Brüder einige Tage später in das Pariser Chinatown im 13. Arrondissement. Wir verbringen ein paar Stunden im chinesischen Supermarkt der Gebrüder Tang: ein Exzess an Waren, Gerüchen, Lebensmitteln, die so ganz anders sind als das, was wir kennen. Die Campanas sind begeistert. Ich erhoffe mir eine Reaktion. Sie kehren nach São Paulo, ich nach Mailand zurück. Ich warte ab. Doch es tut sich nichts. Anfang September beschließe ich, nach São Paulo zu fliegen, um zu einer Lösung zu kommen. Während wir in ihrem Studio sitzen und reden, sehe ich den Katalog *Tropical Modern,* den ich recht gut kenne, auf dem Tisch liegen. Ich beginne ihn durchzublättern und bleibe auf der Seite mit der Aufnahme des Sessels *Favela* hängen, eines Einzelstücks, das sie vor etlichen Jahren für einen Sammlerfreund angefertigt hatten. Plötzlich ist die Idee da. Wie konnten wir bloß ein so außergewöhnliches Objekt vergessen? Ich beschließe, dass wir ein Produkt daraus machen müssen. Und so kommt es auch. *Favela* ist das einzige Objekt der Campanas für Edra, das nicht in Italien hergestellt wird, sondern im Süden Brasiliens in einer Tischlerei, die von Deutschen betrieben wird, die in dieser Gegend sehr zahlreich und rührig sind. Wieder ein »hybrides Wesen«; das bringt unsere Geschichte so mit sich: Das brasilianischste aller Erzeugnisse entsteht in streng teutonischer Maßarbeit ...

Nichts eignet sich so gut wie die Favela, um die Strategie der Campana-Brüder zu beschreiben. Eine Favela, ein brasilianisches Elendsviertel, besteht aus Baracken, die im Eigenbau zum Nulltarif entstehen. Gewiss, hier mag schlimmer Verfall herrschen, zugleich ist es aber ein sehr kreativer Ort. Die Bewohner streifen durch die Stadt und sammeln Abfälle aller Art ein, aus denen sie sich dann ihr Heim zimmern. Genau dies war – in der Kunst – seinerzeit das Prinzip von Kurt Schwitters in Berlin. Es ist dieselbe Methode, nach der die Campana-Brüder ihre Objekte entwickeln. Dieselbe Strategie. Und genauso haben wir auch den Sessel *Favela* gemacht, der ärmlichen Ursprungs ist, uns aber sogleich als imposantes Objekt erschien, als eine Art barbarischer Thron. Für seine Präsentation auf dem Salone Internazionale del Mobile in Mailand 2003 ließ ich einen großen runden Tisch anfertigen, nannte ihn *Camelot* und platzierte zwölf Stühle um ihn herum – für König Artus und seine Ritter.

longs to all of us, even though we try to deny it. In a situation in which all is becoming virtual, the need to stubbornly preserve the manual crafts is a must for everyone – unless we want to lose our sensory faculties forever. Not ostracising ugliness, imperfection, and disgust is a moral imperative for all of us. Favouring the hybrid over consistency is a state of survival. Total Glocal. In short, Fernando and Humberto Campana are not a pair of designers. They are therapy.

Final Bestiary

Three years after its collapse, the roof of the Campana studio has regained its cat population. There is also a new dog, a foundling called Chica. As can be imagined, she is no beauty queen.
At Edra we have developed a special covering for the *Aster Papposus* sofa. I call it 'a wet dog's coat'. It resembles fur but is made of slightly bristling hairs that are clumped together, just like those of a wet dog. It has a remarkable feel.
We have also made a special edition of our *Leatherworks* armchairs for a leading Parisian auction house. They are inlaid with fur and called *Furworks*. They look like sheep that have just passed through the hands of a lousy sheep shearer. The auction was held in November 2008.
Hurrah!

Dem Entwurf von Oscar Niemeyer angemessen, wurde das Präsidialamt in Brasília mit Möbeln der besten Designer der 1950er Jahre ausgestattet, darunter auch die von Charles und Ray Eames. Ich meine, dass der *Favela* heute zu Recht in diesen Räumen Einzug halten müsste. Das ist und bleibt zwar ein frommer Wunsch, doch allein dies zu wünschen erfüllt mich schon mit Zufriedenheit und Stolz.

Glocal

Es gibt eine bestimmte Eigenheit in der Arbeit von Fernando und Humberto Campana, die mir ganz besonders imponiert und die ich derzeit nirgendwo sonst finde: ihre Fähigkeit, absolut lokal und zugleich absolut global zu sein. Ihre Arbeit entsteht im brasilianischen Kontext und schöpft aus ihm, und doch findet sich kein ethnisches Gepräge in ihrem Werk, wie dies leider oft der Fall ist. Ethnisch geprägte Ortsgebundenheit ist fatal, weil sie große Verliebtheit und heftige Enttäuschung gleichermaßen hervorbringen kann. Wie oft kaufen wir, als Beispiel, einen Teppich auf einem orientalischen Basar, bringen das kostbare Stück nach Hause und sind dann peinlich berührt? Mit den Campana-Brüdern ist es anders. Die brasilianische Katastrophe, die sie uns schildern, ist unser aller Katastrophe, auch wenn wir es zu leugnen versuchen. Der beharrliche Versuch, die Handarbeit zu erhalten in einer Zeit, da alles virtuell wird, ist für uns alle eine Notwendigkeit, wenn wir unsere Sinnlichkeit nicht endgültig verlieren wollen. Hässlichkeit, Unvollkommenheit und Ekel nicht auszugrenzen, ist ein ethischer Imperativ, der für alle Menschen gilt. Das Hybride gegenüber dem Kohärenten vorzuziehen, ist eine Voraussetzung für das Überleben. Total Glocal. Auf den Punkt gebracht: Fernando und Humberto Campana sind keine Designer. Sie sind eine Therapie.

Abschließendes Bestiarium

Drei Jahre nach Explosion und Einsturz hat sich das Dach des Studios der Campanas wieder mit Katzen bevölkert. Es gibt auch eine zugelaufene kleine Hündin, die Chica heißt. Unschwer zu erraten, dass sie keine Schönheit ist.
Bei Edra haben wir einen Spezialüberzug für das Sofa *Aster Papposus* entwickelt, den ich »Fell eines nassen Hundes« genannt habe. Es ist ein Bezugsstoff mit unregelmäßig gebündelten, leicht struppigen Borsten, genau wie bei nassen Hunden eben. Es fühlt sich ganz außergewöhnlich an.
Zu guter Letzt haben wir eine Spezialserie der *Leatherworks*-Sessel aus geschichteten Lederstücken für ein großes Pariser Auktionshaus realisiert. Sie heißen *Furworks* und sehen wie Schafe aus, die von einem völlig unfähigen Scherer verunstaltet wurden. Die Auktion hat im November 2008 stattgefunden.
Hurra!

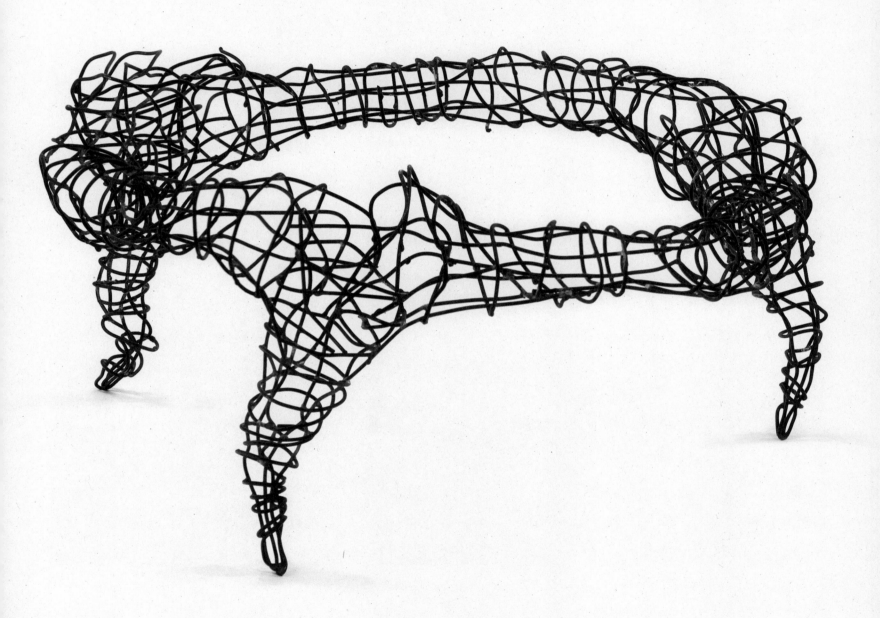

coffee table Couchtisch
Fios (String Schnur)
prototype Prototyp
1990
48×84×95 cm

armchair Armsessel
Anemona (Anemone)
serial model Serienmodell:
Edra spa, Perignano
2000
73×110×87 cm

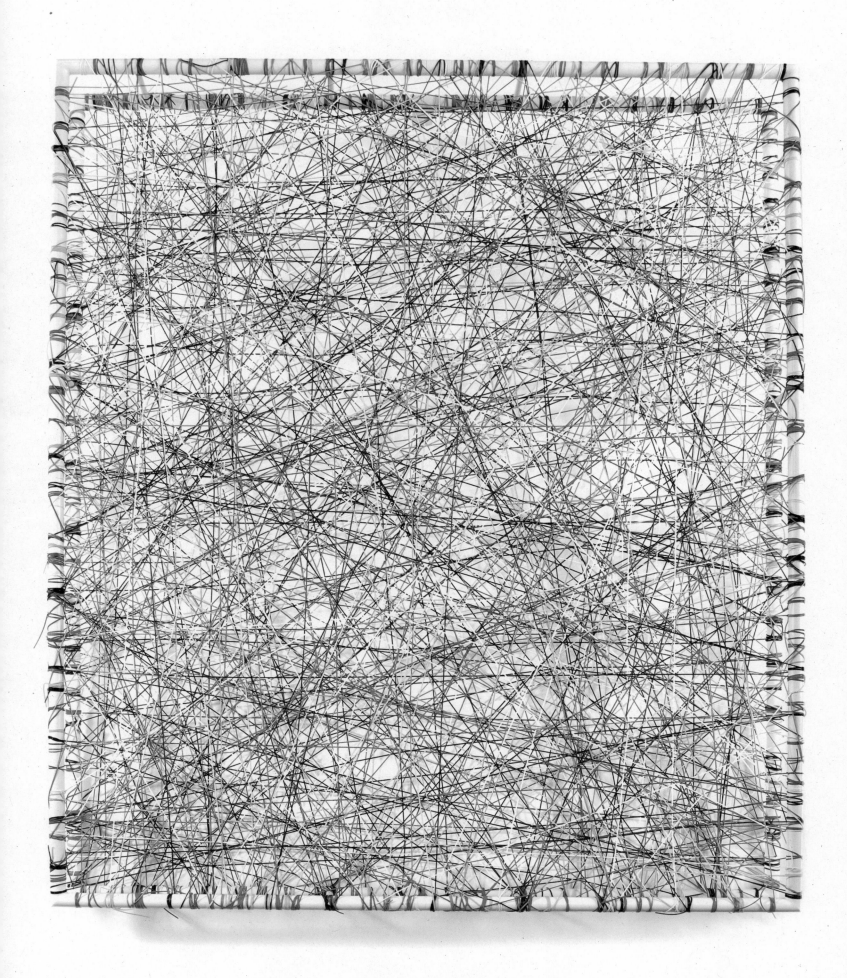

relief Relief
Untitled Ohne Titel
one-off piece Unikat
2005
300×250×35 cm

Humberto Campana
table centrepiece Tafelaufsatz
Tokyo Garden (Tokio Garten)
one-off piece Unikat
2005
22×85×55 cm

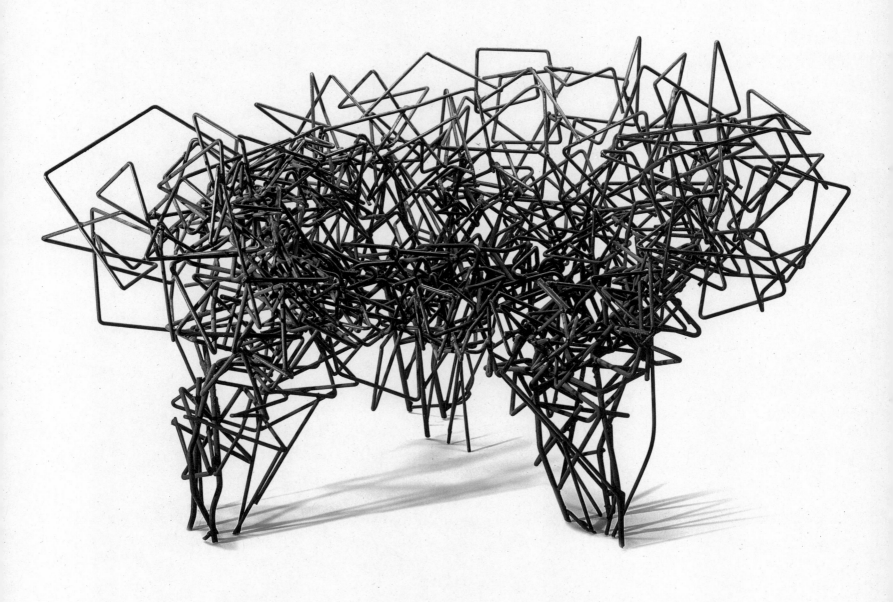

Humberto Campana
mirror frame Spiegelrahmen
(detail Detail)
Untitled Ohne Titel
one-off piece Unikat
1977
74×53×8 cm

Humberto Campana
armchair Armsessel
Bob
one-off piece Unikat
1990
60×120×80 cm

panel Tafel
OSB Masisa Campana,
Stuffed Toys
(Plüschtiere)
prototype Prototyp
2003
185 × 123 × 4 cm

Maria Helena Estrada

Intuition for Guidance, Hands as Tools

Die Intuition als Wegweiser, die Hände als Instrumente

An object is never limited to itself; it bears a constant relationship to the environment, to people, to history, and to a specific materiality.
Andrea Branzi

Brotas

Brotas is the small town in the interior of the state of São Paulo where Humberto and Fernando Campana grew up. The backyard of their house, the lavish vegetation, the trees, the brook – all served as the brothers' first workshop. Twigs, stones, mud, ants, and bees were the materials with which they created their toys. The whole of nature, with its many mysteries, was their everyday cinema, the place where they nurtured their fantasies; and instead of playing football with the other boys, they used to re-create it in their backyard.

Brotas means 'sprout' – as if, by a twist of fate, the name of the brothers' birthplace foretold their future course of life. There are two legends regarding the origin of the town's name. According to one, it stems from the water springs that abound in the surrounding area, each 'sprouting' out of the earth. According to the other, the name goes back to the Bandeirantes, the seventeenth- and eighteenth-century explorers who scoured the Brazilian hinterlands in search of slaves and gold. Leaving from São Paulo, wherever the Bandeirantes passed, they would cut down the entire vegetation; however, whenever they returned, passing through the region now called Brotas, they found that the vegetation had 'sprouted' and grown back again. Thus, whatever its true origin may be, the town's name, Brotas, is emblematic of the fertility that characterizes the spirit of the place.

In an article on the Campana brothers, Cristina Morozzi conveys the significance of this spirit to their work by referring to Plato's dialogues, which are often situated in a specific location. *Phaedrus,* for instance, takes place on the banks of a river, and as Morozzi comments, 'it is not only about two people who communicate with each other but also about two individuals situated in a specific place. It is the location that provides consistency to the beauty and love being discussed.'[1] Such was Brotas for Fernando and Humberto.

Career Start

Brotas was later replaced by São Paulo, the state capital, as the place whose spirit the brothers absorbed. First it was Humberto who moved to the big city. He graduated with a degree in law, as befits – according to tradition – the eldest son of a good Brazilian family, but already in his first days working at a law firm in São Paulo he became horrified and fled to Itabuna, a city in the inner regions of Bahia. There he began creating terracotta objects and little mirrors encrusted with shells, and, like all the local inhabitants, lived off craftsmanship. In a certain way, in Itabuna he realized his childhood dream of becoming a Native Brazilian Indian. He lived there for a couple of years, from 1978 to 1979, during which he reached a final decision regarding the profession he desired for himself: 'I am going to make a living with my hands,' he resolved. Thus, he returned to São Paulo and began pursuing a career as a plastic artist.

Brazilian artist Nazareth Pacheco recounts how she first met Humberto in 1982 at the studio of Portuguese sculptor Santos Lopes, where people from various walks of life – from business administrators to doctors and lawyers – would gather. It was there that she and Humberto became friends. 'It was no coincidence that our paths crossed. Humberto was the most creative and daring student of Lopes. Seeing him daily was my greatest motivation to search for new paths and challenges in plastic art. Humberto was also the one who introduced me to wastes of vulcanized black rubber used in the automobile industry. My first sculptures, tenuous and flexible, were made out of this material.'

1 Cristina Morozzi, 'Il saper fare come spirito del luogo' [Know-how as the spirit of a place], *Campanas,* ed. Maria Helena Estrada (São Paulo: Bookmark, 2003), p. 48.

Das Objekt ist niemals in sich begrenzt, es steht immer in Beziehung zur Umgebung und zu den Menschen, zur Geschichte und zu einem Material.
Andrea Branzi

Brotas

Brotas ist die Kleinstadt im Landesinneren des Bundesstaates São Paulo, in der Humberto und Fernando Campana ihre Kindheit verbrachten. Der Garten hinter dem Haus, die Erde, die eine üppige Vegetation hervorbringt, die Bäume, der Bach – die Natur mit ihren vielen Geheimnissen bildete das erste Laboratorium der Brüder. Aus Zweigen, Steinen, Lehm, Ameisen und Bienen stellten sie ihre Spielzeuge her. Die sie umgebende Natur war ihr tägliches Kino und nährte ihre Fantasien, die sie im Hof ihres Hauses auslebten, statt mit anderen Kindern Fußball zu spielen.

Brotas bedeutet übersetzt »Sprösslinge«, und es scheint, als könnte bereits der Name ihres Geburtsortes als Wink für den Lebensweg der Brüder gedeutet werden. Es gibt zwei Legenden über den Ursprung des Namens. Eine erzählt von den zahllosen Quellen, die aus der Erde sprudeln. Die andere berichtet von den *bandeirantes,* den Eroberern des brasilianischen Hinterlandes, die im 18. Jahrhundert von São Paulo kommend auf der Suche nach Sklaven und Gold sämtliche Vegetation niederschlugen. Als sie aber auf dem Rückweg wieder in diese Region kamen, hatten alle Pflanzen erneut ausgetrieben und die Vegetation war wieder intakt. Wie auch immer es gewesen sein mag, der Name Brotas bringt sinnbildlich die Fruchtbarkeit zum Ausdruck, die den Geist dieses Ortes bestimmt.

Cristina Morozzi erläutert im Buch *Campanas* die Bedeutung des »Geistes des Ortes«, indem sie sich auf die Platonischen Dialoge bezieht, die stets an einem bestimmten Ort angesiedelt sind. Beispielsweise findet im *Phaidros* das Gespräch am Ufer eines Flusses statt. »Es geht dabei nicht einfach um zwei Personen, die sich unterhalten, sondern um zwei Subjekte, die sich an einem Ort befinden. Der Ort ist es, der die Verbindung zum Gesprächsgegenstand, zu Schönheit und Liebe, herstellt«, erklärt Morozzi.[1]

Der Beginn der Karriere

Nach Brotas wurde São Paulo, die große Hauptstadt, der Ort, dessen Geist die Campana-Brüder in sich aufsogen.

Zunächst ging Humberto und machte seinen Abschluss in Rechtswissenschaften, wie es sich in Brasilien für den Erstgeborenen aus guter Familie gehört. Seine ersten Tage in einem Anwaltsbüro aber erfüllten ihn mit Entsetzen – er flüchtete nach Itabuna, eine Stadt im Bundesstaat Bahia, wo er begann, Gegenstände aus Terrakotta und kleine Spiegel mit Muscheleinlagen herzustellen. Er lebte vom Kunsthandwerk wie ein Einheimischer und erfüllte sich damit in gewissem Sinne einen Kindheitstraum – »Wenn ich groß bin, will ich ein Indianer sein.« In Itabuna verbrachte er die Jahre 1978 und 1979 und entschied: »Ich werde meinen Lebensunterhalt mit meinen Händen verdienen.« Die brasilianische Künstlerin Nazareth Pacheco erzählt, dass sie Humberto Campana 1982 in São Paulo kennen gelernt hat, als sie gemeinsam im Atelier des portugiesischen Bildhauers Santos Lopes arbeiteten, in dem Menschen aus den verschiedensten Berufen zusammenkamen, von Betriebswirten bis zu Ärzten und Anwälten. Sie und Humberto wurden Freunde. »Es war kein Zufall, dass unsere Wege sich kreuzten. Humberto war der kreativste und mutigste unter Lopes' Schülern. Diese Zeit mit ihm ermunterte mich mehr als alles andere, neue Wege und Herausforderungen in der plastischen Kunst zu suchen. Humberto war es auch, der mir ein Stück Abfall aus schwarzem vulkanisiertem Gummi brachte, wie man ihn in der Automobilindustrie benutzt. Meine ersten Skulpturen, fadenförmig und biegsam, nutzten dieses Material.«

Während Humberto in der Welt der Kunst und Abstraktion lebte, war der studierte Architekt Fernando eher am Konkreten interessiert. Als er und Humberto sich in São Paulo wiedertrafen, unternahm er gerade die ersten Schritte in der Architektur und begeisterte sich für Möbel. Stets zeichnete

1 Cristina Morozzi: »Il saper fare come spitito del luogo«, in: M. E. Estrada (Hrsg.): *Campanas,* Bookmark, São Paulo 2003, S. 61 ff.

As for Fernando, he graduated in architecture and joined his brother in São Paulo. While Humberto lived in a world of art and abstraction, Fernando, making his first steps as an architect and falling in love with furniture, was interested in the concrete. Always scribbling in a notepad, Humberto sketched improbable shapes that Fernando managed to turn into chairs and tables. Thus, working together, they created their first line of furniture.

When asked how they gained the courage to show these oddly-shaped 'objects', the brothers answer 'by coincidence', or, more precisely, through their chance encounter with the work of English designer Danny Lane. Lane was invited by designer Adriana Adam, owner of the Nucleon 8 gallery, for an exhibition and conference in São Paulo. Upon seeing Lane's carpets, made of intertwined metal wires, the brothers immediately thought: 'If he can do it, so can we.'

This took place at the end of the 1980s – a time when Brazilian designers seemed infatuated with the clean lines that characterized the work of their Italian peers. The brothers decided to show Adriana their first iron pieces and invited her to a presentation they were about to give at the Museu de Arte de São Paulo (MASP), where they wanted to exhibit their work.

Adrian took me along and what we saw not only surprised but also enchanted us! Their furniture pieces had a freshness to them that did not seem diluted by education or formal training: pure inspiration and healthy ingenuity, free from prejudice. Fernando and Humberto Campana's creations appeared to be uncontaminated and bore no similarity to European – or any other – design models. They were plain iron chairs and tables, with high backs of extremely odd shapes, sometimes aggressive. 'I have a wicked, aggressive side', confessed Humberto, 'I like to express brutality.' Such a statement was hardly believable considering his pleasant expression and amiable behaviour. We immediately convinced them to abandon the MASP exhibition for a more avant-garde venue: Nucleon 8, where they had first encountered the work of Danny Lane.

'Today,' says Adriana, 'when I see the *Corallo* chair, or the *Melissa Campana* line,[2] I recall the "intertwinement" that characterized their first fruit bowl, which I saw in 1986 or 1987. At the time, what struck me was the combination of the personal timidity, insecurity, and uneasiness of the Campanas, who were nevertheless full of creative energy, and the unexpected nature of their furniture-sculptures.'

Adriana had just launched in Nucleon 8 a project entitled *Modernos Brasileiros* (Modern Brazilians), which traced the work of the masters of Brazilian design, from Gregori Warchavchik through Flávio de Carvalho and Lina Bo Bardi to Paulo Mendes da Rocha, who later, in 2006, was awarded the Pritzker Prize. It was right after this rediscovery of the legacy of the 1940s and 1950s that Fernando and Humberto Campana arrived on the scene, with a series of chairs and tables that brought with it a gust of fresh air and marked a new direction for Brazilian design.

As far as the name of the exhibition was concerned, we decided to go with the truth: *As Desconfortáveis* (The Uncomfortable Ones) – a line of furniture made of plain iron, without any upholstery, and launched in the middle of a cold winter! As for public relations, my job was to handle the journalists. But instead of the usual presentation for the press, I went by intuition and left Humberto alone with them, without any preliminary rehearsals, preambles, or releases, and also without Fernando, who was travelling abroad. Al-

Humberto auf einem kleinen Block unvorstellbare Entwürfe und Fernando sorgte dafür, dass sie zu Tischen und Stühlen wurden. So entstand ihre erste gemeinsame Möbelkollektion.

Woher nahmen sie den Mut, diese unerhörten »Gebilde« zu zeigen? Ein simpler Zufall brachte sie dazu – die Bekanntschaft mit dem Werk des englischen Designers Danny Lane, der von der Galerie Nucleon 8 der Designerin Adriana Adam zu einer Ausstellung und Konferenz nach São Paulo eingeladen worden war.

Humberto Campana (second from right!) in the Grand Canyon, photographed by Robert Wasilewski, 1987.
Humberto Campana (Zweiter von rechts!) im Grand Canyon, fotografiert von Robert Wasilewski, 1988.

»Was der kann, können wir auch«, dachten die Brüder, als sie Lanes Teppiche aus geflochtenen Metalldrähten sahen.

Das war Ende der 1980er Jahre, in einer Zeit, als die klaren Linien des italienischen Designs die brasilianischen Künstler zu hypnotisieren schienen. Die Brüder Campana beschlossen, Adriana Adam ihre ersten Werke aus Eisen zu zeigen und schickten ihr eine Einladung ins Museu de Arte de São Paulo (MASP), wo sie ihre Arbeit vorstellen wollten.

Adriana nahm mich mit, und was wir sahen, überraschte und begeisterte uns! Diese Möbel zeigten eine Frische, die im positiven Sinne aus mangelnder Ausbildung und Information herrührte. Pure Inspiration und gesunde Naivität, frei von Vorurteilen, ohne die geringsten Anklänge an europäisches Design oder irgendein anderes Modell. Es waren Tische und Stühle aus rohem Eisen, mit hohen Lehnen und äußerst merkwürdigen, mitunter aggressiven Formen. »Ich habe eine bösartige, aggressive Seite«, gesteht Humberto. »Es gefällt mir, Brutalität auszudrücken.« Diese Offenbarung ist fast unglaublich angesichts des Sanftmuts in seinem Ausdruck und Verhalten.

Wir überzeugten die Brüder, das MASP zu verlassen und sich in einem Avantgarde-Showroom zu versuchen, in denselben Ausstellungsräumen von Nucleon 8, wo sie Lane kennen gelernt hatten.

»Wenn ich heute den Stuhl *Corallo* oder die Kollektion *Melissa Campana*[2] sehe fühle ich mich an das ›Geflecht‹ ihres ersten Obstkorbs erinnert, den ich 1986 oder 1987 sah«, sagt Adriana Adam. »Damals begeisterte mich die Mischung aus ihrer persönlichen Schüchternheit, Unsicherheit, Unruhe und kreativen Energie und dem Unerwarteten ihrer Möbel-Skulpturen.«

Adriana hatte gerade in einem Projekt von Nucleon 8 die *Modernos Brasileiros* (Die Brasilianischen Modernen), eine Kollektion von Meistern des Entwurfs, herausgebracht: von Gregori Warchavchik über Flávio de Carvalho bis zu Lina Bo Bardi und dem Architekten und späteren Pritzker-Preisträger Paulo Mendes da Rocha.

Nach dieser Retrospektive und Wiederentdeckung des brasilianischen Designs der 1940er und 1950er Jahre tauchten Fernando und Humberto auf und brachten mit einer Reihe von Tischen und Stühlen frischen Wind in die Szene. Wie sollte die Ausstellung heißen? Wir entschieden uns, die Dinge beim Namen zu nennen: As *Desconfortáveis* (Die Unbequemen). Sie zeigten rohes, nacktes Eisen, mitten im kalten Winter!

Auf ihrer ersten Pressekonferenz übernahm ich nicht wie üblich die Rolle der Moderatorin zwischen den Künstlern und den Journalisten, sondern vertraute meiner Intuition und ließ Humberto allein auf die Menge der Reporter los – ohne Übung, ohne Einleitung, ohne Pressemitteilung, ohne Fernando, der verreist war. Doch von den ersten Sätzen an gewann Humberto die Zuhörer für sich. Die Ehrlichkeit und Einfachheit, die aus seinen Worten sprach (und die

ready with his very first words, Humberto had won them over. The honesty and simplicity with which he spoke (and which he hasn't lost, even after twenty years of success), along with the flood of new perspectives that poured out of him, were more eloquent than any press release or acclamation, prepared beforehand, could have been. Magazines and newspapers all around hailed the good news: a unique project was emerging in Brazil.

'The objects and the shadows they projected on the walls of the gallery left an impression on all those who passed by,' says Adriana. 'Since then, the work of the Campanas has shown much progress and they deserve the considerable international recognition they receive. Instead of a "déjà vu", their work conveys a certain "freshness", an idea that like a cell multiplies and unfolds spatially, gaining complexity and evolving in new forms and materials. This is what accounts, in my opinion, for the strength and success of the work of these designers, who, in Brazil, are still tenderly referred to as "boys".'

The *Desconfortáveis,* however, were successful only in the eyes of the critics. Not one piece was sold. Only years later did the pieces acquire the status of collector's items.

Turning Point

The brothers' breakthrough occurred in 1994, when Marco Romanelli, who at the time was the design critic of the Italian magazine *Domus,* published an article on their work. Romanelli noticed the originality of the young Brazilian brothers' creations and wrote: 'In furniture design too, the function of aesthetic shock needs to be examined. ... I look for such things, chosen on personal principles, in the truth of certain surviving artisan forms, in the bizarreness and extraordinariness of early cabinet-making, in the depth of artistic experience, but also in the borderline territories lying in between all these situations. ... Fernando and Humberto live there, but not, to be sure, by any calculated choice. Theirs has been, for many years now, an incoercible, pure propensity that passes through a love of materials. In a ceaseless blend of old and new, artisan and highly industrialized, and thus with an incredibly Brazilian approach, theirs is an autonomous, autochthonous idiom....'[3]

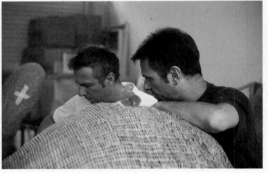

Humberto and Fernando Campana at work on a *Diamantina* seating unit, 2008.
Humberto und Fernando Campana bei der Arbeit an einer *Diamantina*-Sitzinsel, 2008.

Yet how does one give voice to this new language of design in a country in which wooden chairs – traditional to the point of being trite yet acclaimed for their 'Brazilian richness' – control the furniture market? How is it that in their own country the Campana brothers need to swim against the current while in Europe their aesthetics have gained a large following?

The fact is that the most noticeable feature of Fernando and Humberto's approach to design is the valorization of handcrafted production, with its inherent freedom of creation and its use of recyclable materials and wastes. Yet, an uncertainty prevails as to whether the type of craftsmanship found in Brazil today is good enough for mass production, since in most cases it has failed to attain a level of quality that would enable it to compete in the international market.

A case in point is the workshop given by Fernando and Humberto during the 1990s at the Museu Brasileiro da Escultura in São Paulo. Under the brothers' guidance, a group of energetic young students set out to find new possibilities for working with materials that until then had not been utilized in the applied arts (scrap metal, for instance). The result was a very successful exhibition and it seemed as if a new type of high-quality handcrafted design would

3 Marco Romanelli, 'Designs from 1991 to 1994', *Domus* 757 (February 1994), pp. 56, 60.

sich auch nach zwanzig Jahren des Erfolgs nicht verloren hat), die Flut der neuen Perspektiven, waren überzeugender als jede vorbereitete Pressemitteilung oder Lobrede es hätten sein können. Zeitschriften und Zeitungen – alle – verbreiteten die gute Nachricht: In Brasilien entsteht ein einzigartiges Projekt. »Die Objekte und ihre Schatten, die sie an die Wände dieser Ausstellungshalle warfen, bewegten die Gefühle aller, die dort ein- und ausgingen«, erinnert sich die Gründerin von Nucleon 8. »Von damals bis heute war es ein weiter Weg für diese zwei Designer, die ihre internationale Anerkennung so verdient haben. Die ›Frische‹ ihrer Arbeit und nicht das ›déjà vu‹, eine Idee, die sich wie eine Zelle immer weiter teilt, an Komplexität gewinnt und neue Formen und Materialien hervorbringt, pflanzen sich aus meiner Sicht in der Kraft und dem Erfolg dieser Designer fort, die wir in Brasilien noch immer zärtlich ›die Jungs‹ nennen.«

Aber die *Desconfortáveis* erreichten zunächst lediglich einen Erfolg bei der Kritik. Kein einziges Stück wurde verkauft, bis Jahre später in einer erneuten Schau der Ehrgeiz der Sammler erwachte.

Der Wendepunkt

Der Durchbruch der Brüder läßt sich auf 1994 datieren, als Marco Romanelli, damals Design-Kritiker der italienischen Zeitschrift *Domus,* einen Artikel über ihre Arbeit veröffentlichte. Romanelli erkannte die Originalität des Schaffens der jungen Brasilianer und schrieb:

»Auch im Möbeldesign musste die Funktion des ästhetischen Schocks analysiert werden. [...] Ich halte nach solchen Objekten Ausschau, deren Herangehen persönlich ist: in der Aufrichtigkeit gewisser fortlebender Formen des Kunsthandwerks, in der Skurrilität und Exzeptionalität der feinen, alten Möbeltischlerei, in den Tiefen der künstlerischen Erfahrung, aber auch in den Grenzbereichen zwischen all diesen Erscheinungen. [...] Fernando und Humberto Campana leben in diesen Grenzbereichen, aber gewiss nicht aus Berechnung. In ihnen steckt schon seit vielen Jahren eine unbezwingbare und reine Neigung, die sich in der Liebe zum Material ausdrückt, oder besser gesagt, zu den Materialien. In einer unerschöpflichen Verbindung des Alten mit dem Neuen, des Kunsthandwerklichen mit dem Hochindustrialisierten. Eine Herangehensweise also, die unglaublich brasilianisch ist. Ihre Sprache ist unabhängig und bodenständig [...].«[3]

Wie aber kann sich diese neue Sprache im Design in einem Land Gehör verschaffen, in dem traditionellste und banalste Stühle aus Holz, dem sprichwörtlichen »Reichtum Brasiliens«, den Möbelmarkt beherrschen?

Wie kommt es, dass die Campanas in ihrem eigenen Land gegen den Strom schwimmen und man kaum Produkte aus dem »Haus Campana« findet, während in Europa ihre Ästhetik zahlreiche Anhänger hat?

Die sichtbarsten Folgen des Anspruchs, den Fernando und Humberto eingeführt haben, sind die Wertschätzung des Designs aus handwerklichem Ursprung, die Freiheit im Schaffensprozess und die selbstverständliche Verwendung von recyceltem Material und Abfällen. Dennoch herrscht heute Unsicherheit darüber, ob dieses Kunsthandwerk für die industrielle Fertigung taugt, zumal es in der Mehrzahl der Fälle noch nicht die Qualität erreicht hat, um Zugang zum internationalen Markt zu finden.

Nach einem Workshop unter der Anleitung von Fernando und Humberto in den 1990er Jahren im, Museu Brasileiro da Escultura (MUBE) in São Paulo, trat eine Gruppe entschlossener junger Leute auf den Plan und öffnete die Türen

3 Marco Romanelli: »Designs from 1991 to 1994«, in: *Domus,* Nr. 757, Februar 1994, S. 56–61, hier: S. 56 und 60.

be born out of the experience. Unfortunately, however, none of the participants managed to carry on the success and establish a foothold in the furniture market.

Conceptual Refinement

'It is essential to trust one's own intuition,' say Fernando and Humberto in unison. According to them, the intuition they speak of is triggered by the look or the feel of a certain object or material, which, as of that moment, changes the object's or the material's purpose, transforms its nature, and causes it to acquire a new functionality. 'Such was the case, for instance, with our *Jenette* chair,' they say, 'which was inspired by brooms made of piassava fibre.'

Such an attitude towards 'the banal' – namely, seeing an inherent value in a material that is supposedly inferior by nature – seems to be one of the secrets lying behind the brothers' innovative approach to furniture and the starting point of a major current in contemporary design.

To extract the meaning of the trivial, to give soul and expression to objects that most of the time go unnoticed – these are some of the goals towards which the Campanas strive. Today they spend most of their time travelling around the world, as if affirming the very existence of design in Brazil, even if it is based on simple materials and low technology. They have shown that all that is needed is a small push in order for designers to create an original and vigorous vocabulary that will shock old aesthetic patterns and conquer international markets. Plastic jerricans, piassava brooms, bubble wrap, small wooden slats, garden hoses, barbed wire, anti-slip padding for doormats, worn cardboard used in its maximal simplicity and integrity – this universe of re-use, non-waste, and sustainability defines the parameters of the brothers' creations. It is a type of design that, as Mel Byars describes it, goes much beyond formal correction or pleasant aesthetics.[4] Thus, it was a purely poetical gesture when in 1998, for the exhibition *Projects 66* that was held at the Museum of Modern Art in New York, curator Paola Antonelli decided to show the work of a well-known designer – Ingo Maurer – alongside that of the barely known Brazilian brothers.

Keeping Focus

Almost twenty years have passed since the Campana brothers came out with their first collection. During these years, what has changed in their approach, work methods, and perspective on design? 'Everything has changed, has become easier and faster,' replies Fernando, 'yet, at the same time, nothing has changed in essence. We continue to work on a small scale and do not have a huge space or a big team like the large European firms. Our work rhythm has remained the same; the only difference is that now it has an international dimension. But, we always return to the studio in São Paulo, which is also the "lab" where we develop prototypes and limited editions.'

'It is important for us to always return to Brazil,' adds Humberto, 'for it is our primary source of inspiration. Today, much of our work consists of knowing how to stay focused. Because we receive so many interesting proposals – but also others that could be traps – we must keep our minds focused on the most important ones. It is our intuition that must always be kept sharp.'

To work in such close intimacy for over twenty years means alternating between harmony and discord and dealing with mood swings and crises. But, at the moment of creation, the unison between the brothers is so perfect that it becomes impossible to know in which of them originated the initial idea.

4 Mel Byars, 'Does Mies Dance the Samba?', *Tropical Modern: The Designs of Fernando and Humberto Campana,* ed. Mel Byars (New York: Acanthus Press, 1998), p. 7.

für die Arbeit mit Materialien, die bis dahin noch nicht im Design verwendet worden waren, beispielsweise Schrott. Sie zeigten eine sehr erfolgreiche Ausstellung, und es schien, als wäre aus dieser Erfahrung ein neues kunsthandwerkliches Design von Qualität geboren. Leider blieb dieses Projekt ohne nennenswerte Folgen für den Möbelmarkt.

Verfeinerung der Konzepte

»Das Vertrauen in die eigene Intuition ist fundamental«, sagen Fernando und Humberto quasi unisono. »Intuition beginnt mit einer Vision oder der Berührung eines bestimmten Gegenstandes oder Materials, die von diesem Moment an ihre Bestimmung verändern und sich verwandeln, eine neue Natur und Funktion gewinnen, wie im Fall der Palmfaserbesen, die uns zu dem Stuhl *Jenette* inspiriert haben.« Diese »Vision des Banalen«, dieses Erkennen des Reichtums der Möglichkeiten hinter der Armseligkeit des Materials scheint mir eines der Geheimnisse im Herangehen der Brüder und Ausgangspunkt für eine breite Strömung im zeitgenössischen Design zu sein.

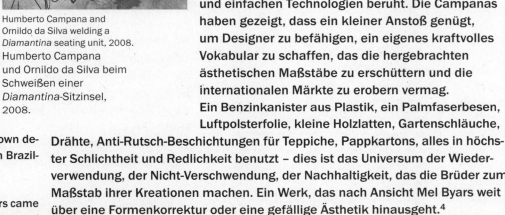

Humberto Campana and Ornildo da Silva welding a *Diamantina* seating unit, 2008. Humberto Campana und Ornildo da Silva beim Schweißen einer *Diamantina*-Sitzinsel, 2008.

Den gewöhnlichen und fast unsichtbaren Gegenständen Seele und Ausdruck zu verleihen, ihre Bedeutung herauszufiltern, das macht den Reichtum im Werk dieser beiden Wanderlustigen aus. Heute verbringen sie einen großen Teil ihrer Zeit damit, als Botschafter durch die Welt zu reisen, wie um zu erklären, dass in Brasilien tatsächlich ein Design existiert, wenn es auch auf simplen Materialien und einfachen Technologien beruht. Die Campanas haben gezeigt, dass ein kleiner Anstoß genügt, um Designer zu befähigen, ein eigenes kraftvolles Vokabular zu schaffen, das die hergebrachten ästhetischen Maßstäbe zu erschüttern und die internationalen Märkte zu erobern vermag.

Ein Benzinkanister aus Plastik, ein Palmfaserbesen, Luftpolsterfolie, kleine Holzlatten, Gartenschläuche, Drähte, Anti-Rutsch-Beschichtungen für Teppiche, Pappkartons, alles in höchster Schlichtheit und Redlichkeit benutzt – dies ist das Universum der Wiederverwendung, der Nicht-Verschwendung, der Nachhaltigkeit, das die Brüder zum Maßstab ihrer Kreationen machen. Ein Werk, das nach Ansicht Mel Byars weit über eine Formenkorrektur oder eine gefällige Ästhetik hinausgeht.[4]

Und so war es auch von Paola Antonelli eine sehr poetische Geste, 1998 in der Werkschau *Projects 66* im Museum of Modern Art (MoMA) einen bereits anerkannten Designer – Ingo Maurer – mit den fast unbekannten Brasilianern zusammen in einer Ausstellung zu zeigen.

Ein gut gesetzter Schwerpunkt

Fast zwanzig Jahre sind seit ihrer ersten Kollektion vergangen. Was hat sich seither an ihrem Herangehen, an ihrer Arbeitsweise und ihrer Perspektive auf das Design verändert?

»Alles hat sich geändert, es ist leichter geworden, schneller; und zugleich hat sich im Kern nichts verändert«, erklärt Fernando. »Wir arbeiten weiter in kleinem Rahmen, wir haben weder eine große Werkstatt noch einen Mitarbeiterstab wie die großen europäischen Ateliers; unser Arbeitsrhythmus ist derselbe geblieben – nur dass sich jetzt alles auf internationaler Ebene abspielt. Aber immer wieder kehren wir in dieses Atelier in São Paulo zurück, das auch das Labor ist, in dem wir die Prototypen und die limitierten Editionen entwickeln.«

4 Mel Byars: »Does Mies Dance the Samba?«, in: Ders. (Hrsg.): *Tropical Modern. The Designs of Fernando und Humberto Campana,* Acanthus Press, New York 1998, S. 7.

'Along these twenty-something years, we have passed through different phases,' says Humberto. 'First, we began developing our own language, working on a semi-industrial scale or, in the case of limited editions, producing pieces that were entirely handcrafted. Then, we moved on to large pieces and installations, consolidating the language we had developed. And today, it seems our work is entering a new phase, oriented towards interior architecture and design: a hotel in Athens, the Camper store in Berlin, a showroom for avant-garde design pieces in São Paulo, a café for the Musée d'Orsay in Paris.'

Fernando Campana working on the poster *Camper together with Campana*, 2006.
Fernando Campana bei der Arbeit am Poster *Camper together with Campana*, 2006.

How do the brothers manage to coordinate themselves among all these projects, setting up a large installation at the British Museum in London while planning another that is to be exhibited in Russia and, at the same time, preparing for a big exhibition at the Vitra Design Museum in Germany? And where do they find inspiration and focus to work, in the mean time, on a series of fashion products, such as the *Melissa Campana* line that they designed for Grendene?

'Today things happen more easily,' explains Fernando. 'Maybe this is exactly what has changed. Not only the organization of the studio, which is still small, but the ideas themselves: we feel as if they are within closer reach, as if all it takes is a single gesture or look in order for us to know where to start and in what direction to head.'

Leo Kim, who is responsible for the studio's legal and commercial affairs, follows the brothers' activities closely and can therefore shed some light on the inner dynamics of this 'laboratory of ideas'. 'We are a young, multicultural team,' he explains. 'The "elders" are around 35 years old and the educational background is quite varied, from those who have attained only a basic education to bilingual, trilingual, even polyglot postgraduates. The team is highly motivated and quite versatile and everybody at the studio participates in one stage or another of the development of each project. The range of activities can be divided into two main orientations: products developed for the industry, on the one hand, and the projects of Estúdio Campana, on the other. We are few in number, but Fernando and Humberto are always involved, with open eyes and four hands on everything.'

Today, many of the brothers' pieces are commissioned by museums and galleries and, besides product design, the work at Estúdio Campana encompasses architecture and interiors, curator work, set design, and art direction. However, even the products developed for industry are not entirely machine made, be it for conceptual reasons or due to the complexity of the projects and the level of craftsmanship demanded.

All the pieces are designed at the studio in São Paulo. When a piece is sent to a client abroad and is accepted for serial production, the first model always remains at the company. If it is rejected, it gets sent back and is also stored at the studio: 'One day it will find its destination,' says Humberto. 'The situation today is different from the time of the *Desconfortáveis* chairs, when not a single piece was sold for three years. Today we are in a position to create any folly that enters our minds and see it accepted as a unique piece or super-limited edition. That was the case, for instance, with the *Multidão* (Crowd) armchair, which is made of ragdolls, or the *Banquete* (Feast) armchair, which is made of stuffed animals.'

The employees of Estúdio Campana and the dog Chica in the courtyard of the studio, early 2009.
Die Mitarbeiter des Estúdio Campana und der Hund Chica im Innenhof des Ateliers, Anfang 2009.

»Es ist wichtig, immer wieder hierher zurückzukommen, denn Brasilien ist und bleibt die Hauptquelle unserer Inspiration«, ergänzt Humberto. »Die Arbeit von heute besteht darin, Schwerpunkte setzen zu können. Weil wir so viele interessante und wichtige Angebote erhalten, aber auch andere, die Fallstricke sein können, müssen wir den Kopf für das Wichtigste frei haben, das ist der Schwerpunkt. Es ist die Intuition, die immer geschärft sein muss.«

In mehr als zwanzig Jahren der Nähe und Zusammenarbeit bleiben bei aller Harmonie Streitigkeiten, Stimmungsschwankungen und Krisen nicht aus. Aber im Moment des Schaffensprozesses ist die Abstimmung so perfekt, dass es unmöglich ist, zu sagen, auf wen eine Idee letztlich zurückgeht. »In diesen Jahren durchschritten wir verschiedene Etappen«, sagt Humberto. »Zunächst begannen wir eine eigene Sprache zu entwickeln; dann arbeiteten wir nicht nur an Möbeln – in halbindustrieller Produktion oder, bei limitierten Auflagen, in komplett handwerklicher Herstellung –, sondern auch an großen Stücken, an Installationen, die diese Sprache verfestigt haben. Und jetzt scheinen wir auf dem Weg zur Innenarchitektur und zum Interior Design zu sein: ein Hotel in Athen, das Geschäftslokal von Camper in Berlin, ein Showroom für Avantgarde-Design in São Paulo, der Vorentwurf für ein Café im Musée d'Orsay in Paris.«

Wie organisieren sie sich, um diese Reisen zu ermöglichen, große Objekte im British Museum in London zu installieren und andere, für Russland bestimmte, fertig zu stellen, während sie eine große Ausstellung im Vitra Design Museum in Deutschland vorbereiten? Und wie finden sie Inspiration und Konzentration, um zur selben Zeit an Modeentwürfen zu arbeiten, wie der Kollektion *Melissa Campana* von Grendene?

»Wir können sagen, dass die Dinge heute viel einfacher vonstatten gehen. Vielleicht ist es das, was sich wirklich geändert hat. Nicht nur die Organisation der Werkstatt, die nach wie vor klein ist, sondern die Ideen: Es scheint uns so, als ob sie schon eher zu greifen sind; es reicht ein Wink, ein Blick, um zu wissen, wo der Ausgangspunkt ist und in welche Richtung der Weg führt, den wir im Moment gehen müssen«, sagt Fernando.

Leo Kim, verantwortlich für die juristischen und kommerziellen Aspekte des Ateliers, erklärt die Dynamik in diesem Laboratorium der Ideen, in dem vielseitige Begabungen zusammenkommen: »Wir sind ein junges, multikulturelles Team. Die ›Ältesten‹ sind um die 35, und der Bildungsstand ist sehr unterschiedlich, von Hauptschülern bis zu Uni-Absolventen, von zweisprachigen bis zu vielsprachigen Mitarbeitern. Dieses Team ist hoch motiviert, vielseitig einsetzbar und jeder Mitarbeiter im Atelier ist zu irgendeinem Zeitpunkt an der Projektarbeit beteiligt [...] Die Bandbreite der Aktivitäten folgt hauptsächlich zwei Richtungen: eine wendet sich an die Industrie und die andere bearbeitet die Projekte des Estúdio Campana. Wir sind wenige, aber Humberto und Fernando sind stets mit wachen Augen und vier Händen an allem beteiligt«, erklärt Leo.

Im Estúdio Campana werden selbst die für die Industrie bestimmten Stücke niemals vollständig maschinell hergestellt, sei es aus Gründen der Konzeption oder wegen der Komplexität der Projekte und der erforderlichen handwerklichen Fertigkeiten. Heute sind viele der bestellten Stücke für Museen und Galerien bestimmt. Die Arbeit des Ateliers umfasst neben Produktdesign, Architektur und Inneneinrichtung Tätigkeiten als Kuratoren, Szenografen und künstlerische Leiter.

Regarding *Multidão* and its ragdolls, Ruth Cardoso mentioned them in an interview she gave only a few days before she died in June 2008.[5] Cardoso, the wife of former President Fernando Henrique Cardoso and founder of Artesanato Solidário, a non-governmental organization devoted to the development of handicrafts in destitute communities, spoke of the success of the ragdolls and how they are made according to a tradition that was kept alive by a single artisan in Paraíba. The goal of the organization she founded was to provide revenue to poor communities all over Brazil by stimulating craftsmanship and, as a result, to restore the self-respect and dignity of these populations. Through a workshop conducted by the organization, the number of people making the ragdolls rose to more than forty, and, as Cardoso remarked, by choosing these dolls for one of their most famous creations, Fernando and Humberto Campana had made the work of these artisans known all over the world.

Julia Roque Santos Ribeiro sewing together the dolls for a *Multidão* stool from the *Leatherworks* series, 2008.
Julia Roque Santos Ribeiro beim Zusammennähen der Puppen für einen *Multidão*-Hocker der *Leatherworks*-Serie, 2008.

Recognition, Step by Step

Sonia Diniz, a leading figure in São Paulo's design scene, first met Fernando and Humberto in 1994, when she opened Firma Casa on São Paulo's interior decoration street, Alameda Gabriel Monteiro da Silva. 'At the time, everybody was interested in the clean, minimalistic lines of Italian design,' she recalls. 'How could anyone understand what these boys were making? It was the opposite of what fashion or trends dictated. From a piece of wire, twisted by hand, arose vases and fruit bowls, full of small curves. How difficult to understand – and sell – such design! The *Ninho* (Nest) series was the first product made by the boys that I sold.'

It was then that Diniz decided that every product the Campana brothers designed abroad would be sold at Firma Casa; and today she believes that this decision had a considerable influence on the range of products sold at the store. The collaboration began with the *Vermelha* (Red), *Azul* (Blue), and *Verde* (Green) armchairs that the brothers designed for Edra; and every year since then, another Edra-novelty designed by Fernando and Humberto has been added to the store's collection.

'I recall,' Sonia recounts, 'how they got stressed each time they were interviewed in Europe. To walk beside them at the Salone del Mobile in Milan was like walking next to Richard Gere: endless harassment. The trajectory of the brothers' career had been launched and there was no way of stopping it. Throughout the years, my biggest thrill was when I visited their studio and saw the *Sushi, Banquete,* and *Multidão* armchairs. I knew they would become objects of desire.'

'Today, after all these years of working together,' she concludes, 'I am grateful for having been so lucky as to be able to follow the brothers' career so closely and see their work progress and reach a milestone: the development of the Campana Design signature mark – products that even when industrialized maintain a handmade quality. Like in nature, each Campana piece is always singular and unique.'

For twenty years the Campana brothers have followed their intuition and broken all barriers, including geographic, to become – with their typical simplicity – a pioneering influence in contemporary design. Recognition? After exhibiting in dozens of museums and cultural institutions all over the world, they recently received the Designer of the Year award at the 2008 Design Miami show. The tension between poor and primitive Brazil, which serves as their source of inspiration, and the aesthetics of the great international centres of the world is a unique quality of the brothers' work

5 Ruth Cardoso, unpublished video interview by Dora Kaufmann, 14 June 2008. Copy in possession of Campana brothers.

Alle Objekte werden in der Werkstatt in São Paulo projektiert. Wenn ein Stück zu einem Kunden ins Ausland geschickt und für die Serienproduktion akzeptiert wird, bleibt das erste Modell dort im Unternehmen. Wird ein Objekt von einem ausländischen Hersteller abgelehnt, wird es zurückgeschickt und in der Werkstatt aufbewahrt. »Eines Tages wird es seine Bestimmung finden«, sagt Humberto. »Die Situation ist heute anders als zu Zeiten der *Desconfortáveis,* als drei Jahre vergingen, ohne dass ein einziges Stück verkauft wurde. Heute können wir es uns leisten, jede Verrücktheit zu schaffen, die unseren Köpfen entspringt, und sie als Einzelstück oder super-limitierte Auflage abzusetzen. Das ist zum Beispiel bei dem Sessel *Multidão* (Menschenmenge) der Fall, der aus Stoffpuppen besteht, und bei *Banquete* (Gelage), der aus Stofftieren gemacht ist.«

Den *Multidão* und die Stoffpuppen, aus denen er gearbeitet ist, erwähnte Ruth Cardoso in einem Interview, das sie im Juni 2008, wenige Tage vor ihrem Tod, gab.[5] Die Ehefrau des früheren brasilianischen Präsidenten Fernando Henrique Cardoso und Gründerin der Hilfsorganisation Artesanato Solidário spricht darin vom Erfolg der Stoffpuppen aus Paraíba, deren traditionelle Herstellungstechnik nur noch eine einzige Frau beherrschte. Das Ziel ihrer Hilfsorganisation sei es gewesen, sehr armen Kommunen in Brasilien eine Einnahmequelle zu verschaffen, indem das Kunsthandwerk gefördert und, vor allem, das Selbstwertgefühl und die Würde dieser Menschen wiederhergestellt worden sei. So seien nunmehr nach einem von Artesanato Solidário veranstalteten Workshop über vierzig Frauen mit der Herstellung der Puppen beschäftigt. Indem Fernando und Humberto Campana diese Puppen für eine ihrer berühmtesten Kreationen verwendeten, hätten sie die Arbeit der Puppenmacherinnen in der ganzen Welt bekannt gemacht.

Anerkennung, Schritt für Schritt

Sonia Diniz, eine wichtige Vermittlerin in der Design-Szene São Paulos, lernte Fernando und Humberto 1994 kennen, als sie die Firma Casa in der Alameda Gabriel Monteiro da Silva eröffnete, einer Straße in São Paulo, wo sich die Geschäfte für Innenausstattung konzentrieren. Damals interessierten sich alle nur für das klare, minimalistische Design aus Italien. »Wie sollte man da verstehen, was diese Jungs machten?«, erinnert sie sich. »Das war das Gegenteil dessen, was die Mode oder die Strömungen diktierten. Aus einem Stück handgebogenen Drahts mit vielen Windungen entstanden Vasen und Obstschalen. Wie schwer war es, dieses Design zu verstehen! Zu verstehen und zu verkaufen! Die Serie *Ninho* (Nest) war das erste Produkt, das die Jungs über mich verkauft haben.«

Damals entschloss sich Sonia Diniz, alle Produkte, die die Campanas außerhalb Brasiliens herstellten, über die Firma Casa zu verkaufen. Diese Entscheidung, so scheint ihr heute, hatte einen großen Einfluss auf die Palette der Produkte, die in ihrem Geschäft verkauft wurden. Begonnen habe es mit dem Vertrieb von Edra-Produkten, den Stühlen aus Schnüren, *Vermelha* (Rot), *Azul* (Blau) und *Verde* (Grün). Seither bietet sie jedes Jahr Edra-Neuheiten von Fernando und Humberto an.

»Ich erinnere mich«, erläutert Sonia Diniz, »wie gestresst sie jedes Mal waren, wenn sie Interviews in Europa gaben. Auf dem Salone del Mobile in Mailand an ihrer Seite zu gehen, das ist wie an der Seite Richard Geres – ein totaler Ansturm. Der Erfolgsweg der Campanas hatte begonnen. Sie waren nicht mehr aufzuhalten. Am stärksten von Gefühlen überwältigt war ich in all diesen Jahren, als ich in ihrer Werkstatt die Sessel *Sushi, Banquete* und *Multidão* sah. Ich wusste, dass sie sich in Objekte der Begierde verwandeln würden.«

5 Ruth Cardoso, unveröffentlichtes Interview mit der Journalistin Dora Kaufmann am 14. Juni 2008. Kopie des Videos im Besitz der Campana-Brüder.

and one of their greatest feats. To be sure, Fernando and Humberto never had a clear and elaborated vision of making design intersect with art. They rediscovered materials and connected between them in a way contrary to aesthetic trends or worldwide fashions; they knowingly selected scraps and transformed existing objects; and they never strayed far from the path of handcrafted production, at times assisting it only slightly with machinery.

The brothers' sensitive handling of materials is brought to light, for example, in their recurrent use of cords. Every conceivable type of cord is featured in their work – from strings to metal wires, from piassava fibres through plastic hoses to, most recently, wicker, as in their new line of chairs, *Transplastics.*

This latest series consists of cheap plastic chairs – the ones found in bars and popular beaches all over the world – covered in wickerwork. The material's sensuality and its continuously random intertwinement enlarge the volume of the chairs and, in a mysterious way, transform them into couches or even shelters, similar to the hideouts built by children. Thus, once again, the Campanas have managed, through an apparently casual gesture, to extract the meaning of trivial, almost invisible materials and objects and give them soul and expression.

The office of Humberto Campana, 2008.
Das Büro von Humberto Campana, 2008.

Heute, nach all diesen Jahren der Zusammenarbeit, bin ich dankbar, dass ich das Glück hatte, die Entwicklung ihrer Arbeit zur Marke, die das Design des Estúdio Campana heute ist, begleiten zu dürfen, [eines Designs], das, auch wenn es industriell hergestellt wird, die Charakteristik des Kunsthandwerks bewahrt. So wie in der Natur ist jedes Campana-Stück stets einzigartig, ein Unikat.«

Zwanzig Jahre folgten die Brüder Campana ihrer Intuition und durchbrachen alle Barrieren, einschließlich der geografischen. Und sie wurden, mit der sie auszeichnenden Einfachheit, wegweisend im zeitgenössischen Design. Die Anerkennung? Nachdem sie in Dutzenden von Museen und kulturellen Institutionen in aller Welt ausgestellt hatten, wurden sie schließlich auf der Messe Design Miami zu Designern des Jahres 2008 gewählt.

Das Austarieren der Spannung zwischen dem noch immer armen und primitiven Brasilien als Quelle ihrer Inspiration und ihren Auftritten in den großen internationalen Design-Zentren ist eine einzigartige Qualität im Werk der Brüder und eine ihrer »Heldentaten«.

Doch sicherlich war es nie eine klar ausgearbeitete Idee von Humberto und Fernando, das Design an die Schnittstelle zur Kunst zu bringen. Sie entdeckten Materialien wieder und verknüpften sie auf eine Weise, die der herkömmlichen Ästhetik oder den Modeströmungen der Welt fremd waren. Sie wählten bewusst Schrott und Lumpen aus und verwandelten bereits existierende Objekte. Niemals verließen sie diesen Weg und auch nicht die kunsthandwerkliche Produktion, die lediglich einige Male maschinelle Unterstützung erfuhr.

Ihr einfühlsamer Umgang mit Material zeigt sich zum Beispiel daran, wie sie Fäden und Schnüre handhaben. Sie bedienen sich aller erdenklichen Arten von Fasern, vom Bindfaden bis zum Metalldraht, von Palmfasern bis zum Plastikschlauch und zu Weidenruten. Letztere nutzen sie, um den billigsten aller Stühle zu umwickeln, den Plastikstuhl, wie man ihn in allen Kneipen und an allen Badestränden dieser Welt sieht, um eine neue Kollektion zu schaffen – die *Transplastics.* Die Sinnlichkeit des Materials förderte die Entwicklung der Serie und ihre Übertragung in große Volumina, oft mit mysteriösen Formen, die ein Sofa oder auch einen Zufluchtsort darstellen können – wie bei spielenden Kindern, die sich eine Höhle bauen. Auch hier scheinen sie wie beiläufig die Bedeutung der Dinge herauszuarbeiten, geben sie Materialien und Gegenständen, die so banal, quasi unsichtbar sind, eine Seele und einen Ausdruck.

armchair Armsessel
Multidão Mulata (A Crowd of Mulattos
Ein Haufen Mulatten)
one-off piece Unikat
2004
67×97×90 cm

fruit bowl Fruchtschale
Untitled Ohne Titel
prototype Prototyp
2008
55×47×8.5 cm

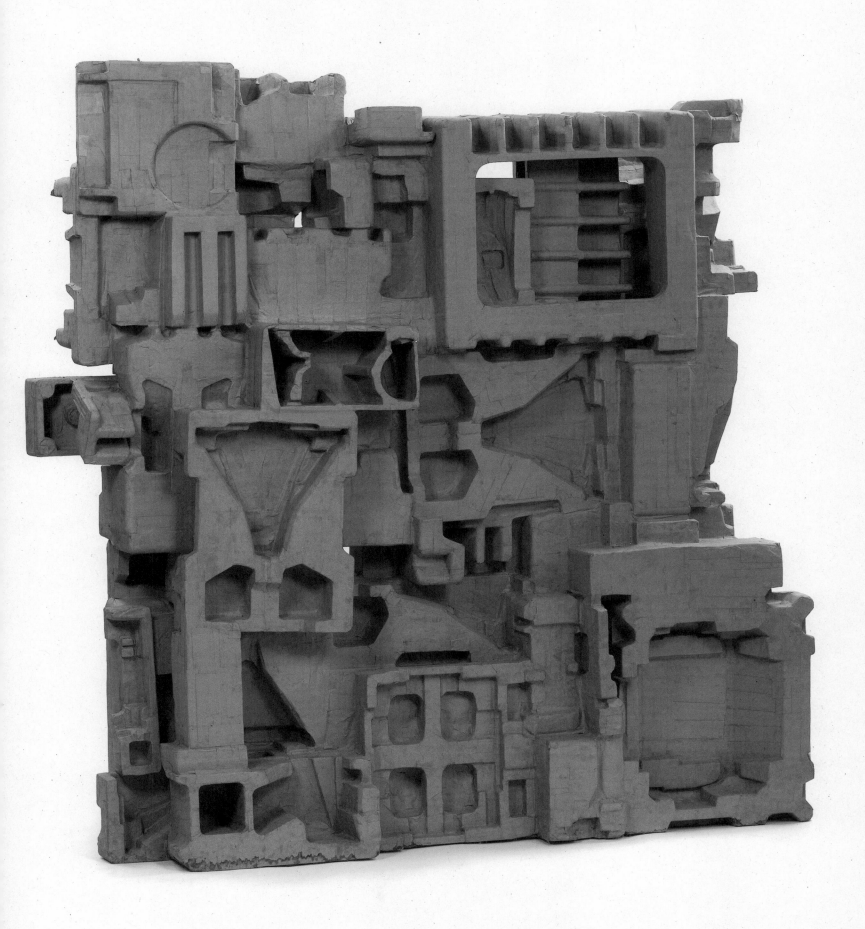

screen Wandschirm
Untitled Ohne Titel
one-off piece Unikat
2006
200 × 200 × 40 cm

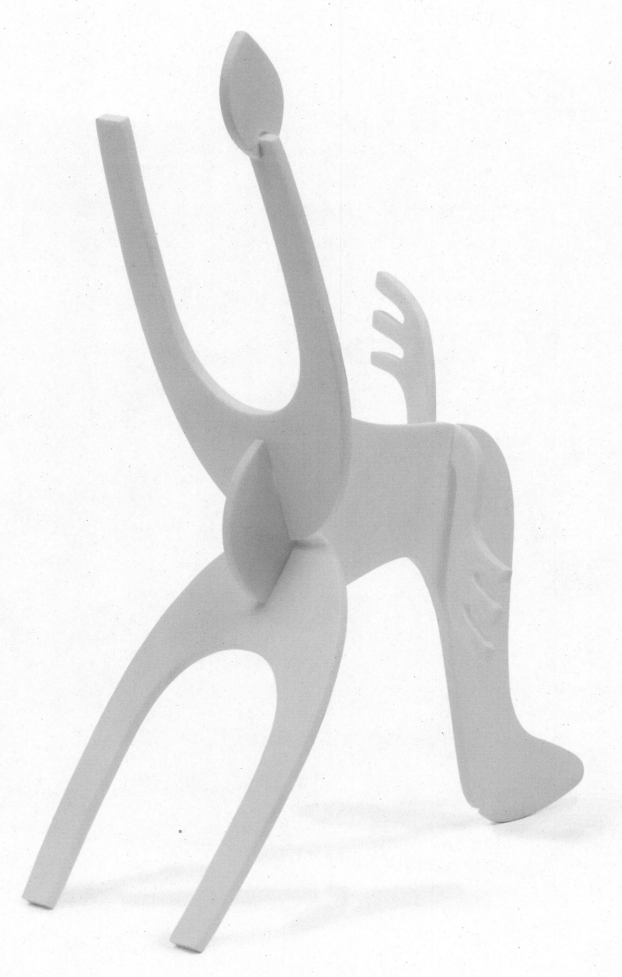

Fernando Campana
sculpture Plastik
Bambi
2006
41×12×31 cm

screen Wandschirm
Natureza Morta (Still Life Stillleben)
one-off piece Unikat
1990
193 × 24 × 113 cm

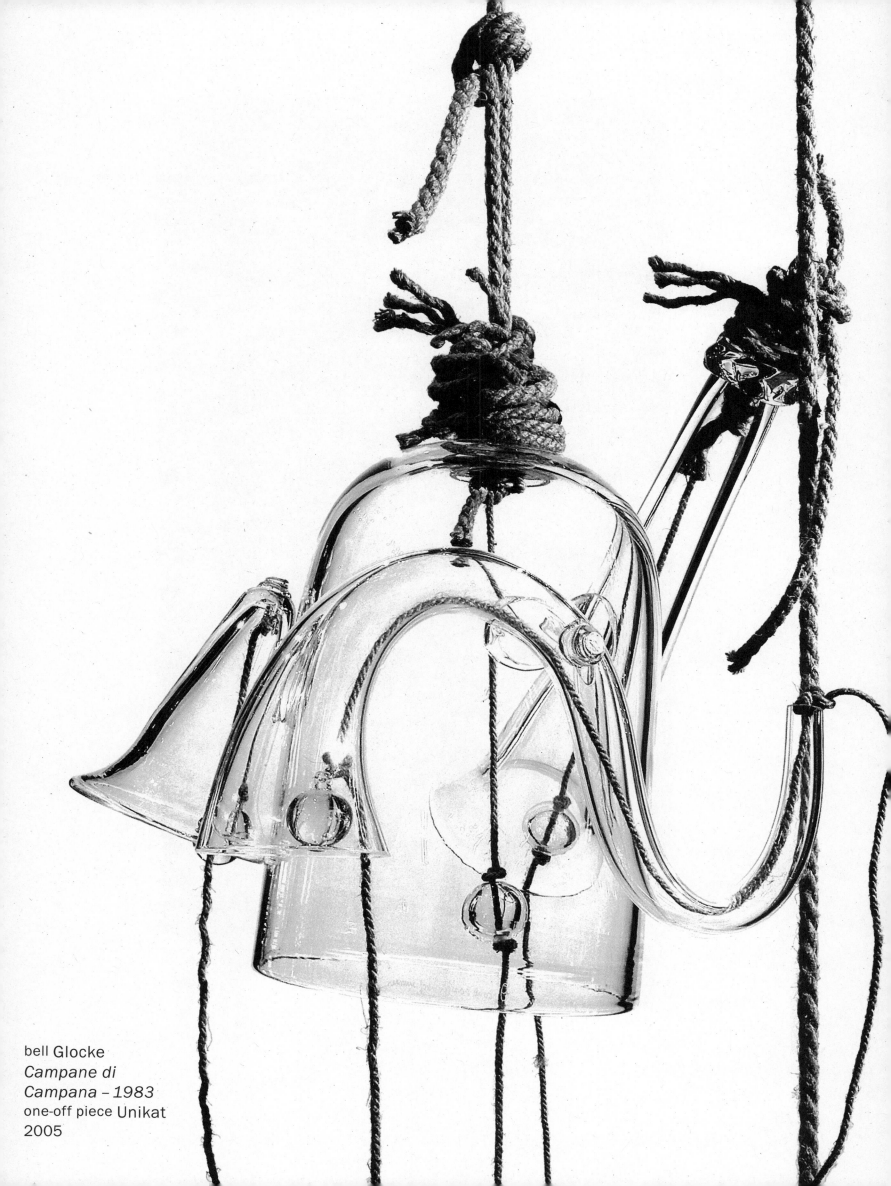

bell Glocke
*Campane di
Campana – 1983*
one-off piece Unikat
2005

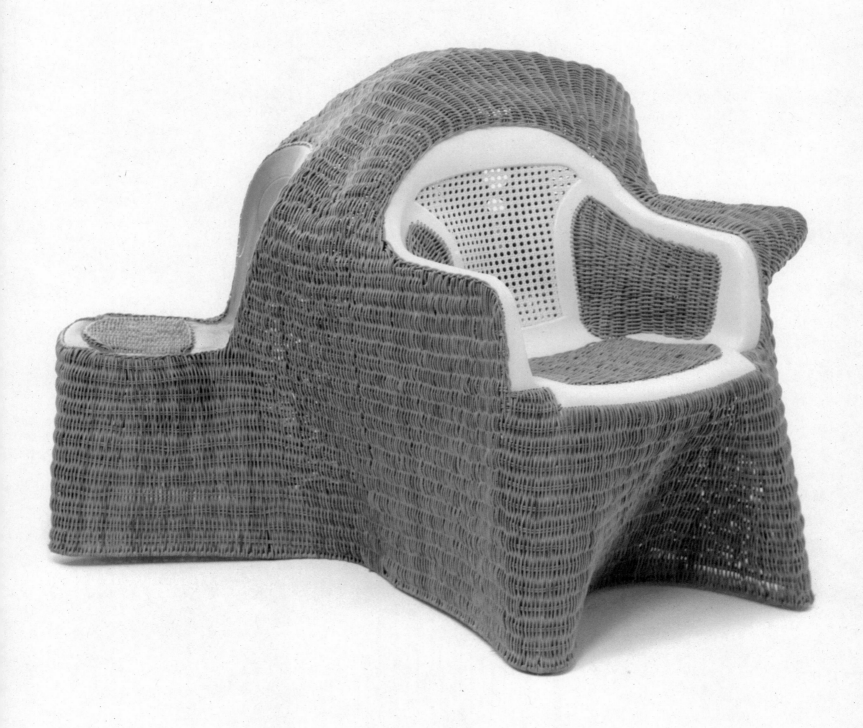

suite Sitzgruppe
Una Famiglia
(One Family Eine Familie)
one-off piece Unikat
2006
140×87×78 cm

chandelier Kronleuchter
Prived Oca
(Own House Eigenes Haus)
one-off piece Unikat
240 cm × 100 × 100 cm

fruit bowl Fruchtschale
Untitled Ohne Titel
one-off piece Unikat
1993
9 × 53 × 40 cm

Adélia Borges

Popular Culture in Contemporary Brazil
Populärkultur im heutigen Brasilien

stool Hocker
Vitória Régia (detail Detail)
unlimited edition, numbered per year (prototype)
unlimitierte Auflage, numeriert pro Jahr (Prototyp)
2002
58 × 100 × 100 cm

A decisive factor in Fernando and Humberto Campana's work is the strong inspiration they draw from the country in which they were born and chose to live. From the limpid rivers of their childhood to the congested chaos of today's biggest cities; from exuberant forests to asphalted urban jungles; from modernist dreams of formal clarity to the over-decorated kitsch objects of the middle class – all the attributes of the natural, cultural, and socioeconomic environment in which the brothers live, including especially its contradictions and noises, are digested by them and returned in a form of design that has a strong Brazilian flavour to it.

But what type of Brazil is this? The country expressed by the Campana brothers in their work is certainly not the common stereotype of samba, football, and beaches. One could mention the vastness of the country, namely its 8.5 million square kilometres, inhabited by 190 million people who share the same language, Portuguese. One could discuss the fact that it has been announced – along with Russia, India, and China – as one of the four major emerging markets in worldwide economy (the so-called BRIC economies). One could also mention the huge social inequalities that afflict the country – children begging for food on the streets while at the same time record sales of brands such as Prada, BMW, and Louis Vuitton are registered. One could – why not? – talk about the tropics; about samba and 'The Girl from Ipanema'; about the magical football passes of the likes of Pelé and Ronaldo; about the utopia of Brasília, the capital city built in the heart of the country …

The aspect dealt with in this essay, however, consists of a Brazil in which the sum of all the attributes mentioned above – and many others – results in a perfect blend of creative energy. This is the Brazil of popular culture, wherein people transform invention into a survival strategy; and it is exactly this cultural DNA that is strongly present in the work of the Campana brothers.

To see this country of invention among so many other Brazils is not always easy. Sometimes we are so close to something that we need to close our eyes to see it better; or, we need to leave and then come back in order to contemplate it with a clear vision.

Against the 'Flattening of the World'

The first university design course in Brazil was founded in 1964, in Rio de Janeiro. The Escola Superior de Desenho Industrial (ESDI) followed essentially the same curricular programme as that of the Ulm School of Design in Germany, from which some of the professors came, bringing with them the Bauhaus ideal of 'good form'. The principles introduced in Rio spread throughout the country. Adherence to the International style and the principle of 'form follows function' became the dominant force in the education and, consequently, the practice of design in Brazil. The schools also trained their students in mass-production techniques, typical of big industries.

Everything that happens during infancy – be it of a person, an institution, or a movement – leaves a strong and profound mark. These close ties with Ulm and its functionalist principles separated Brazilian design from the cultural roots of the country, which were deemed irrelevant and viewed as a symbol of regression that needed to be abandoned in order to assure for the nation a privileged spot on the international scene. Combined with the inferior-

The exhibition *Indigenous Seats: Between Function and Ritual* held in 2006 at the Museu da Casa Brasileira, curated by Adélia Borges and Cristiana Barreto.
Ausstellung *Indigenous Seats: Between Function and Ritual,* 2006 im Museu da Casa Brasileira, kuratiert von Adélia Borges und Cristiana Barreto.

Die entscheidenden Inspirationen für ihre Arbeit empfangen Fernando und Humberto Campana aus den Gegebenheiten Brasiliens, des Landes, in dem sie geboren sind und das sie zu ihrem Lebensmittelpunkt gewählt haben. Alles nehmen sie in sich auf: die sauberen Flüsse ihrer Kindheit ebenso wie das Verkehrschaos der heutigen Großstädte, die üppig wuchernden Wälder genau wie den Asphaltdschungel der Großstädte, die formale Klarheit der Träume des aufgeklärten Modernismus sowie den Hang der Mittelklasse zu Überdekoration und Kitsch. Alle diese Attribute des natürlichen, kulturellen und sozioökonomischen Umfeldes, in dem sie leben, auch und gerade seine Widersprüche und Geräusche, spiegeln sich in ihrer Arbeit, die in Brasilien zu einem starken Markenzeichen geworden ist, wieder.

Aber was für ein Brasilien ist es, das sich in der Arbeit der Campanas ausdrückt? Sicherlich sind es nicht die platten Stereotype »Samba, Fußball und Strand«. Man könnte die Größe Brasiliens nennen, die einem Kontinent gleichkommt, wo sich 190 Millionen Menschen auf 8,5 Millionen Quadratkilometern in einer Sprache, Portugiesisch, verständigen. Man könnte die Tatsache erwähnen, dass Brasilien – neben Russland, Indien und China – zu den aufstrebenden Mächten der Weltwirtschaft gehört, den so genannten BRIC-Staaten. Man könnte über die enormen sozialen Unterschiede im Land sprechen, über die Kinder, die durch die Straßen ziehen und um Nahrung betteln, während die Verkaufszahlen von Marken wie Prada, BMW und Luis Vuitton Rekorde erreichen. Man könnte – warum eigentlich nicht? – über die Tropen sprechen, über Samba und das »Girl from Ipanema«, über die magischen Pässe von Fußballspielern wie Pelé und Ronaldo, über die Utopie Brasília, die Hauptstadt, die im Herzen des Landes gebaut wurde.

Aber der Aspekt, um den es in diesem Essay geht, ist der eines Brasiliens, in dem die Summe vieler Attribute zu einer perfekten Mixtur von kreativer Energie führt. Es geht um die Populärkultur Brasiliens, in der die Bevölkerung aus der Erfindungsgabe eine Überlebensstrategie macht – und das ist der kulturelle genetische Code, der seinen kraftvollen Ausdruck in der Arbeit der Brüder Campana findet.

Es ist nicht immer einfach, das Land der Erfindungen im Durchschnittsbrasilien zu entdecken. Manchmal kommt man einer Sache so nahe, dass man die Augen schließen oder einen Schritt zurücktreten muss, um besser sehen zu können.

Gegen die »Verflachung der Welt«

Der erste universitäre Designkurs entstand in Brasilien im Jahre 1964 in Rio de Janeiro. Der Lehrplan der Hochschule für Industriedesign (Escola Superior de Desenho Industrial, ESDI) folgte im Wesentlichen dem Studienplan der Hochschule für Gestaltung in Ulm in Deutschland. Von dort kamen auch einige Lehrer, die zur Entstehung des brasilianischen Designs als akademischer Disziplin das Bauhausideal der »guten Form« beisteuerten. Die Ideenwelt, die in Rio eingepflanzt wurde, breitete sich über das ganze Land aus. Das funktionalistische Gebot »die Form folgt der Funktion« und die Anbindung an den International Style bestimmten den Design-Unterricht und folglich auch die Design-Praxis Brasiliens. Die Schulen bereiteten ihre Studenten also auf den Markt der großindustriellen Massenproduktion vor.

Alle frühen Prägungen – sei es bei einer Person, einer Institution oder einer Bewegung – hinterlassen tiefe Spuren. Im Bereich des Designs führte die enge Bindung an die funktionalistischen Regeln aus Ulm zur Loslösung von den kulturellen Wurzeln des Landes. Sie erschienen nicht relevant, sondern wurden vielmehr als Symbol für eine Rückständigkeit angesehen, die es zu überwinden galt, wenn man der Nation mit neuen Gestaltungsvorhaben einen Platz auf der internationalen Bühne sichern wollte. Dieser spezifische Einfluss im Bereich

ity complex of a colonized people, who place greater value on whatever comes from abroad, the result was a type of design that took its points of reference from outside the local reality.

There were, however, a number of influential voices that spoke against this self-alienating attitude. One of the most expressive was Italian architect Lina Bo Bardi (1914–1992), who, not by chance, is the first name cited by the Campana brothers when asked about their influences. Bo Bardi had worked in Milan with Gio Ponti and had directed the *Domus* magazine before moving to Brazil in 1946 together with her husband, Pietro, who had been invited to establish a museum of modern art in São Paulo. 'In the New World she fell in love with the exuberance of tropical nature – the vegetation – and with the Brazilian people, with their relaxed attitude and their unique ingenuousness "not yet contaminated by arrogance or money", as she used to say,' recalls one of her collaborators, architect and designer Marcelo Ferraz.[1]

Besides her restless activity as architect and designer, Bo Bardi organized exhibitions and established institutions dedicated to the research of this 'popular aristocracy', as she termed it. Among her many projects was the foundation, in 1959, of the Museu de Arte Popular (Museum of Popular Art) in Salvador, the capital of Bahia, a state in the northeast of Brazil. 'We call it Museum of Popular Art – and not Museum of Folklore – because folklore is a static and regressive legacy, guided paternalistically by the ones responsible for culture; while popular art (we use the word "art" not only for its artistic meaning but also in reference to the technical deed itself) defines the progressive attitude of a popular culture linked to real problems,' she wrote. Her vision was deliberately focused on the present and the future: 'This museum aims to be an invitation for young people to consider the problem of simplification (and not indigence) in today's world; which is a necessary gateway, inside technical humanism, towards a new poetic art.'[2]

Bo Bardi said she found in peripheral popular culture 'forms full of vital electricity', thus full of potentialities. 'To search attentively for the cultural bases of a country (whichever they are: poor, miserable, popular) … does not mean to preserve forms and materials; it means to evaluate original creative possibilities. Modern materials and production systems will, later on, take the place of primitive means, maintaining not the forms but the profound structure of these possibilities.'[3]

After the dark years of dictatorship, during which a number of civil rights were suspended and cultural manifestations were severely censored, the beginning of political distension found another potent voice to defend the need for recognizing the popular roots of Brazilian culture. It was Aloísio Magalhães (1927–1982), a plastic artist and designer, who was much involved in the development of corporate identities for large Brazilian companies and who played an active role in formulating public policies for Brazilian culture. Magalhães was concerned with what he called the 'flattening of the world' – 'a kind of aversion, a monotony, a depreciation of values' caused by the accelerated industrialization process undergone by the Western world. In his view, 'cultural erosion' was threatening

Handcrafted wickerwork in front of a shop in Belém.
Handgearbeitete Korbwaren vor einem Laden in Belém.

1 Marcelo Ferraz, 'Lina Bardi e a Tropicália' [Lina Bardi and Tropicália], *ProjetoDesign* 337 (March 2008), p. 87.
2 Lina Bo Bardi, 'Civilização do Nordeste' [Northeast Civilization], in *Tempos de grossura: o design no impasse* [Times of abundance: Design at an impasse] (São Paulo: Instituto Lina Bo Bardi e P. M. Bardi, 1994), p. 37.
3 Ibid.

der Gestaltung, verbunden mit dem atavistischen Minderwertigkeitskomplex eines kolonisierten Volkes, das alles Ausländische höher schätzt als die eigenen Werte, ergab ein Design, das seine Bezugspunkte außerhalb der lokalen Realität suchte.

Einige einflussreiche Stimmen erhoben sich gegen diese intellektuelle Attitüde der Selbstentfremdung. Eine der ausdrucksvollsten war die der italienischen Architektin Lina Bo Bardi (1914–1992), die die Campanas nicht zufällig an erster Stelle nennen, wenn sie nach prägenden Einflüssen gefragt werden. Lina Bo Bardi hatte schon in Mailand mit Gio Ponti zusammengearbeitet und die Zeitschrift *Domus* geleitet, als sie 1946 zusammen mit ihrem Mann Pietro nach Brasilien kam, der damit betraut wurde, ein Museum für Moderne Kunst in São Paulo zu errichten. »In der Neuen Welt verliebte sie sich in den Überfluss der tropischen Natur«, so erinnert sich einer ihrer Mitarbeiter, der Architekt und Designer Marcelo Ferraz, »in das Grün – und in das brasilianische Volk mit seiner Gelassenheit und seiner ganz eigenen und, wie sie zu sagen pflegte, ›noch nicht vom Hochmut und vom Geld infizierten‹ Art von Unbefangenheit.«[1]

Neben ihrer rastlosen Arbeit als Architektin und Designerin begann Lina Bo Bardi Ausstellungen zu organisieren und Einrichtungen zu gründen, die dem Wissen über diese »Volksaristokratie«, um wiederum einen ihrer Ausdrücke zu benutzen, Wertschätzung entgegenbrachten. So gründete sie im Jahr 1959 das Museu de Arte Popular (Museum der Volkskunst) in Salvador, der Hauptstadt des Bundesstaats Bahia im Nordosten des Landes. »Wir nennen es Museum der Volkskunst und nicht der Folklore, weil Folklore ein statisches und regressives Erbe ist, das paternalistisch von den Kulturverantwortlichen gestützt wird, während die Volkskunst (wobei wir den Begriff Kunst nicht nur im künstlerischen Sinne, sondern auch im Sinne der technischen Fertigkeit benutzen) eine fortschrittliche Einstellung der Populärkultur bezeichnet, die an realen Problemen ausgerichtet ist«, schrieb sie. Ihre Vision war einfach und an Gegenwart und Zukunft orientiert: »Dieses Museum will eine Einladung an die Jungen sein, den Aspekt der Simplifizierung (nicht der Dürftigkeit) in der heutigen Welt in Betracht zu ziehen; ein notwendiger Weg, um innerhalb des technischen Humanismus eine Lehre der Poesie zu finden.«[2]

Bo Bardi sagte, sie finde in den populären Randkulturen »Formen voller vitaler Elektrizität« und deshalb voller Möglichkeiten. »Aufmerksam die kulturellen Grundlagen eines Landes suchen, mögen sie auch arm, elend und volkstümlich sein [...], bedeutet nicht, die Formen oder die Materialien zu bewahren, sondern es bedeutet, die originalen kreativen Möglichkeiten zu schätzen. Die modernen Materialien und Produktionssysteme treten an die Stelle der primitiven Mittel; nicht die Formen werden bewahrt, sondern die tiefere Struktur dieser Möglichkeiten.«[3]

Nach den dunklen Jahren der Diktatur, in denen zahlreiche Bürgerrechte außer Kraft gesetzt waren und die kulturellen Aktivitäten des Landes unter einer strengen Zensur litten, wies zu Beginn der politischen Entspannung eine andere mächtige Stimme auf die Notwendigkeit hin, sich auf die Wurzeln der Volkskultur zu besinnen. Diese Stimme gehörte Aloísio Magalhães (1927–1982), der als bildender Künstler und Designer manchem großen brasilianischen Unternehmen zu einer Corporate Identity verholfen hatte und an der Gestaltung der öffentlichen Kulturpolitik Brasiliens beteiligt war.

Magalhães beobachtete besorgt Tendenzen, die er als »Verflachung der Welt« bezeichnete. Er diagnostizierte eine »Art von Überdruss, Monotonie und Nivel-

1 Marcelo Ferraz: »*Lina Bardi e a Tropicália*«, in: *Projeto Design,* Nr. 337, März 2008, S. 87.
2 Lina Bo Bardi: »Civilização do Nordeste«, in: *Tempos de grossura: o design no impasse,* hrsg. v. Instituto Lina Bo Bardi e P. M. Bardi, São Paulo 1994, S. 37.
3 Ebenda.

'spontaneous cultural processes' and in order to preserve them he advocated a plunge into the past of Brazilian culture.[4]

According to Magalhães, the further one delved into the past, the stronger the impulse one had towards the future. For this reason, in 1975 he coordinated the foundation of the Centro Nacional de Referência Cultural (National Centre for Cultural Reference) at the Federal Ministry of Industry and Commerce, where research was conducted into different aspects of popular culture – the production of ceramics, weaving, indigenous handicraft, beverage labels, popular brands, the recycling of industrial leftovers – with the aim of implementing the results in the search for the distinct identity of Brazilian design. Just like Bo Bardi, Magalhães was not concerned with preserving the forms of the past at all costs but focused rather on reviving its strengths, which, in his opinion, were important for the future of the country.

Melting Pot of Cultures

Besides impeding ongoing processes, the sudden death of Magalhães in 1982 deprived the movement for the acknowledgment of popular cultural in Brazil of one of its strongest and most confident articulators. However, although models of reference continued to be sought in the Northern Hemisphere (mainly in Italy), during the 1980s a deliberate search for a typically Brazilian style of design began to emerge. Pioneered by such designers as Sergio Rodrigues and his followers, Carlos Motta, Maurício Azeredo, and Marcelo Ferraz, this movement continued to gain ground in the 1990s, when along with the consolidation of democracy in the country and the economic improvement that followed 'shame' (of being Brazilian instead of part of the First World) was replaced by hope. These internal developments joined the changes occurring throughout the world, globalization leading paradoxically to a valorization of multiculturalism, thus creating a suitable environment for the flourishing of a form of Brazilian design that cherished its own cultural roots. Fernando and Humberto Campana may be the most famous and successful representatives of this current but they are by no means the only ones. In the field of fashion design, Lino Villaventura, Ronaldo Fraga, and Carlos Miele are a few names that can be mentioned along with them; while, in the field of graphic design, one should not forget the contributions of Rico Lins, Enéas Guerra, and Marcelo Drummond.

Street grill made of waste material in the state of Ceará. Straßengrill aus dem Bundesstaat Ceará, hergestellt aus Abfallmaterial.

These designers view the 'disadvantage' of Brazilian culture – namely, its alleged 'lack' of tradition as opposed to that of more ancient civilizations, such as the European – as an advantage. For them, the fact that everything in Brazil is anyway new means that everything can also be newly invented and, thus, can undoubtedly be brought about with a certain freedom and lightheartedness.

A further feature of their work is mixture – perhaps an expression of the synthesis that characterizes Brazilian culture. Initially inhabited by native Indians, Brazil was 'discovered' in 1500 by the Portuguese and sustained by African slaves. Adding to this triple eth-

4 Zoy Anastassakis, 'Sobre Aloísio Magalhães e o Centro Nacional de Referência Cultural: algumas considerações entre o design e a antropologia' [About Aloísio Magalhães and the National Centre for Cultural Reference: Some considerations between design and anthropology], Revista Design em Foco 4, no. 2 (2007), p. 74. See also Aloísio Magalhães, É triunfo? A questão dos bens culturais no Brasil [Is it a triumph? The issue of cultural assets in Brazil] (Rio de Janeiro: Nova Fronteira and Fundação Roberto Marinho, 1997).

lierung der Werte«, die er als Folge des »beschleunigten und komplexen Industrialisierungsprozesses« ansah, den die westliche Welt erlebte. Nach seiner Meinung fand eine »kulturelle Erosion« statt, die die »spontanen kulturellen Prozesse« bedrohte.[4]

Um dieser Erosion entgegenzuwirken, forderte Aloísio Magalhães das Eintauchen in die Vergangenheit der brasilianischen Kultur. Je weiter diese Rückbesinnung gehe, umso stärker sei, nach seiner Ansicht, der Impuls für die Planung der Zukunft. Aus diesem Grund leitete er 1975 die Gründung des Centro Nacional de Referência Cultural (Nationales Kulturzentrum) im Industrie- und Handelsministerium der Bundesregierung, das die Aufgabe übernahm, Forschungen anzustoßen und zu koordinieren. Schwerpunkte waren dort die Textilweberei, das indianische Kunsthandwerk, die Keramikproduktion, das Erscheinungsbild bekannter Marken, der Entwurf von Getränkeetiketten und die Wiederverwertung industrieller Abfälle. Die Resultate sollten bei der Entwicklung einer eigenen Physiognomie für brasilianische Produkte und brasilianisches Design Verwendung finden. Wie Lina Bo Bardi ging es Aloísio Magalhães nicht darum, um jeden Preis Formen aus der Vergan-genheit zu bewahren, sondern Kräfte ans Licht zu bringen, die aus seiner Sicht wichtig für die Zukunft des Landes waren.

Schmelztiegel der Kulturen

Mit dem plötzlichen Tod von Aloísio Magalhães verlor die Bewegung zur Wertschätzung des volkskulturellen Erbes 1982 einen starken und entschiedenen Fürsprecher und die damals angelaufenen Prozesse gerieten ins Stocken.

Obwohl die Bezüge für das Design nach wie vor in der nördlichen Hemisphäre gesucht wurden, vor allem in Italien, kam im Laufe der 1980er Jahre allmählich eine entschlossene Suche nach den Attributen des Brasilianischen in Gang, die dann beispielsweise ihren Ausdruck in den Arbeiten des Design-Pioniers Sergio Rodrigues und der seiner Anhänger, wie etwa Carlos Motta, Maurício Azeredo und Marcelo Ferraz, fand. Diese Bewegung verstärkte sich in den 1990er Jahren, als die Konsolidierung der Demokratie im Land und die wirtschaftliche Stabilisierung dazu führten, dass das Gefühl der »Scham« (Scham, Brasilianer zu sein und nicht zur »Ersten Welt« zu gehören) durch ein Gefühl der Hoffnung ersetzt wurde. Zu diesen landesinternen Phänomenen kommen Veränderungen im internationalen Umfeld, da die Globalisierung paradoxerweise zu einer Vielfalt der kulturellen Strömungen und zur Wertschätzung des Multikulturalismus führt. In diesem günstigen Ambiente blüht im brasilianischen Design eine Einstellung auf, die sich auf die eigenen kulturellen Wurzeln besinnt. Die bekanntesten Vertreter dieser Denkrichtung sind Fernando und Humberto Campana, aber sie sind nicht die einzigen. In der Mode zählen Designer wie Lino Villaventura, Ronaldo Fraga und Carlos Miele dazu, und im Grafikdesign sind es Rico Lins, Enéas Guerra und Marcelo Drummond, um nur einige Namen zu nennen.

Diese Designer begannen das, was gemeinhin als »Nachteil« der brasilianischen Kultur galt – ihren vermeintlichen Mangel an Tradition im Vergleich zu älteren Zivilisationen wie der europäischen –, geradezu als ihren prinzipiellen »Vorteil« anzusehen. Da hier ohnehin alles neu ist, muss auch alles neu erfunden werden, was zweifellos der Freiheit und Unbeschwertheit zugute kommt.

Eine andere brasilianische Eigenheit, die man schätzen gelernt hat, ist die Vermischung. Und das ist vielleicht das grundlegendste Attribut der Kultur unseres Landes, das ursprünglich von Indianern bewohnt, im Jahr 1500 von den Portugiesen »entdeckt« und mit der Arbeitskraft der Afrikaner, die als Sklaven hierher kamen, bewirtschaftet wurde. Zu dieser dreifachen ethnischen Zusammensetzung Brasiliens kamen ab Ende des 19. Jahrhunderts viele Einwandererströme, vor allem aus Europa. Auch im 21. Jahrhundert hält

4 Zoy Anastassakis: »Sobre Aloísio Magalhães e o Centro Nacional de Referência Cultural: algumas considerações entre o design e a antropologia«, in: Revista Design em Foco, Bd. 4, Nr. 2, 2007, S. 74. Siehe auch: Aloísio Magalhães: É triunfo? A questão dos bens culturais no Brasil, Nova Fronteira und Fundação Roberto Marinho, Rio de Janeiro 1997.

nicity are the immigrants that began arriving in the country at the end of the nineteenth century, mainly from Europe, and continue to do so to this very day, most recently from Bolivia and Korea. Nevertheless, unlike other countries, where immigrants remain in segregated ghettos, in Brazil cultures are amalgamated. The skin colour of Brazilians ranges from the whitest of white to the blackest of black, with all variations in between, from blond Japanese to green-eyed dark-skinned people.

Due to the composition of its population, the mixture of races is an essential feature of Brazilian culture. The melting pot of habits, religions, and accents is in constant fluctuation and resignification, and involves a high level of permeability between so-called 'high' and 'low' cultures. 'The greatest assets of Brazil are these oscillating boundaries interpreting themselves, this permanent mixture,' says art critic and poet Lélia Coelho Frota.[5]

Despite initial apprehensions to the contrary, democracy did not cause the traditional and popular manifestations of Brazilian culture to stagnate, deteriorate, or disappear in a way similar to that of indigenous cultures elsewhere; rather, they were revived and developed, incorporating within them a number of innovations. Thus, today, with democratization diffusing information via new technologies, Brazilians of various social classes enjoy a higher self-esteem and experience a fertile state of creative explosion.

For sure, hybridism and reciprocal influences occur more often in some mediums than in others. They are determining factors in music, certainly the strongest and most diverse cultural expression in Brazil, continuously unfolding in new rhythms and sounds across the country. However, they are also present in dance and theatre, and, lately, show greater prominence in the field that interests us most here – namely, that of the applied arts.

A walk through Brazilian cities, big or small, or through rural communities across the country can teach one precious lessons in design. Not everyone discerns or values; not everyone pays attention; but for those who have eyes and are willing to see, behind the misery and precariousness that characterize the lives of most Brazilians, there are ingenious solutions and unequivocal manifestations of creative wisdom. In this sense, the Campana brothers are true 'antennas', capturing and apprehending these 'encoded messages' of popular creativity and drawing from them the inspiration for a great number of their projects, a fact repeatedly mentioned in their lectures. 'Just around the corner from our studio lives a beggar who makes trousers and turbans from plastic. He would make John Galliano jealous,' jokes Humberto.

Much Beyond Function

The interiors of Brazilian homes teach many lessons in popular creativity. However, since the domestic scene is essentially an intimate space, forbidden to foreign eyes, we can suffice ourselves with what can be learnt from the urban landscape.

5 Lélia Coelho Frota, 'Cultura do Brasil' [Brazilian Culture], *Raiz* 1 (2006), p. 53.

Fernando Campana in the shop of street artist Getulio Damato in Rio de Janeiro, 2007.
Fernando Campana am Laden des Straßenkünstlers Getulio Damato in Rio de Janeiro, 2007.

Popó, Leo, Betolo, and *Falcão,* figures by the Rio de Janeiro street artist Getulio Damato, 2007.
Popó, Leo, Betolo und *Falcão,* Figuren des Straßenkünstlers Getulio Damato aus Rio de Janeiro, 2007.

der Zuzug von Ausländern, vornehmlich aus Korea und Bolivien, an. Aber im Gegensatz zu anderen Ländern, wo die Einwanderer getrennt voneinander in Ghettos leben, vermischen sich in Brasilien die Ethnien. Die Hautfarben der Brasilianer reichen vom weißesten Weiß bis zum schwärzesten Schwarz über alle Variationen, vom blonden Japaner bis zur Mulattin mit grünen Augen. Infolge dieser Vielfalt der Bevölkerungsgruppen ist die Vermischung auch ein fundamentaler Teil der brasilianischen Kultur. Im großen Kessel der Gebräuche, Religionen und Ausdrucksformen herrschen ständig Bewegung und Werden und eine unaufhörliche Neubestimmung mit einer großen Durchlässigkeit zwischen jenen Kulturen, die man für gewöhnlich als »high« oder »low« bezeichnet. »Der große Reichtum Brasiliens sind diese unscharfen Grenzen, die sich überschneiden, diese ständige Vermischung«, sagt Lélia Coelho Frota, eine angesehene Dichterin und Kunstkritikerin.[5]

Entgegen allen Befürchtungen stagnierten die traditionellen und populären Manifestationen der Kultur wie auch die Kulturen der indigenen Völker nicht. Sie verfielen nicht und noch weniger starben sie aus, sondern erfuhren vielmehr eine Wiederbelebung unter Einbeziehung verschiedener Innovationen. Die neuen virtuellen Technologien brachten eine Demokratisierung in der Informationsverbreitung mit sich, die den Brasilianern ein nie gekanntes Selbstwertgefühl vermittelte. Die Brasilianer, gleich welcher sozialen Schicht sie angehören, erleben heute eine fruchtbare Phase kreativer Explosion.

Hybridität und wechselseitige Beeinflussung prägen mehr oder weniger alle kulturellen Äußerungen in Brasilien. Sie sind bestimmend in der Musik, der mit Sicherheit stärksten und vielfältigsten brasilianischen Ausdrucksform, die sich unablässig mit neuen Rhythmen und Klängen landauf, landab verbreitet. Sie sind im Tanz und im Theater gegenwärtig und nehmen in den vergangenen Jahren auch in dem Bereich zu, der uns hier vor allem interessiert: bei den visuellen Kreationen und vor allem bei der angewandten Kunst.

Spaziergänge durch brasilianische Städte, egal ob kleine oder große, oder durch ländliche Gemeinden können wertvolle Design-Lektionen abgeben. Nicht jeder vermag das wahrzunehmen oder wertzuschätzen, nicht jeder bringt die nötige Aufmerksamkeit mit. Aber, wer Augen hat zu sehen, wird erkennen, dass aus dem Elend und dem Mangel im Leben der meisten Brasilianer geniale Lösungen erwachsen, die untrüglicher Ausdruck kreativer Weisheit sind. Die Brüder Campana sind wahre »Antennen«, sie fangen diese Botschaften ein und lernen aus ihnen. Viele ihrer Projekte sind, darauf weisen sie in ihren Vorträgen hin, von diesen volkstümlichen Lösungen inspiriert. »Hier um die Ecke von unserem Atelier lebt ein Bettler, der Hosen und Kopfbedeckungen aus Plastik herstellt. Da würde John Galliano neidisch werden«, lacht Humberto.

Weit mehr als nur Funktion

Wahrscheinlich verbergen sich im Inneren der Häuser ebenfalls viele dieser kreativen Lehrstücke. Da aber der häusliche und vor allem der intime Bereich fremden Augen verborgen ist, müssen wir uns damit begnügen, die zahlreichen Lösungen zu schätzen, die wir auf der Bühne der städtischen Landschaft finden.

5 Lélia Coelho Frota: »Cultura do Brasil?«, in: *Raiz,* Nr. 1, 2006, S. 53.

For a start, there are the people who make the streets their work-place: street vendors, assembling and disassembling in a matter of seconds boards on which they display an assortment of goods, ranging from Ray Ban glasses to mobile phone batteries; street peddlers, walking between cars stuck in the traffic of big cities and offering mineral water, Chinese toys, or roasted peanuts to stranded drivers; sellers of flowers or candy, making their way through restaurant clients; shoe shiners, offering comfortable chairs for their patrons to sit in; and even junk collectors – always present in big Brazilian cities – gathering paper, aluminium, and other valuable wastes, thus relieving the public authorities of their garbage collection and recycling duties.

There are some recurrent features in the objects made and sold by these people, who, as a rule, have but a few years of formal education. The first thing that draws attention is the perfect functionality obtained in their, at once, simple and intelligent solutions, manifesting what Aloísio Magalhães used to call 'patrimonial technology'[6] and what the late Fausto Alvim Jr., researcher at the National Centre for Cultural Reference, explained as the 'technical knowledge incorporated by and embedded within specific social groups'.[7] These techniques, transmitted over generations, show a remarkable capacity to utilize all possible means, resources, and elements in order to transform the surrounding environment. Corn husks and reeds are mixed with cotton in the weaver's loom to make textiles; plant seeds become curtains; soda bottle caps are transformed into door mats, efficient as any industrially manufactured ones; plastic bottles turn into brooms; and twigs are used to make furniture, as is evinced, with rare mastery, in the work of Fernando Rodrigues of Ilha do Ferro in Alagoas.

Second, a noticeable feature of Brazilian popular design is that form transcends function so as to follow the heart and express emotion. There is no fear of ornaments, bright colours, or decorative exaggerations. This feature was first noticed and formulated by Gustavo Amarante Bonfim and Lia Monica Rossi. Impressed by the formal freedom and the elaborate chromatic vocabulary of objects sold in the street markets of the small cities surrounding Campina Grande in northeastern Brazil, they described this characteristic of Brazilian popular design in an article that posed the provocative question, 'Was Sottsass inspired by Campina Grande?'[8]

The third recurring element is sustainability. Even before the word 'ecology' existed in dictionaries, Brazilian people were already ecological. To make full use of the raw materials that the local environment has to offer and to take advantage of wastes and leftovers is a common attitude in Brazilian society, including that of the middle class. Fernando and Humberto, for instance, make a point of mentioning their grandmother in this regard and how she would never threw anything away, making plates out of used cans and inventing new uses for leftovers. The epitome of this ability to transform waste into something new is patchwork.

A shoeshine stand in São Paulo, 2008.
Stand eines Schuhputzers in São Paulo, 2008.

Mobile stall for selling coffee, designed by Gilberto Santana from Salvador in the state of Bahia.
Mobiler Verkaufsstand für Kaffee, entworfen von Gilberto Santana aus Salvador im Bundesstaat Bahia.

Als erstes wären da die Legionen von Menschen zu nennen, die ihren Arbeitsplatz auf den Straßen haben. Das sind die Straßenhändler, die in Sekunden ihre Stände auf- und abbauen, auf denen sie Rayban-Brillen und Handy-Batterien anbieten. Es sind die Straßenverkäufer, die in den Megastaus der Großstadtstraßen zwischen den Fahrzeugen umherlaufen und ihre Waren feilbieten, vom Mineralwasser bis zum chinesischen Spielzeug, ja sogar geröstete Erdnüsse aus tragbaren Öfen. Es sind die Blumen- und Süßwarenverkäufer, die sich zwischen den Restaurantbesuchern hindurchschlängeln. Es sind die Schuhputzer, die den Kunden einladen, auf prächtigen Stühlen Platz zu nehmen. Und dann noch die Müllsammler, allgegenwärtige Gestalten in den großen brasilianischen Städten, die Papier, Aluminium und andere verwertbare Abfälle einsammeln und dabei einen Teil der öffentlichen Aufgaben der Müllsammlung und Mülltrennung erfüllen und die Materialien der Wiederverarbeitung zuführen.

Diese Personen mit ihrer geringen Schulbildung stellen Gegenstände her, die sich allesamt durch gewisse Eigenschaften auszeichnen: An erster Stelle erweckt die perfekte Funktionalität Aufmerksamkeit, die in den so einfachen wie intelligenten Lösungen steckt. Aloísio Magalhães bezeichnete das als »technologisches Gemeingut«[6] und Fausto Alvim Jr., Forscher am Centro Nacional de Referência Cultural, erklärte es als »technisches Wissen, das in spezifischen sozialen Gruppen verborgen und verwurzelt ist«.[7] In den von Generation zu Generation weitergegebenen Techniken zeigt sich eine beachtliche Fähigkeit, sich die umgebende Natur unter sparsamstem Einsatz der Mittel, Ressourcen und Elemente anzueignen. Reste aus Maisstroh oder Schilf werden auf dem Webstuhl mit Baumwolle vermischt, um Stoffe herzustellen; die Samen verschiedener Pflanzen werden zu Vorhängen verarbeitet; Flaschenverschlüsse verwandeln sich in Fußabtreter, die in nichts den industriell gefertigten nachstehen; Reste von Plastikflaschen werden zu Besen; Äste verwandeln sich in Möbel, wie sie mit großer Meisterschaft Fernando Rodrigues aus Ilha do Ferro in Alagoas herstellt.

An zweiter Stelle ist festzuhalten, dass im populären brasilianischen Design die Form, wenn sie in die Funktion übergeht, auch der Emotion und dem Herzen folgt. Es gibt keine Angst vor Ornamenten, kräftigen Farben und dekorativen »Übertreibungen«; darauf haben Gustavo Amarante Bonfim und Lia Monica Rossi als erste hingewiesen. Beeindruckt beschrieben sie in einem Artikel die Freiheit der Formen und das reiche farbliche Vokabular der volkstümlichen Design-Objekte, die sie in den 1980er Jahren auf den Märkten der kleinen Städte um Campina Grande im Nordosten Brasiliens gefunden hatten, und stellten die provo-zierende Frage: »Hat sich Sotsass in Campina Grande inspirieren lassen?«[8]

6 Anastassakis, 'Sobre Aloísio Magalhães', p. 77.

7 Fausto Alvim Jr., as quoted by Clara Alvim in interview with the author, 7 October 2008.

8 Gustavo Amarante Bonfim and Lia Monica Rossi, 'Moderno e pós-moderno, a controvérsia: Caminhos de uma discussão sobre a estética e a semântica do produto industrial' [Modern and post-modern, the controversy: Paths towards a discussion of the aesthetics and semantics of the industrial product], *Revista Design e Interiores* 3, no. 19 (1990), pp. 20–26.

6 Anastassakis, a.a.O., S. 77 (Anm. 4).

7 Fausto Alvim Jr., zitiert nach einer Äußerung seiner Tochter Clara Alvim im Interview mit der Autorin am 7. Oktober 2008.

8 Gustavo Amarante Bonfim und Lia Monica Rossi: »Moderno e pós-moderno, a controvérsia: Caminhos de uma discussão sobre a estética e a semântica do produto industrial«, in: *Revista Design e Interiores* 3, Nr. 19, 1990, S.20–26.

Finally, the fourth feature dominant in Brazilian popular design is diversity. This feature stems from the obvious fact that this form of design is embedded within completely local traditions and arises from conditions that vary from region to region across a vast country. It is noticeable in indigenous craftwork, such as basketry and feather work, and exemplified in the utensils and other domestic tools found in the huts of native societies.

A simple example can help understand this dynamics of functionality, formal freedom, sustainability, and diversity. In the centre of Salvador, capital of Bahia, coffee is sold on the streets by vendors using wheeled wooden carts. Each vendor designs his own cart, employing elaborate graphisms and colours and often adding accessory components, such as music. Each one strives to differentiate himself from the other in order to attract clientele, unaware that he is making use of one of the basic rules of design: to confer an identity to a product or service that distinguishes them from similar ones.[9]

Celebrations and Colours in Urban Space

The public space of Brazilian cities is not all work; it is also play. The ability to enjoy oneself and celebrate is an essential component of Brazilian culture, whether it be manifested in sacred or profane contexts, or, not unusually, in a mixture of both. From *congado* dances in the interior of Goiás to the *maracatu* rhythms of rural Pernambuco, from the *bumba-meu-boi* in Maranhão to the *jongo* samba of the country side of Rio de Janeiro, Brazilian popular festivities are true aesthetic experiences. But, above all, it is carnival that comprises the privileged moment in which to observe the Brazilian creative spirit, whether it be celebrated in simple block parties, in which people improvise costumes (the most common being men dressing up as women), or in the huge parades of Olinda, Salvador, and Rio de Janeiro, where it has become a show of splendour.

In an analysis of the parades of Rio de Janeiro's samba schools, Lélia Coelho Frota remarks that 'the show-like status acquired by the schools strengthens the visual component while blurring the musical element.'[10] However, the musical theme is dramatized by the club members not only through dance but also through costumes and parade floats, and in the past four decades the role of a professional set designer has become prominent. One should mention, in this regard, the work of Joãozinho Trinta, ballet dancer at the Rio de Janeiro Municipal Theatre. During the 1970s, Trinta began developing 'an operatic conception of samba-school parades, seeking a general harmony of all elements of the parade,

Das dritte konstante Element ist die Nachhaltigkeit. Lange bevor das Wort »Ökologie« Eingang in unsere Wörterbücher fand, war das brasilianische Volk schon umweltbewusst. Etwas im Einklang mit dem lokalen Ambiente zu erschaffen, sorgsam mit den vorhandenen Rohstoffen umzugehen oder Reste und Abfälle wiederzuverwenden, das ist eine verbreitete Einstellung in der brasilianischen Gesellschaft, einschließlich der Mittelklasse. Fernando und Humberto erinnern sich an ihre Großmutter, die nichts wegwarf, die aus Resten neue Dinge erfand und beispielsweise die Konservendosen in Teller verwandelte. Der Inbegriff dieser Gabe, Abfälle in etwas Neues zu verwandeln, ist die Flickendecke.

Mobile stand for a vendor of sweets and beverages in the state of Alagoas, 2008. Mobiler Stand eines Verkäufers von Süßigkeiten und Getränken im Bundesstaat Alagoas, 2008.

Das vierte gemeinsame Charakteristikum des kreativen Volksschaffens ist die Vielfalt, denn die strikt lokal gebundenen Traditionen und Lebensbedingungen in diesem riesigen Land variieren von Region zu Region stark. Dieser Wesenszug rührt aus der indianischen Tradition her, wie man an den Körben, dem Federschmuck, dem Kochgeschirr und den Haushaltsgegenständen aus den Indianerhütten feststellen kann.

Ein einfaches Beispiel soll helfen, diese Dynamik der Funktionalität, Poesie, Nachhaltigkeit und Vielfalt besser zu verstehen. Im Zentrum von Salvador, der Hauptstadt Bahias, bieten Straßenhändler Kaffee zum Verkauf an, wobei sie Holzkarren mit Rädern verwenden. Jeder Verkäufer gestaltet seinen eigenen Verkaufskarren, dekoriert ihn aufwendig mit Grafiken, mit Farben und fügt dem Gegenstand häufig neue Funktionen hinzu, etwa indem er ihn Musik spielen lässt. Im Bestreben, die Kundschaft anzulocken, ist jeder Händler bemüht, sich von den anderen zu unterscheiden. Ohne sich dessen bewusst zu sein, machen die Händler Gebrauch von einer der Grundregeln des Designs, nämlich einem Produkt oder einer Dienstleistung eine Identität zu geben, die sie von ähnlichen unterscheidet.[9]

Feste und Farben im städtischen Raum

Der öffentliche Raum brasilianischer Städte dient nicht nur als Arbeitsplatz, sondern auch als Festplatz. Die Gabe zu scherzen, sich zu freuen und Feste zu feiern ist ein wesentlicher Zug der brasilianischen Kultur, der in Veranstaltungen kirchlichen oder weltlichen Charakters – nicht selten in einer Mixtur aus beidem – seinen Ausdruck findet. Die brasilianischen Volksfeste, von den *congados* im tiefen Goiás bis zum ländlichen *maracatu* in Pernambuco, vom *bumba-meuboi* in Maranhão bis zum *jongo* im Landesinneren von Rio de Janeiro, sind wahrhaftige

Dancers in São Paulo's carnival in 1999. Tänzer beim Karneval 1999 in São Paulo.

ästhetische Erfahrungen. Doch zu keinem Zeitpunkt kann man die kreativen Fähigkeiten der Brasilianer so gut beobachten wie beim Karneval, wenn sie in Blöcken mit improvisierten Kostümen durch die Straßen der kleinen und großen Städte des Landes ziehen – am häufigsten sieht man übrigens auf groteske Weise als Frauen verkleidete Männer. In Olinda, Salvador und Rio de Janeiro erreicht der Karneval die Dimension wahrer Spektakel.

9 These coffee carts caused great repercussions within the professional design community when they were put on display in an exhibition entitled *Design Popular da Bahia* (Popular design from Bahia), held in 2004 at the Museu da Casa Brasileira in São Paulo. For one enthusiastic response, see Mario Botta, 'Anonymous design in points of sales', *Ottagono* 174 (October 2004), p. 70.

10 Lelia Coelho Frota, *Pequeno dicionário da arte do povo brasileiro* [Small dictionary of the art of Brazilian people] (Rio de Janeiro: Aeroplano, 2005), p. 99.

9 Diese Kaffeewagen fanden in der professionellen Design-Szene große Resonanz, als sie 2004 in der Ausstellung *Design Popular da Bahia* im Museu da Casa Brasileira in São Paulo gezeigt wurden. Eine der begeisterten Reaktionen stammt von Mario Botta: »Anonymous design in points of sales«, in: *Ottagono,* Nr. 174, Oktober 2004, S. 70.

including its music, and – to a large extent – a complete integration of the arts, as envisaged centuries earlier by the Baroque.'[11]
An exhibition held in 2008 at the Edison Carneiro Folklore Museum in Rio de Janeiro served as an opportunity to contemplate this fugacious art, prepared throughout an entire year but displayed only during the few days of carnival, from Saturday to Tuesday, and gone by Ash Wednesday. The exhibition focused on the Styrofoam sculptures that adorn the floats of the parade, but displayed them stripped of their decorations and ornamentations so as to allow the beauty of their bare forms to be appreciated. They were described as 'excellent examples of what is currently defined as popular art. It is a type of art not necessarily folkloric, of unknown authorship and bound to deep roots, but established as an articulation point for several tensions and influences, directed to contemporary issues, and involving concepts of reproducibility, authorship, publicity, fragmentation, originality, collaboration, and massification, amongst others.'[12]
Besides the functional creativity involved in work and festivities, another important feature of Brazilian urban space is public art, especially graffiti, which adds colour to the country's big cities. Art critic Sérgio Poato describes it as 'colourful, loose, free, and blending together a diversity of artistic styles',[13] ranging from pop art to Japanese mangas and from surrealism to Mexican murals – all mixed together in a process of reinterpretation of popular cultural traditions. Os Gêmeos (The Twins) – the most famous Brazilian graffiti artists working today – often cite or recreate folkloric dances, garments, and legends from the countryside; while the work of another well-known street artist, Calma, is inspired by the São João (Saint John) festival, celebrated throughout Brazil during the winter month of June with bonfires, paper garlands, and traditional *forró* dances (a derivative of the English expression 'for all').

These street artists 'react to the city not only in a violent or hostile way but in a curious mix of aggression and lyricism. It is not unusual to see half-human half-machine figures, skulls pouring tears, delicate girls holding knifes, caricaturistic faces – yet all of them are at the same time appealing.'[14] In recent years, Brazilian graffiti has enjoyed increasing international recognition. In England alone, London-based publisher Thames & Hudson published in 2005 the book *Graffiti Brasil,* while in 2008 Tate Modern commissioned Brazilian graffiti artists to exhibit on the building's facade.[15]

The Power of Hands
Another aspect of contemporary Brazilian design is the ongoing attempts at bridging the gap between designers and artisans. The impervious division that set these two practices apart in the past

Graffiti in São Paulo, 2008.
Ein Graffito in São Paulo, 2008.

Wenn man den Aufmarsch der Sambaschulen Rio de Janeiros analysiert, so Lélia Coelho Frota, sei zu bemerken, dass »der showartige Charakter, den ihre Spektakel erreicht haben, die visuelle Komponente stark betont, zu Lasten der musikalischen«.[10] Das musikalische Motto und seine Themen werden von den Mitgliedern der Sambaschulen nicht nur mit tänzerischen Mitteln in Szene gesetzt, sondern auch durch die Kostüme und die allegorischen Wagen, und so haben in den letzten vier Jahrzehnten die professionellen Szenografen immer mehr an Bedeutung gewonnen. Als Beispiel hierfür ist Joãozinho Trinta zu nennen, der berühmte Tänzer des Stadttheaters von Rio de Janeiro, der in den 1970er Jahren »auf der Suche nach einer allgemeinen Harmonie aller Elemente des Aufmarschs, inklusive der musikalischen, eine opernhafte Konzeption für die Aufzüge der Sambaschulen« entwickelte »und in gewisser Weise eine totale Integration der visuellen Künste, wie Jahrhunderte zuvor im Barock, anstrebte«.[11]
Eine Ausstellung, die 2008 im Museu de Folclore Edison Carneiro (Museum für Volkskunst Edison Carneiro) in Rio de Janeiro gezeigt wurde, bot eine Gelegenheit, diese so flüchtige Kunst kennen zu lernen. Sie wurde das ganze Jahr vorbereitet, um lediglich für die kurze Zeit des Karnevals zu bestehen, von Samstag bis Dienstag – und am Aschermittwoch war schon alles vorbei. Die Ausstellung konzentrierte sich auf die Skulpturen aus Styropor, bevor der Schmuck und die Verzierungen angebracht wurden, damit man auf diese Weise die Schönheit ihrer reinen Formen bewundern konnte, die als »ausgezeichnete Beispiele dessen« angesehen werden, »was man gegenwärtig als Populärkultur bezeichnet. Es ist nicht notwendigerweise eine folkloristische Kunst, von unbekannter Urheberschaft und an tiefe Wurzeln gebunden, sondern eine Kunst, die sich als Raum für den Ausdruck verschiedener Spannungen und Einflüsse entwickelt, die auf Gegenwartsfragen hindeutet und Begriffe wie Reproduzierbarkeit, Urheberschaft, Öffentlichkeit, Fragmentierung, Originalität, Zusammenarbeit und Verbreitung unter vielen anderen einschließt.«[12]
Neben diesem funktionsgebundenen Schöpfertum aus dem Kontext der Arbeit und des Feierns verdient eine andere Erscheinung der Kunst im städtischen Raum Erwähnung, und zwar die Graffiti, die den brasilianischen Großstädten Farbe geben. Der Kunstkritiker Sérgio Poato beschreibt die brasilianischen Graffiti als »bunt, gelöst, frei und eine Mixtur verschiedener künstlerischer Stilrichtungen«[13], von der Pop-Art bis zum japanischen Manga, vom Surrealismus bis zur mexikanischen Wandmalerei unter Wiederbelebung der alten Traditionen der Volkskultur. Os Gêmeos (Die Zwillinge), in Brasilien die bekanntesten Graffiti-Künstler der Gegenwart, zitieren oder verarbeiten in ihren Arbeiten häufig Elemente des Volkstanzes, der ländlichen Kleidung und Legenden. Calma, ein anderer gefeierter Künstler, bekennt sich zu seiner Inspiration durch die Feste des São João (Johannisfeste), die in ganz Brasilien im Juni, dem brasilianischen Wintermonat, gefeiert werden – mit Holzfeuern, Papiergirlanden und typischen Tänzen zum Rhythmus des *forró,* einer Abwandlung des englischen *for all.*
Diese Straßenkünstler »reagieren auf die Stadt nicht nur auf gewalttätige Weise, so als ob sie die Feindseligkeit zurückgeben wollten, sondern mit einer

11 Ibid.
12 Felipe Ferreira, 'Arte efêmera?' [Ephemeral art?], in *Carnaval em branco: esculturas em isopor para escolas de samba* [White carnival: Styrofoam sculptures for samba clubs] (Rio de Janeiro: Edison Carneiro Folklore Museum, 2008), p. 14. Exhibition catalogue.
13 Sérgio Poato, *Graffiti na Cidade de São Paulo* [Graffiti in the city of São Paulo] (São Paulo: Laboratório do Inconsciente, 2006), as quoted in Daniel Piza, 'Grafites paulistanos' [Paulistano graffiti], *O Estado de S. Paulo,* 2 November 2008.
14 Piza, 'Grafites paulistanos'.
15 Lost Art, Caleb Neelon, and Tristan Manco, *Graffiti Brasil* (London: Thames & Hudson, 2005); *Street Art,* Tate Modern, London, 23 May–25 August 2008.

10 Lelia Coelho Frota: *Pequeno dicionário da arte do povo brasileiro,* Aeroplano, Rio de Janeiro 2005, S. 99.
11 Ebenda.
12 Felipe Ferreira: »Arte efêmera?«, in: *Carnaval em branco: esculturas em isopor para escolas de samba,* Ausst.-Kat. zur gleichnamigen Ausstellung im Museu do Folclore Edison Carneiro in Rio de Janeiro, 2008, S. 14.
13 Sérgio Poato: *Graffiti na Cidade de São Paulo,* Laboratório do Incosciente, 2006, zitiert nach: Daniel Piza: »Grafites paulistanos«, in: *O Estado de São Paulo,* 2. November 2008.

was largely due to the industrial orientation of Brazilian design schools, whose curricular programmes focused on serial production. This caused the labour market to be flooded with newly-graduated professional designers, from about four hundred higher-education design courses existent in Brazil, whereas handcrafted production remained confined to rural areas, thus suffering an accentuated loss of cultural significance.

The elaborate traditions of manual production, according to which communities used to design products for their own consumption, began to deteriorate as competition with industrial products imported from China became harsher. Artisans began copying industrial forms or adopting foreign stereotypes in the production of their wares. As a result, alien motifs began recurring in handcrafted objects all over Brazil: gnomes, pyramids, the flora and fauna of cold countries, all reproduced from magazines.

In the last two decades, however, a change in the situation has begun to evolve due to the efforts of organizations, such as Sebrae and Central ArteSol/Artesanato Solidário, devoted to the stimulation of craftsmanship as a source of income for destitute populations. These organizations have sponsored workshops throughout Brazil in which designers have worked with local artisans on improving the technical and aesthetical quality of their crafts. One of these projects relates directly to the ragdolls used by the Campana brothers in their *Multidão* armchair. Made from leftover fabrics, these dolls were originally produced by a woman, Dona Socorro, living in Esperança (Portuguese for 'hope'), a town in the interior of Paraíba. Had it not been for a revitalization project coordinated by ArteSol in 1999, the singular technique by which Dona Socorro manufactured her dolls would have been lost upon her death. Fortunately, however, the project was a success and the number of people now producing the dolls has grown to forty.

Another example is the project initiated by Maria Teresa Leal in Rocinha, one of the largest favelas in Rio de Janeiro. Leal, who heads the Cooperativa de Trabalho Artesanal e de Costura (Cooperative Society for Handicrafts and Sewing), sought to improve the technical skills of the favela's craftswomen by introducing them to designers, stylists, and plastic artists who, in turn, would be able to use the women's wares in their own productions. Commercial partnerships were established with Brazilian and international designers and artists, such as Carlos Miele, Fernando Jaeger, Ernesto Neto, and Tord Boontje, thus improving the lives of the original sixteen craftswomen involved in the project. Today, their number has risen to about one hundred.

At the core of all these projects lies the challenge of convincing the designers who work in these communities to acquire – through an honest and reciprocal exchange – a respectful attitude towards the work of the artisans in question. In this regard, the methodology followed by the Laboratório Piracema de Design (Piracema Design Laboratory) – a centre for the research of Brazilian design that conducts workshops for artisans and designers throughout the country – is guided by the idea that 'the artisan is sovereign, a starting and finishing point for all intervention.'[16] The origin of the laboratory's

16 Laboratório Piracema de Design (Piracema Design Laboratory), internal documents.

kuriosen Mischung aus Aggressivität und Lyrismus. Häufig sieht man Figuren, halb Mensch, halb Maschine, Tränen vergießende Totenschädel, zarte Mädchen, die Messer zücken, und verzerrte Gesichter – und doch wirken alle zugleich anziehend.«[14]

Die brasilianische Graffitikunst gewinnt übrigens wachsende Anerkennung beim Kunstestablishment, speziell den internationalen Galerien. Der Londoner Verlag Thames & Hudson brachte 2005 das Buch *Grafitti Brasil* heraus und die Tate Modern lud 2008 einige Brasilianer ein, die Außenflächen des Gebäudes mit Graffiti zu versehen.[15]

Die Kraft der Hände

Eine andere Tendenz im brasilianischen Kunstschaffen der vergangenen Jahre ist die schrittweise Annäherung zwischen Designern und Kunsthandwerkern. Die hermetische Abschottung dieser beiden Aktivitäten war die Folge eines akademischen Lehrprogramms, das sich auf die industrielle Serienproduktion fokussiert hatte. So fehlte es zum einen an Arbeitsplätzen für die jungen Absolventen aus den circa 400 Kursen der Design-Hochschulen im Land. Zum anderen wurde die kunsthandwerkliche Produktion in den armen ländlichen Regionen durch den rapiden Verfall ihrer kulturellen Bedeutung vernichtet.

Die reichen Traditionen der Handarbeit, in der die Kommunen Produkte für ihren eigenen Bedarf

Women from Esperança in the state of Paraíba with their hand-sewn rag dolls.
Frauen aus Esperança im Bundesstaat Paraíba mit ihren handgenähten Puppen.

herstellten, litten unter der Konkurrenz der chinesischen Importe, und die Kunsthandwerker begannen, die industriellen Formen zu kopieren und/oder Stereotype in ihre Produktion aufzunehmen. Gleich, in welche Region Brasiliens man schaute, man sah praktisch immer dieselben »Motive«: Zwerge, Pyramiden oder die Flora und Fauna der kalten Länder, die aus irgendeiner Zeitschrift abgezeichnet waren.

Unter der Schirmherrschaft verschiedener Organisationen – unter ihnen die Sebrae, die sich um die kleinen und mittelständischen Unternehmen Brasiliens kümmert, und die Central ArteSol/Artesanato Solidário, eine Institution, die Kunsthandwerkern Anreize bietet, damit sie Einkommensquellen für Not

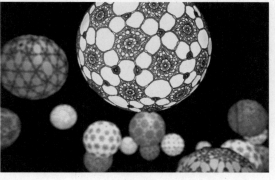

Cristal de Luz lamps, designed by TT Leal and manufactured together with the Rocinha Craftwork Cooperative in Rocinha.
Cristal de Luz-Leuchten, entworfen von TT Leal und hergestellt zusammen mit der Rocinha Craftwork Cooperative aus Rocinha.

leidende Bevölkerungsgruppen schaffen – haben die Designer in den vergangenen zwei Jahrzehnten abgelegene Landesteile besucht und Workshops veranstaltet, die die technische und ästhetische Qualität des Kunsthandwerks verbessern sollen. Eine dieser Aktivitäten betraf die Herstellung von Stoffpuppen in der Stadt Esperança – *esperança* ist das portugiesische Wort für »Hoffnung« – im Staat Paraíba. Es sind dieselben Puppen, die Fernando und Humberto Campana in ihrem Sessel *Multidão* verwendet haben. Damals, als das Kunsthandwerk allmählich wieder belebt wurde, im Jahre 1999, stellte nur noch eine einzige Frau, Dona Socorro, diese Puppen aus Stoffresten her – und mit ihrem Tod wäre ihre Handwerkstechnik untergegangen, da ja schon die Kinder der Gemeinde lieber mit den Plastikpuppen aus China spielten. Dank des von ArteSol koordinierten Projekts beteiligen sich nunmehr 40 Kunsthandwerkerinnen an der Puppenherstellung.

14 Ebenda.

15 Lost Art, Caleb Neelon und Tristan Manco: *Graffiti Brasil,* Thames & Hudson, London 2005. Ausstellung *Street Art,* Tate Modern, London, 23. Mai–25. August 2008.

name reveals its founding principle. In the Tupi language (an important Native Brazilian linguistic stem), the word *piracema* designates the upstream migration of fish for reproductive needs. 'For reasons known only by nature, fish are bound to come back to their birthplace in order to secure a future through spawning. This image of a return to origins in order to establish an avant-garde is the laboratory's source of inspiration and structural approach: to drink tradition and transpire contemporaneity.'[17]

The Production of Happiness

Adopting creativity as a survival strategy may be considered one of the foremost attributes of the Brazilian people. Aloísio Magalhães considered this inventive capacity as also 'closely related to their capacity for tolerance.'[18] With the increase in the number of meeting points between designers of different origins and social classes, reciprocal fertilizations are potentialized and multiplied. Thus, when São Paulo musician Tom Zé says, 'I am in love with the ability of Brazilian people to produce beauty and joy,'[19] he is actually summarizing the contribution of designers such as Fernando and Humberto Campana to the development of Brazil's image as a place of much more than samba, football, and beaches.

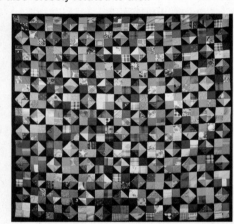

Patchwork quilt designed and sewn by Christina Ribeiro de Paiva of Recife in the state of Pernambuco, 2008.
Flickendecke, entworfen und genäht von Christina Ribeiro de Paiva aus Recife im Bundesstaat Pernambuco, 2008.

17 Ibid.
18 Aloísio Magalhães, *É Triunfo?*, p.178.
19 Tom Zé, interview in *O Estado de S. Paulo,* 9 March 2008.

Ein anderes Beispiel für diese Art von Projekten ist die Cooperativa de Trabalho Artesanal e de Costura da Rocinha (Kooperative für Kunsthandwerk und Näherei von Rocinha), in einer der größten Favelas Rio de Janeiros. Als Koordinatorin der Institution förderte Maria Teresa Leal seit 1982 einerseits die technischen Fertigkeiten der Kunsthandwerkerinnen und suchte andererseits Gespräche mit Designern, Stilisten und plastischen Künstlern, damit diese die kunsthandwerklichen Stücke in ihre eigene Produktion aufnehmen konnten. Es wurden Geschäftspartnerschaften mit brasilianischen Designern und Künstlern wie Carlos Miele, Fernando Jaeger und Ernesto Neto und sogar mit ausländischen Designern wie Tord Boontje geschlossen. Diese Bemühungen trugen reiche Früchte und verbesserten die Lebensbedingungen der Frauen von Rocinha. Anfänglich bestand die Gruppe aus sechzehn Kunsthandwerkerinnen, heute sind es etwa hundert.

Für die Designer, die mit diesen Gemeinschaften zusammenarbeiten, ist es eine Herausforderung, der Arbeit der Kunsthandwerker Respekt zu zollen und einen wahrhaften Dialog entstehen zu lassen. Das Laboratório Piracema de Design (Laboratorium Piracema für Design), das sich als ein Forschungszentrum für die Form in der brasilianischen Kultur versteht, betrachtet es als ein methodisches Grundprinzip, dass »der Kunsthandwerker unabhängig ist, Ausgangs- und Endpunkt jeder Intervention«.[16]

Der Name des Laboratoriums ist indianischen Ursprungs und von Bedeutung, um sein Gründungsprinzip zu verstehen. In der Sprache *tupí* (einer wichtigen Sprachfamilie innerhalb der brasilianischen Indianersprachen), bezeichnet *piracema* das Naturphänomen, wenn die Fische stromaufwärts zu den Quellen der Flüsse wandern, um sich fortzupflanzen. »Aus Gründen, die nur die Natur kennt, werden die Fische dazu getrieben, zu dem Ort, an dem sie geboren wurden, zurückzukehren, um dort mit dem Ablaichen die Zukunft zu bestimmen. Dieses Bild des Eintauchens in die Ursprünge, um von dort aus die Avantgarde zu schaffen, ist Quelle der Inspiration und die Leitlinie für das Laboratorium. Von der Tradition trinken und die Gegenwart ausschwitzen«, sagen sie.[17]

Produktion von Freude

Schöpfertum als Überlebensstrategie ist ein Wesenszug der brasilianischen Menschen. Nach Aloísio Magalhães ist diese Erfindungsgabe »auch sehr stark mit der Fähigkeit zur Toleranz verbunden«.[18] Mit der Zahl der Begegnungen zwischen Akteuren verschiedener Herkunft und sozialer Klassen vervielfachen sich die wechselseitigen Befruchtungen. »Ich bin beeindruckt von der Fähigkeit der Brasilianer, Schönheit und Freude zu produzieren«, sagt Tom Zé, ein in São Paulo lebender Musiker aus Bahia,[19] und fasst damit eine Eigenschaft zusammen, die von Schöpfern wie Fernando und Humberto Campana verkörpert wird und alles mit sich bringt, um aus Brasilien mehr zu machen, als nur einen Ort für »Samba, Fußball und Strand«.

16 Laboratório Piracema de Design (interne Dokumente).
17 Ebenda.
18 Magalhães, a.a.O., S. 178 (vgl. Anm. 4).
19 Tom Zé im Interview für die Zeitung *Estado de S. Paulo,* 9. März 2008.

List of exhibited works Verzeichnis der ausgestellten Werke

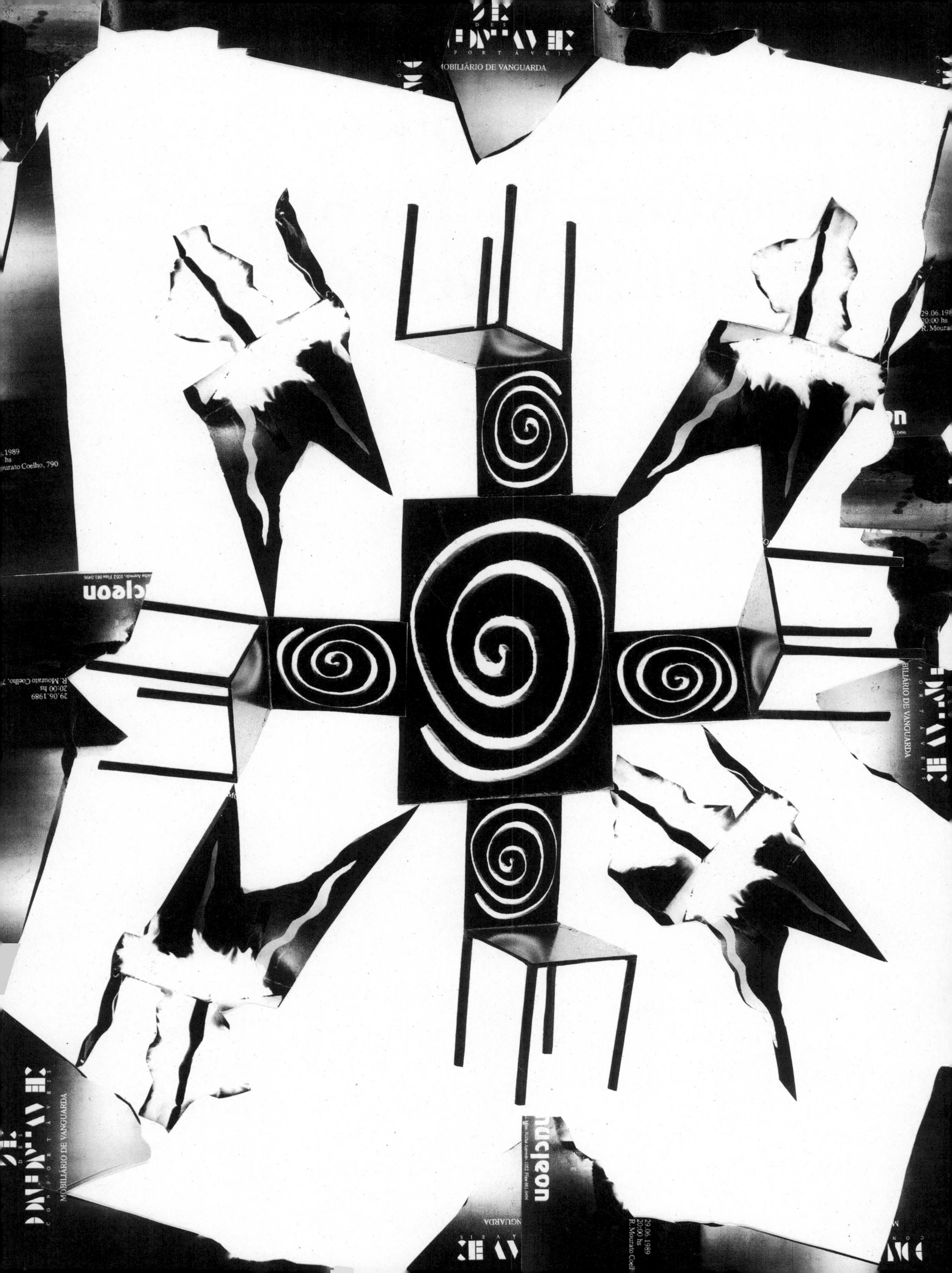
MOBILIÁRIO DE VANGUARDA

Humberto Campana
chair Stuhl
Negativo (Negative Negativ)
one-off piece Unikat
1988
110×50×50 cm
steel Stahl
loan Leihgabe: Dan Fialdini, São Paulo

On a 1988 white-water rafting trip in Arizona, USA, Humberto Campana discovered spiral-patterned drawings by Native Indians and later that night dreamt of being swallowed up by a spiral. The next day, his boat capsized and he came very close to drowning. Back in São Paulo, he created this chair as a reaction to his experience. His brother Fernando countered by using Humberto's cut-out spiral as the backrest for a chair of his own, which he named *Positivo*. The distinct work method intimated in these early works has remained characteristic of the Campanas.

1988 bei einer Wildwasserfahrt in Arizona, USA, hatte Humberto Campana spiralförmige Indianerzeichnungen entdeckt und träumte nachts, eine Spirale würde ihn verschlingen. Tags darauf kenterte sein Boot und er entkam nur knapp dem Ertrinken. Zurück in São Paulo schuf er diesen Stuhl als Reaktion auf sein Erlebnis. Sein Bruder Fernando konterte, indem er Humbertos ausgeschnittene Spirale als Rückenlehne für einen eigenen Stuhl verwendete, den er *Positivo* nannte. Die unterschiedlichen Arbeitsweisen, die sich damals andeuteten, blieben typisch für die Campanas.

Clusters
Haufen

Humberto Campana
mirror frame Spiegelrahmen
Untitled Ohne Titel
one-off piece Unikat
1977
74×53×8 cm
wood, mirror glass, seashells, glue Holz, Spiegelglas, Muscheln, Klebstoff
loan Leihgabe: Robert Wasilewski, São Paulo

Humberto Campana's first artistic works were mirror frames lavishly decorated with seashells he had collected himself – a motif prevalent in the Baroque style imported by the Spanish and Portuguese conquerors as well as in the artisanal traditions of Native Indians.

Humberto Campanas erste künstlerische Arbeiten waren Rahmen, die er über und über mit selbst gesammelten Muscheln verzierte – ein Motiv, das sowohl auf den barocken Stil verweist, den die spanischen und portugiesischen Eroberer importierten, als auch auf das Handwerk der indianischen Ureinwohner.

Fernando & Humberto Campana
easy chair Sessel
Sonia Diniz
limited edition of 12 copies (prototype) limitierte Auflage von 12 Exemplaren (Prototyp)
2003
83×70×76 cm
carpet, rubber, ethylene vinyl acetate (EVA), fabric, wood, stainless steel Teppich, Gummi, Ethylenvinylacetat (EVA), Textilgewebe, Holz, Edelstahl
loan Leihgabe: Estúdio Campana, São Paulo

Created from assorted textiles that have been rolled and cut into pieces, this mix of materials constitutes a wholly new form of decorative upholstery padding and covering.

Die Materialmischung aus gerollten und dann geschnittenen Stücken unterschiedlicher Textilien stellt eine völlig neuartige, dekorative Form von Polsterung beziehungsweise Bezugsstoff dar.

Fernando & Humberto Campana
chair Stuhl
Harumaki
unlimited edition, numbered per year (prototype) unlimitierte Auflage, numeriert pro Jahr (Prototyp)
2004
92×66×55 cm
carpet, rubber, ethylene vinyl acetate (EVA), fabric, brushed aluminium Teppich, Gummi, Ethylenvinylacetat (EVA), Textilgewebe, gebürstetes Aluminium
loan Leihgabe: Estúdio Campana, São Paulo

Humberto Campana
table centrepiece Tafelaufsatz
Tokyo Garden (Tokio Garten)
one-off piece Unikat
2005
30×85×55 cm
glass, ethylene vinyl acetate (EVA), rubber, carpet, fabric Glas, Ethylenvinylacetat (EVA), Gummi, Teppich, Textilgewebe
loan Leihgabe: Estúdio Campana, São Paulo

Invited by the Japanese design magazine Casa Brutus to create an ideal garden, Humberto Campana conceived this model for a hanging garden as an hommage to Japanese rock gardens and bonsai – microcosms for meditations on nature.

Auf Einladung des japanischen Designmagazins *Casa Brutus,* einen idealen Garten zu entwerfen, entstand dieses Modell eines hängenden Gartens als Hommage an japanische Steingärten und Bonsais – Mikrokosmen zur Besinnung auf die Natur.

Fernando & Humberto Campana
fruit bowl Fruchtschale
Sushi
unlimited edition, numbered per year (prototype) unlimitierte Auflage, numeriert pro Jahr (Prototyp)
2002
20×56×56 cm
rubber, felt, carpet, canvas, ethylene vinyl acetate (EVA) Gummi, Filz, Teppich, Segeltuch, Ethylenvinylacetat (EVA)
loan Leihgabe: Estúdio Campana, São Paulo

Fernando & Humberto Campana
armchair **Armsessel**
Banquete (Feast Gelage)
limited edition of 150 copies (prototype) **limitierte
Auflage von 150 Exemplaren (Prototyp)**
2002
85×100×140 cm
plush animals, stainless steel **Plüschtiere, Edelstahl**
loan **Leihgabe: Estúdio Campana, São Paulo**

Fernando & Humberto Campana
armchair **Armsessel**
Multidão Mulata (A Crowd of Mulattos **Eine Menge Mulatten**)
one-off piece **Unikat**
2004
67×97×90 cm
cotton dolls, stainless steel **Baumwollpuppen, Edelstahl**
loan **Leihgabe: Estúdio Campana, São Paulo**

This chair pays homage to Brazil's colourful mix of ethnicities and
translates the proverbial sea of people, as most vividly experienced during the
Brazilian carnival, into a unique armchair. By using hand-sewn rag dolls, the
Campanas support traditional artisanry in the northeastern town of Esperança.
**Der Sessel ist eine Hommage an das bunte Völkergemisch
Brasiliens und übersetzt das sprichwörtliche Bad in der Menge,
das man zu keinem Zeitpunkt so eindrucksvoll erleben
kann wie beim brasilianischen Karneval, in einen einzigartigen
Sessel. Indem sie die handgenähten Puppen verwenden,
unterstützen die Campanas das traditionelle Kunsthandwerk
im Städtchen Esperança im Nordosten des Landes.**

Fernando & Humberto Campana
stool **Hocker**
Vitória Régia
unlimited edition, numbered per year (prototype) **unlimitierte Auflage,
numeriert pro Jahr (Prototyp)**
2002
58×100×100 cm
powder-coated steel, ethylene vinyl acetate (EVA), rubber, fabrics
**pulverbeschichteter Stahl, Ethylenvinylacetat (EVA), Gummi,
Textilgewebe**
loan **Leihgabe: Estúdio Campana, São Paulo**

The name comes from a type of water lily found in the Amazon.
**Der Name stammt von einer Seerosenart aus dem
Amazonasgebiet.**

Fernando & Humberto Campana
stool **Hocker**
Vitória Régia
prototype **Prototyp**
2002
59×63×63 cm
brushed stainless steel, ethylene vinyl acetate (EVA), rubber,
fabrics **gebürsteter Edelstahl, Ethylenvinylacetat (EVA),
Gummi, Textilgewebe**
loan **Leihgabe: Estúdio Campana, São Paulo**

Fernando & Humberto Campana
armchair **Armsessel**
Sushi IV
limited edition of 35 copies (prototype) **limitierte Auflage von
35 Exemplaren (Prototyp)**
2003
83×110×95 cm
stainless steel, carpet, rubber, ethylene vinyl acetate (EVA), various
fabrics **Edelstahl, Teppich, Gummi, Ethylenvinylacetat
(EVA), verschiedene Textilgewebe**
loan **Leihgabe: Estúdio Campana, São Paulo**

Fernando & Humberto Campana
costume **Kostüm**
Untitled **Ohne Titel**
one-off piece **Unikat**: Ballet National de Marseille,
Marseille
2007
85×46×36 cm (variable **variabel**)
velcro, cotton **Klettband, Baumwolle**
loan **Leihgabe: Ballet National de Marseille, Marseille**

Fernando & Humberto Campana
armchair Armsessel
Sushi
serial model Serienmodell: Edra spa, Perignano
2002
60×95×85 cm
polyurethane foam, elastic belt, etylene vinyl acetate (EVA),
felt, plastic, fabrics Polyurethanschaum, elastisches
Band, Ethylenvinylacetat (EVA), Filz, Kunststoff,
verschiedene Textilgewebe
loan Leihgabe: Edra spa, Perignano

The predecessor of this armchair was designed by the Campanas
for a party sponsored by a textile manufacturer to promote its synthetic fabrics. The colourful bundled strips of cloth can also be found
in traditional hats such as those worn in some parts of Brazil for the
congado folk dance.
Den Vorläufer zu diesem Objekt entwarfen die Campanas
für eine Party, bei der ein Textilunternehmen für seine
synthetischen Stoffe warb. Die bunten, gebündelten
Stoffstreifen findet man auch in traditionellen Hüten, wie
man sie in einigen Gegenden Brasiliens zum Volkstanz
congado trägt.

Fernando & Humberto Campana
vase Vase
Buriti
unlimited edition, numbered per year (prototype) unlimitierte Auflage,
numeriert pro Jahr (Prototyp)
2003
35×30×30 cm (variable variabel)
glass, carpet, rubber, ethylene vinyl acetate (EVA), fabrics Glas,
Teppich, Gummi, Ethylenvinylacetat (EVA), Textilgewebe
loan Leihgabe: Estúdio Campana, São Paulo

The name is taken from a type of Brazilian palm tree.
Der Name ist einer brasilianischen Palmenart entlehnt.

Fragments
Fragmente

Fernando & Humberto Campana
armchair Armsessel
Favela (Slum Elendsviertel)
one-off piece Unikat
2009
85×74×65 cm
wooden boards, nails Holzbretter, Nägel
loan Leihgabe: Estúdio Campana, São Paulo

The Campanas adapted the aesthetic and technique of hammered-
together shacks for an armchair made of scrap wood, which they gave
the form of a throne – in honour and recognition of the ingenuity
found in the Brazilian slums. The first *Favela* armchair was a one-off
piece that served as the model for Edra's later serial production.
The version shown here was created especially for the *Antibodies*
exhibition.
Die Technik und Ästhetik von Bretterbuden adaptierten
die Campanas für einen Sessel aus Abfallholz, dem
sie die Form eines Throns gaben – als Würdigung des
Erfindungsreichtums in den brasilianischen Slums.
Der erste *Favela*-Sessel war ein Unikat, das zum Vorbild
für Edras spätere Serienproduktion wurde. Die hier
gezeigte Fassung entstand für die *Antikörper*-Ausstellung.

Fernando & Humberto Campana
hanging lamp Hängeleuchte
Favela (Slum Elendsviertel)
prototype Prototyp
2004
60×53×12 cm
wooden boards, nails Holzbretter, Nägel
loan Leihgabe: Estúdio Campana, São Paulo

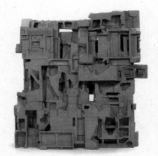

Fernando & Humberto Campana
screen Wandschirm
Untitled Ohne Titel
one-off piece Unikat
2006
200×200×40 cm
polystyrene, wrapping paper Styropor, Packpapier
loan Leihgabe: Estúdio Campana, São Paulo

This model for a screen was to have been realized from papier mâché
in collaboration with the Vitra Design Museum. To simulate the
structure and surface of the object, the Campanas fit various units
of polystyrene packaging into one another and covered them with
plain brown wrapping paper. The result is a powerful sculptural work
that reflects the technoid chaos of an urban metropolis.
Dieses Modell für einen Wandschirm sollte in Zusammenarbeit mit dem Vitra Design Museum aus Pappmaché
entwickelt werden. Um Struktur und Oberfläche des Objekts zu simulieren, fügten die Campanas unterschiedliche
Styroporverpackungen ineinander und beklebten sie
mit Packpapier.
Das Ergebnis ist eine kraftvolle Raumplastik, die das
technoide Chaos einer Großstadt reflektiert.

Humberto Campana
sculpture Plastik
Untitled Ohne Titel
1982
80×40×40 cm
terracotta Terrakotta
loan Leihgabe: Marta Maria Guimarães Furtado,
São Paulo

Fernando & Humberto Campana
stage prop Bühnenrequisite
Peter and the Wolf; Wolf (Peter und der Wolf; Wolf)
one-off piece Unikat
2008
59×45×136 cm
wood, glue Holz, Klebstoff
loan Leihgabe: Estúdio Campana, São Paulo,

The following figures were created for the Campanas' set of
a production of Sergei Prokofiev's musical fable *Peter and the Wolf*
performed at New York's Guggenheim Museum during the 2008
Christmas season.
Die folgenden Figuren entstanden für ein Bühnenbild der
Campanas zu Sergei Prokofjews musikalischem Märchen
Peter und der Wolf, das zu Weihnachten 2008 im
Guggenheim Museum in New York aufgeführt wurde.

Fernando & Humberto Campana
stage prop Bühnenrequisite
Peter and the Wolf; Peter (Peter und der Wolf; Peter)
one-off piece Unikat
2008
133×37×24 cm
wood, nails, glue Holz, Nägel, Klebstoff
loan Leihgabe: Estúdio Campana, São Paulo

Fernando & Humberto Campana
stage prop Bühnenrequisite
Peter and the Wolf; Cat (Peter und der Wolf; Katze)
one-off piece Unikat
2008
77×35×45 cm
wood, glue Holz, Klebstoff
loan Leihgabe: Estúdio Campana, São Paulo

Fernando & Humberto Campana
stage prop Bühnenrequisite
Peter and the Wolf; Duck (Peter und der Wolf; Ente)
one-off piece Unikat
2008
51×35×77 cm
wood, glue Holz, Klebstoff
loan Leihgabe: Estúdio Campana, São Paulo

Fernando & Humberto Campana
stage prop Bühnenrequisite
Peter and the Wolf; Bird (Peter und der Wolf; Vogel)
one-off piece Unikat
2008
26×44×14 cm
wood, glue Holz, Klebstoff
loan Leihgabe: Estúdio Campana, São Paulo

Fernando & Humberto Campana
architectural model Architekturmodell (1:20)
Volcano (Vulkan)
study Studie
2003
30×16×16 cm
wood, glue Holz, Klebstoff
loan Leihgabe: Estúdio Campana, São Paulo

In their *Ideal House* for the Cologne furniture fair, the original idea
was to create some sort of enclosed space within the house. During
their preparations, the Campanas came across the raffia-covered huts
of Brazil's Native Indians and adapted their design accordingly.
In ihrem *Ideal House* für die Kölner Möbelmesse sollte
ein abgeschirmter Raum innerhalb des Hauses entstehen – dies ist die erste Idee dazu. Während ihrer Vor-
bereitungen wurden die Campanas in Brasilien auf
die mit Raffia gedeckten Hütten der Indios aufmerksam
und änderten ihren Entwurf entsprechend.

Fernando & Humberto Campana
poster Plakat
Camper together with Campana (Camper
zusammen mit Campana)
2006
112×77 cm
paper, marker Papier, Filzstift
loan Leihgabe: Estúdio Campana, São Paulo

The poster was created to advertise a Camper shoe store in Berlin
for which the Campanas had lined the interior walls with multiple
layers of variously coloured papers. The idea was to integrate customers
in a continuing design process by inviting them to tear off layer
after layer. This inversion of the collage technique frequently employed
by the Campanas results in ever-changing decors.
Das Poster entstand als Ankündigung eines Camper-
Schuhgeschäfts in Berlin, dessen Innenwände die
Campanas mit mehreren Lagen verschiedenfarbiger
Papiere verkleideten. Die Idee ist, Kunden in die Fortset-
zung der Gestaltung zu integrieren, indem sie immer
neue Lagen aufreißen dürfen. So entstehen, in
Umkehrung der von den Campanas häufig verwendeten
Collagetechnik, ständig wechselnde Dekors.

Fernando & Humberto Campana
fruit bowl Fruchtschale
Untitled Ohne Titel
study for *Nazareth* Studie für *Nazareth*
2006
22×47×48 cm
merged parts of plastic dolls, lacquer verschmolzene
Teile von Plastikpuppen, Lack
loan Leihgabe: Estúdio Campana, São Paulo

Fernando & Humberto Campana
table centrepiece Tafelaufsatz
Nazareth (Bronze)
limited edition of 10 copies limitierte Auflage von
10 Exemplaren: Bernardaud, Paris
2008
19×36×42 cm
porcelain Porzellan
loan Leihgabe: Bernardaud, Paris

The piece refers to the crowd theme explored earlier in the *Multidão* armchair. Allusions to the cannibalism of indigenous Brazilian populations, the voodoo magic of African slaves, and Christian votive offerings are also suggested. Yet above all, the object pays homage to the Campanas' artist friend Nazareth Pacheco, who in her work treats physical pain as an integral part of her identity.

Die Schale nimmt Bezug auf die schon im *Multidão*-Sessel thematisierte Menschenmenge. Auch Anspielungen auf den Kannibalismus brasilianischer Ureinwohner, den Voodoo-Zauber der afrikanischen Sklaven und auf christliche Votivgaben klingen an. Vor allem aber ist das Objekt eine Hommage an die mit den Campanas befreundete Künstlerin Nazareth Pacheco, die in ihrem Werk den physischen Schmerz als Teil ihrer Identität verarbeitet.

Fernando & Humberto Campana
fruit bowl Fruchtschale
Untitled Ohne Titel
study Studie
2007
16×52×50 cm
leather, glue Leder, Klebstoff
loan Leihgabe: Estúdio Campana, São Paulo

Fernando & Humberto Campana
bar stool Barhocker
Untitled Ohne Titel
one-off piece Unikat
2006
73×34×34 cm
wood, leather, foam Holz, Leder, Schaumstoff
loan Leihgabe: Estúdio Campana, São Paulo

Fernando & Humberto Campana
seat shell for the *Aguapé* armchair Sitzschale für
den Armsessel *Aguapé*
prototype Prototyp
2007
42×135×95 cm
leather, glue Leder, Klebstoff
loan Leihgabe: Estúdio Campana, São Paulo

The thick raw leather petals recall the displays of a butcher's shop. Originally, the seat shell was supposed to rest on legs of twisted leather, however the idea could not be executed due to structural reasons.

Die dicken, rohen Lederlappen erinnern an die Auslagen einer Metzgerei. Ursprünglich sollte die Sitzschale auf Beinen aus gedrehtem Leder ruhen. Diese Idee ließ sich aus konstruktiven Gründen jedoch nicht umsetzen.

Fernando & Humberto Campana
wastebasket Papierkorb
Untitled Ohne Titel
study Studie
2007
55×30×34 cm
leather, glue Leder, Klebstoff
loan Leihgabe: Estúdio Campana, São Paulo

Fernando & Humberto Campana
wastebasket **Papierkorb**
Untitled **Ohne Titel**
study **Studie**
2008
52×38×36 cm
leather, glue, polyamide thread **Leder, Klebstoff,
Polyamidfaden**
loan **Leihgabe: Estúdio Campana, São Paulo**

Fernando & Humberto Campana
planting pot **Pflanzgefäß**
Untitled **Ohne Titel**
study **Studie**
2008
30×18×18 cm (variable **variabel**)
leather, glue, polyamide thread **Leder, Klebstoff,
Polyamidfaden**
loan **Leihgabe: Estúdio Campana, São Paulo**

In the same way that the Campanas' *Transplastics* series creates
an interpenetration of organic and inorganic materials, here
a living compound of animal leather and substances from the earth
is sought.
So wie die Campanas in ihrer *Transplastics*-Serie
eine Durchdringung organischer und anorganischer
Materialien schaffen, suchen sie hier nach einer
lebendigen Verbindung von tierischem Leder mit den
Substanzen in der Erde.

Fernando & Humberto Campana
planting pot **Pflanzgefäß**
Untitled **Ohne Titel**
study **Studie**
2008
40×21×22 cm (variable **variabel**)
leather, glue, polyamide thread **Leder, Klebstoff,
Polyamidfaden**
loan **Leihgabe: Estúdio Campana, São Paulo**

Fernando & Humberto Campana
planting pot **Pflanzgefäß**
Untitled **Ohne Titel**
study **Studie**
2008
20×13×11 cm (variable **variabel**)
leather, glue, polyamide thread **Leder, Klebstoff,
Polyamidfaden**
loan **Leihgabe: Estúdio Campana, São Paulo**

Fernando & Humberto Campana
planting pot **Pflanzgefäß**
Untitled **Ohne Titel**
study **Studie**
2008
20×18×18 cm (variable **variabel**)
leather, glue, polyamide thread **Leder, Klebstoff,
Polyamidfaden**
loan **Leihgabe: Estúdio Campana, São Paulo**

Fernando & Humberto Campana
fruit bowl **Fruchtschale**
Untitled **Ohne Titel**
study **Studie**
2008
15×38×38 cm
leather, glue, polyamide thread **Leder, Klebstoff,
Polyamidfaden**
loan **Leihgabe: Estúdio Campana, São Paulo**

Fernando & Humberto Campana
chair Stuhl
Untitled Ohne Titel
one-off piece Unikat
1989
106×55×66 cm
stainless steel Edelstahl
loan Leihgabe: Mariangela Martinelli, Recife

The off-centre form and polished surface of this early object might have been inspired by the furniture sculptures of Ron Arad or Danny Lane. What makes it distinctly original, however, is its particular sculptural quality. Moreover, it is the first object in the Campanas' œuvre that was built from fragments of industrial materials.

Die exzentrische Form und die polierte Oberfläche dieses frühen Objekts sind möglicherweise noch den Möbelplastiken Ron Arads oder Danny Lanes entlehnt. Von eigenständiger Originalität ist jedoch die plastische Qualität, und zum ersten Mal in ihrem Werk bauten die Campanas hier ein Möbel aus Fragmenten industrieller Materialien.

Fernando & Humberto Campana
ceiling lamp Deckenleuchte
Espelhos (Mirror Spiegel)
prototype Prototyp
2008
25×120×115 cm
acrylic mirror, light bulb, cabelling Acrylspiegel, Leuchtmittel, Verkabelung
loan Leihgabe: Estúdio Campana, São Paulo

Fernando & Humberto Campana
necklace Halskette
Untitled Ohne Titel
study Studie
2007
31×24 cm
leather, polyamide thread Leder, Polyamidfaden
loan Leihgabe: Estúdio Campana, São Paulo

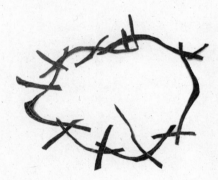

Fernando & Humberto Campana
necklace Halskette
Untitled Ohne Titel
study Studie
2007
35×35 cm
leather, polyamide thread Leder, Polyamidfaden
loan Leihgabe: Estúdio Campana, São Paulo

Fernando & Humberto Campana
necklace Halskette
Untitled Ohne Titel
study Studie
2007
39×31 cm
fur, polyamide thread Fell, Polyamifaden
loan Leihgabe: Estúdio Campana, São Paulo

Fernando & Humberto Campana
necklace Halskette
Untitled Ohne Titel
study Studie
2007
37×30 cm
leather, polyamide thread Leder, Polyamidfaden
loan Leihgabe: Estúdio Campana, São Paulo

Fernando & Humberto Campana
necklace Halskette
Untitled Ohne Titel
study Studie
2007
35×19 cm (variable variabel)
leather, magnets, polyamide thread Leder, Magnete,
Polyamidfaden
loan Leihgabe: Estúdio Campana, São Paulo

Fernando & Humberto Campana
necklace Halskette
Untitled Ohne Titel
study Studie
2008
25×25 cm (variable variabel)
aluminium sheet, magnets Aluminiumblech, Magnete
loan Leihgabe: Estúdio Campana, São Paulo

Organics
Organik

Fernando & Humberto Campana
vase Vase
Galho (Branch Zweig)
one-off piece Unikat
2001
21×71×27 cm
glass Glas
loan Leihgabe: Estúdio Campana, São Paulo

Fernando & Humberto Campana
Campane di Campana – 1983
one-off piece Unikat: Venini, Murano
2005
44×43×46 cm
mouth-blown glass, hemp rope mundgeblasenes Glas, Hanfseil
loan Leihgabe: Moss Gallery, New York

Featuring motifs from Brazil's natural environment, these two
glass bells are from a series of 175, commissoned by Murray Moss
and created by the Campanas in collaboration with the glass-
blowers of Venini in Murano. For the 2005 Christmas season, all the
Campane di Campana (Italian: Bells of the Campanas) were
presented in a spectacular installation along the wall of the Moss
Gallery.
Die beiden hier gezeigten Glocken mit Motiven aus der
brasilianischen Natur entstammen einer Reihe von
insgesamt 175 Glasglocken, die die Campanas auf Initia-
tive von Murray Moss und zusammen mit den Glas-
bläsern von Venini in Murano schufen. Zu Weihnachten
2005 wurden sämtliche *Campane di Campana* (ital.:
Glocken der Campanas) in einer spektakulären Installation entlang einer Wand der Moss Gallery präsentiert.

Fernando & Humberto Campana
Campane di Campana – 1969
one-off piece Unikat: Venini, Murano
2005
49×40×30 cm
mouth-blown glass, hemp rope mundgeblasenes Glas,
Hanfseil
loan Leihgabe: Moss Gallery, New York

Fernando & Humberto Campana
ashtray Aschenbecher
Untitled Ohne Titel
study Studie
1992
14×14×4 cm
aluminium Aluminium
loan Leihgabe: Estúdio Campana, São Paulo

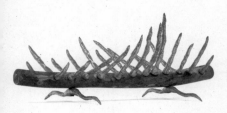

Fernando & Humberto Campana
fruit bowl Fruchtschale
Costela (Rib Rippe)
one-off piece Unikat
1990
22×53,5×22 cm
aluminium, jabuticabeira wood Aluminium,
Jabuticabeira-Holz
loan Leihgabe: Adriana Adam, São Paulo

This object belongs to the early *Organicos* series in which the Campanas intersected found pieces of wood and metal to create motifs of nature in transformation.
Das Objekt gehört zur frühen Serie der *Organicos,* in der die Campanas gefundene Holzstücke und Metall zu Motiven einer sich verändernden Natur gekreuzt haben.

Fernando & Humberto Campana
fruit bowl Fruchtschale
Bola (Beet Rübe)
one-off piece Unikat
1990
47×40×25 cm
aluminium, wood Aluminium, Holz
loan Leihgabe: Pedro Useche, São Paulo

This unusual fruit dish suggests the structure of the *Vermelha* armchair, which was produced three years later.
Die ungewöhnliche Schale deutet die Struktur des *Vermelha*-Sessels an, der drei Jahre später entstand.

Fernando & Humberto Campana
candle holders Kerzenhalter
Raiz (Root Wurzel)
one-off pieces Unikate
1990
42×12×15 cm
cast brass, Jabuticaba wood, acrylic paint gegossenes
Messing, Jabuticaba-Holz, Acrylfarbe
loan Leihgabe: Robert Wasilewski, São Paulo

Fernando & Humberto Campana
Pe de Galinha (Chicken Foot Hühnerfuß)
study Studie
2008
11×10×10 cm
plaster Gips
loan Leihgabe: Estúdio Campana, São Paulo

Fernando & Humberto Campana
wall pockets Wandtaschen
Drosera Copper & Drosera Velvet
limited edition of 24 copies limitierte Auflage von
24 Exemplaren: Vitra AG, Basel
2007
(2×) 80×90×30 cm (variable variabel)
copper, velvet Kupfer, Samt
Collection Vitra Design Museum, Weil am Rhein

Fernando & Humberto Campana
screen Wandschirm
Amarelo (Yellow Gelb)
one-off piece Unikat
2006
225×160×30 cm (variable variabel)
aluminium wire, fabric Aluminiumdraht, Textil
loan Leihgabe: Estúdio Campana, São Paulo

Fernando & Humberto Campana
study for the *Kaiman Jacarè* sofa Studie für das Sofa
Kaiman Jacarè
model Modell
2006
16×70×43 cm (variable variabel)
polystyrene, canvas Styropor, Segeltuch
loan Leihgabe: Estúdio Campana, São Paulo

Fernando & Humberto Campana
sofa Sofa
Kaiman Jacarè
serial model Serienmodell: Edra spa, Perignano
2006
100×700×500 cm (variable variabel)
leather, foam Leder, Schaumstoff
loan Leihgabe: Edra spa, Perignano

Explorations of the Brazilian rainforest led to the idea for this design, which was inspired by the caimans of the Amazon basin that can grow to a length of six metres. Part of the *Historia Naturalis* series developed with Edra, the seating elements can be assembled and re-assembled at will and also used individually.

Nach Erkundungen des brasilianischen Urwalds entstand die Idee zu diesem Entwurf, für den die bis zu sechs Meter langen Kaimane aus dem Amazonasbecken Pate standen. Die Elemente dieses Möbels aus der mit Edra entwickelten Serie *Historia Naturalis* können nach Belieben zusammengestellt oder auch einzeln benutzt werden.

Fernando & Humberto Campana
study for the *Aster Papposus* sofa Studie für das frei stehende Sofa *Aster Papposus*
model Modell
2005
56×170×170 cm
polystyrene, canvas Styropor, Segeltuch
loan Leihgabe: Estúdio Campana, São Paulo

The study was produced in collaboration with Edra for a free-standing sofa whose name is taken from a type of starfish.

Die Studie entstand in Zusammenarbeit mit Edra für ein freistehendes Sofa, dessen Name einer Seesternart entlehnt ist.

Fernando & Humberto Campana
sofa Sofa
Boa
serial model Serienmodell: Edra spa, Perignano
2002
60×190×355 cm
polyurethane foam, velvet Polyurethanschaum, Samt
loan Leihgabe: Edra spa, Perignano

The motif of the knot dates back to the earliest furniture designs of the Campanas. In a 1991 art installation for the São Paulo Pinacoteca, they translated it into an abstract formation that evokes the figure of a snake in the branches. These explorations ultimately led to this piece of furniture.

Das Motiv des Knäuels findet sich schon in den frühesten Möbelentwürfen der Campanas. In einer Kunstinstallation 1991 für die Pinakothek in São Paulo übersetzten sie es in ein abstraktes Gebilde, das an eine Schlange im Geäst erinnert. Später entwickelte sich dieses Möbel daraus.

Fernando & Humberto Campana
sitting cube Sitzwürfel
Dado Couro (Leather Cube Lederwürfel)
one-off piece Unikat
2007
50×50×50 cm
wood, coconut fibre, leather Holz, Kokosfaser, Leder
loan Leihgabe: Estúdio Campana, São Paulo

The precursor of this design, whose blister-like protrusions were intended to invite a tactile exploration of its surface, was covered with Tactel – a pleasant-feeling fabric that the sitting cubes were meant to showcase at a promotional party.

Der Vorläufer dieses Entwurfs, dessen Beulen dazu provozieren, die Oberfläche zu ertasten, war mit Tactel bespannt – einem angenehmen Textil, auf das während einer Werbeparty mit den Sitzwürfeln aufmerksam gemacht werden sollte.

Fernando & Humberto Campana
textile figure Stofffigur
Mandacaru Formiga (Ant Cactus Ameisen-Kaktus)
prototype for Prototyp für:
Alessi spa, Omegna Crusinallo
2006
15×24×15 cm (variable variabel)
fabric, foam, aluminium wire Textil, Schaumstoff, Aluminiumdraht
loan Leihgabe: Estúdio Campana, São Paulo

Fernando & Humberto Campana
textile figure Stofffigur
Mandacaru (Cactus Kaktus)
prototype for Prototyp für:
Alessi spa, Omegna Crusinallo
2006
33×19×10 cm (variable variabel)
fabric, foam, aluminium wire Textil, Schaumstoff, Aluminiumdraht
loan Leihgabe: Estúdio Campana, São Paulo

Fernando & Humberto Campana
textile figure Stofffigur
Mandacaru Boto (Amazon River Dolphin Cactus
Amazonasdelfin-Kaktus)
prototype for Prototyp für:
Alessi spa, Omegna Crusinallo
2006
25×40×30 cm (variable variabel)
fabric, foam, aluminium wire Textil, Schaumstoff,
Aluminiumdraht
loan Leihgabe: Estúdio Campana, São Paulo

Fernando & Humberto Campana
textile figure Stofffigur
Unstructured Pieces (Unstrukturierte Teile)
2006
31×26×12 cm (variable variabel)
fabric, foam, aluminium wire Textil, Schaumstoff,
Aluminiumdraht
loan Leihgabe: Estúdio Campana, São Paulo

Fernando & Humberto Campana
textile figure Stofffigur
Mandacaru Curupira (Little Forest Spirit Cactus
Kleiner-Waldgeist-Kaktus)
prototype for Prototyp für:
Alessi spa, Omegna Crusinallo
2006
41×25×25 cm (variable variabel)
fabric, foam, aluminium wire Textil, Schaumstoff,
Aluminiumdraht
loan Leihgabe: Estúdio Campana, São Paulo

Fernando & Humberto Campana
textile figure Stofffigur
Mandacaru Curupira (Little Forest Spirit Cactus
Kleiner-Waldgeist-Kaktus)
prototype for Prototyp für:
Alessi spa, Omegna Crusinallo
2006
16×32×18 cm (variable variabel)
fabric, foam, aluminium wire Textil, Schaumstoff,
Aluminiumdraht
loan Leihgabe: Estúdio Campana, São Paulo

Fernando & Humberto Campana
textile figure Stofffigur
Mandacaru Saci (Goblin Cactus Kobold-Kaktus)
prototype for Prototyp für:
Alessi spa, Omegna Crusinallo
2006
33×18×21 cm (variable variabel)
fabric, foam, aluminium wire Textil, Schaumstoff,
Aluminiumdraht
loan Leihgabe: Estúdio Campana, São Paulo

Fernando & Humberto Campana
textile figure Stofffigur
Mandacaru (Cactus Kaktus)
study for Studie für:
Alessi spa, Omegna Crusinallo
2006
27×15×13 cm (variable variabel)
fabric, foam, aluminium wire Textil, Schaumstoff,
Aluminiumdraht
loan Leihgabe: Estúdio Campana, São Paulo

Fernando & Humberto Campana
textile figure Stofffigur
Mandacaru Tatá (Water Snake Cactus
Wasserschlangen-Kaktus)
prototype for Prototyp für:
Alessi spa, Omegna Crusinallo
2006
20×14×15 cm (variable variabel)
fabric, foam, aluminium wire Textil, Schaumstoff,
Aluminiumdraht
loan Leihgabe: Estúdio Campana, São Paulo

Flexed Planes
Gebogene Flächen

Humberto Campana
sculpture Plastik
Untitled Ohne Titel
1982
25×31×15 cm
terracotta Terrakotta
loan Leihgabe: Estúdio Campana, São Paulo

Long before Humberto Campana designed furniture together with his brother, he had attended seminars and visited studios of other artists to become familiar with various techniques. It was during this period that he created this terracotta sculpture, which seems inspired by the curving forms of Oscar Niemeyer.
Lange bevor Humberto Campana zusammen mit seinem Bruder Möbel entwarf, hatte er sich in Seminaren und Ateliers anderer Künstler mit deren Techniken vertraut gemacht. Damals entstand auch diese Terrakottaplastik, die von den schwungvollen Formen Oscar Niemeyers inspiriert scheint.

Fernando Campana
Sculpture Plastik
Bambi
2006
41×12×31 cm
Corian
loan Leihgabe: Estúdio Campana, São Paulo

For this figure, Fernando Campana arranged the individual parts of another object in a new configuration.
Für diese Figur hat Fernando Campana die Einzelteile eines anderen Objektes neu zusammengesteckt.

Fernando & Humberto Campana
Gangorra (Seesaw Wippe)
one-off piece Unikat
1997
92×117×49 cm
powder-coated steel pulverbeschichteter Stahl
loan Leihgabe: Estúdio Campana, São Paulo

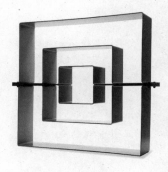

Fernando & Humberto Campana
storage rack Regal
Labirinto (Labyrinth)
prototype Prototyp
1997
140×140×30 cm
brushed aluminium sheet gebürstetes Aluminiumblech
loan Leihgabe: Estúdio Campana, São Paulo

Fernando & Humberto Campana
Carpet Teppich
Numeros (Numbers Nummern), n°7
small series Kleinserie
1999
160×220 cm
acrylic fibre Acrylfaser
loan Leihgabe: Leo Kim, São Paulo

Fernando & Humberto Campana
Carpet Teppich
Numeros (Numbers Nummern), n°5
small series Kleinserie
1999
160×220 cm
acrylic fibre Acrylfaser
loan Leihgabe: Estúdio Campana, São Paulo

The reduced black-and-white graphics of these carpets recalls the tiled promenades designed by landscape architect Roberto Burle Marx in Rio de Janeiro and other Brazilian cities.
Die reduzierte, schwarzweiße Grafik dieser Teppiche erinnert an die Pflasterung der Gehwege, die der Landschaftsarchitekt Roberto Burle Marx in Rio de Janeiro und anderen Städten Brasiliens angelegt hat.

Fernando & Humberto Campana
chair Stuhl
Curvas (Bows Bögen)
proof copy, produced by Belegexemplar, produziert von: Arredamento, São Paulo
1997
91×40×63 cm
stainless steel, polycarbonate sheeting Edelstahl, Polykarbonatfolie
loan Leihgabe: Estúdio Campana, São Paulo

Fernando & Humberto Campana
floor lamp Bodenleuchte
Pillow (Kissen)
prototype Prototyp
1997
22×53×53 cm
nylon fabric, polycarbonate, acrylic blanket, fluorescent
lamp Nylongewebe, Polykarbonat, Acrylteppich,
fluoriszierende (glimmende) Lampe
loan Leihgabe: Estúdio Campana, São Paulo

For this object, Fernando and Humberto were inspired by the view
of São Paulo from an airplane when the sky is covered with clouds or
smog and the city lights glimmer through the haze.
Der Blick aus dem Flugzeug auf São Paulo, wenn der
Himmel von Wolken oder Abgasen bedeckt ist und die
Lichter der Stadt durch den Nebel leuchten, hat
Fernando und Humberto zu diesem Objekt inspiriert.

Fernando & Humberto Campana
hanging lamp Hängeleuchte
Trapo (Cloth Lappen)
one-off piece Unikat
1997
106×45×15 cm
rubber, PVC, light bulb, cabelling Gummi, PVC, Leuchtmittel,
Verkabelung
loan Leihgabe: Jacqueline Terpins, São Paulo

Fernando & Humberto Campana
table lamp Tischleuchte
Untitled Ohne Titel
study Studie
2000
45×46×19 cm
acrylic, sunblind, light bulb, cabelling Acryl,
Sonnenschutzschirm, Leuchtmittel, Verkabelung
loan Leihgabe: Estúdio Campana, São Paulo

Fernando & Humberto Campana
table lamp Tischleuchte
Jequitibá
small series Kleinserie: La Lampe, São Paulo
2000
51×45×19 cm
acrylic, light bulb, cabelling Acryl, Leuchtmittel, Verkabelung
loan Leihgabe: Estúdio Campana, São Paulo

Fernando & Humberto Campana
side table Beistelltisch
Inflável (Inflatable Aufblasbar)
one-off piece Unikat
1995
48×43×43 cm
anodized aluminium, PVC film eloxiertes Aluminium,
PVC-Folie
loan Leihgabe: Estúdio Campana, São Paulo

Between two round aluminium pizza pans, the Campanas glued
a section of an oversized inflatable plastic beer can they had found
advertising a brewery. Letting the air out of the balloon, the
side table transforms into its own package – an inversion of their
works of furniture made from packaging material like corrugated cardboard or bubble wrap.
Zwischen zwei Pizzaformen aus Aluminium klebten die
Campanas ein Stück einer überdimensionierten
Bierdose aus Plastik, die sie als Werbemittel einer Braue-
rei fanden. Lässt man die Luft aus dem Ballon, verwandelt sich der Beistelltisch in seine eigene Verpackung
– eine Umkehrung ihrer Möbel aus Verpackungsmaterial
wie Wellpappe oder Luftpolsterfolie.

Fernando & Humberto Campana
side table Beistelltisch
Inflável (Inflatable Aufblasbar)
small series Kleinserie: Museum of Modern Art,
New York
1998
8×43×43 cm
anodized aluminium, PVC film eloxiertes Aluminium,
PVC-Folie
loan Leihgabe: Estúdio Campana, São Paulo

Fernando & Humberto Campana
mirror Spiegel
Espello Elétrico (Electric Mirror Elektrischer Spiegel)
prototype Prototyp
2000
52×30×10 cm
acrylic, mirror glass Acryl, Spiegelglas
loan Leihgabe: Dorival Pereira Barbosa, São Paulo

The *Elétrico* series, which in addition to the piece shown here includes
a larger mirror as well as vases, fruit dishes, and other vessels of
varying sizes, owes its name to the iridescent effect of the cut edges
of the acrylic.
Die Serie *Elétrico*, zu der neben diesem auch ein
größerer Spiegel sowie Vasen, Fruchtschalen und andere
Gefäße unterschiedlicher Größe gehören, verdankt
ihren Namen dem irisierenden Effekt an den Schnittkanten des Acryls.

Fernando & Humberto Campana
armchair with ottoman **Armsessel mit Fußschemel**
Cone (Trichter)
serial model **Serienmodell: Edra spa, Perignano**
1997
77×107×84 cm / 45×66×65 cm
powder-coated steel, acrylic glass **pulverbeschichteter
Stahl, Acryl**
Collection Vitra Design Museum, Weil am Rhein
(armchair **Armsessel**)
loan **Leihgabe: Edra spa, Perignano**
(ottoman **Fußschemel**)

Fernando & Humberto Campana
table lamp **Tischleuchte**
Estela (Stele)
serial model **Serienmodell: Oluce srl, Milano**
1997
40×30×26 cm
laquered stainless steel, ethylene vinyl acetate (EVA), light bulb,
cabelling **lackierter Edelstahl, Ethylenvinylacetat (EVA),
Leuchtmittel, Verkabelung**
loan **Leihgabe: Estúdio Campana, São Paulo**

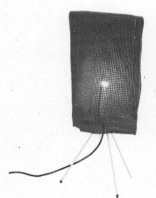

Fernando & Humberto Campana
table lamp **Tischleuchte**
Estela (Stele)
serial model **Serienmodell: Oluce srl, Milano**
1997
66×33×26 cm
lacquered stainless steel, ethylene vinyl acetate (EVA), light bulb,
cabelling **lackierter Edelstahl, Ethylenvinylacetat (EVA),
Leuchtmittel, Verkabelung**
Collection Vitra Design Museum, Weil am Rhein

Paper Pieces
Papierobjekte

Fernando & Humberto Campana
side table **Beistelltisch**
Papel (Paper Papier)
one-off piece **Unikat**
1993
54×48×48 cm
corrugated cardboard, aluminium, glue, acrylic paint **Wellpappe,
Aluminium, Klebstoff, Acryllackfarbe**
loan **Leihgabe: Estúdio Campana, São Paulo**

Fernando & Humberto Campana
standing lamp **Stehleuchte**
Papel (Paper Papier)
one-off piece **Unikat**
1993
105×25×25 cm
corrugated cardboard, aluminium, glue, dichroic bulb, cabelling
**Wellpappe, Aluminium, Klebstoff, zweifarbiges Leucht-
mittel, Verkabelung**
loan **Leihgabe: Claudio Elisabetsky, Perdizes**

Fernando & Humberto Campana
chair **Stuhl**
Papel (Paper Papier)
small series **Kleinserie**
1995
87×40×52 cm
corrugated cardboard, stainless steel, glue, acrylic paint
Wellpappe, Edelstahl, Klebstoff, Acryllackfarbe
Collection Vitra Design Museum, Weil am Rhein

Fernando & Humberto Campana
sofa Sofa
Papel (Paper Papier)
prototype Prototyp
1993
72×159×70 cm
corrugated cardboard, stainless steel, glue Wellpappe,
Edelstahl, Klebstoff
loan Leihgabe: Estúdio Campana, São Paulo

Fernando & Humberto Campana
screen Wandschirm
Papel (Paper Papier)
one-off piece Unikat
2003
170×120×5 cm
corrugated cardboard, steel wire Wellpappe,
Stahldraht
loan Leihgabe: Estúdio Campana, São Paulo

A stack of cardboard sheets, used by São Paulo's homeless as insulation mats, seat pads or as parts of their huts, gave the Campanas the idea of utilizing an unanticipated property of the material: the transparency that only becomes evident when viewing the cut edges at a right angle.

Ein Stapel aus Pappe, wie sie São Paulos Straßenbewohner für Isoliermatten, Sitzunterlagen oder Teile ihrer Hütten verwenden, brachte die Campanas auf die Idee, eine unerwartete Eigenschaft des Materials zu nutzen: die Transparenz, die man nur bemerkt, wenn man im rechten Winkel auf die Schnittkanten blickt.

Fernando & Humberto Campana
screen Wandschirm
Papel (Paper Papier)
small series Kleinserie
1995
175×56×28 cm
chromium-plated steel, corrugated cardboard, glue
Stahl verchromt, Wellpappe, Klebstoff
loan Leihgabe: Estúdio Campana, São Paulo

Fernando & Humberto Campana
panel Tafel
Papel II (Paper II Papier II)
one-off piece Unikat
2001
180×50×5 cm
corrugated cardboard, glue, wood Wellpappe,
Klebstoff, Holz
loan Leihgabe: Estúdio Campana, São Paulo

Fernando & Humberto Campana
chair Stuhl
Untitled Ohne Titel
study Studie
2006
87×76×32 cm
cardboard, glue, wrapping paper Pappe, Leim, Packpapier
loan Leihgabe: Alexander von Vegesack, Lessac-Confolens

Fernando & Humberto Campana
child's chair Kinderstuhl
Untitled Ohne Titel
study Studie
2006
78×60×23 cm
corrugated cardboard, wrapping paper, glue
Wellpappe, Packpapier, Leim
loan Leihgabe: Estúdio Campana, São Paulo

Initial sketches for a house made of cardboard ultimately led to these corrugated cardboard models produced in cooperation with the Vitra Design Museum: design proposals for seating furniture made of multiple layers of papier mâché nested like egg cartons.

Aus den ersten Überlegungen zu einem Haus aus Pappe entstanden in Zusammenarbeit mit dem Vitra Design Museum schließlich diese Modelle aus Wellpappe: Entwürfe für Sitzmöbel aus mehreren Lagen Pappmaché, die wie Eierkartons ineinander gesteckt werden.

Fernando & Humberto Campana
fruit bowl Fruchtschale
Untitled Ohne Titel
prototype Prototyp
2008
55×47×9 cm
paper, glue Papier, Kleister
loan Leihgabe: Estúdio Campana, São Paulo

The bowl was produced as a collaboration with the Vitra Design Museum on the development of industrial products from paper pulp – a recycled material that in turn can be recycled itself or composted. The prototype here shows how well the three-dimensional formability of papier mâché accommodates the sculptural work of the Campanas, even though the manufacturing process only permits curved surfaces.

Die Schale entstand im Rahmen einer Kooperation mit dem Vitra Design Museum zur Entwicklung von Industrieprodukten aus Papierpulpe – einem recycelten Material, das selbst wieder recycelbar oder kompostierbar ist. Das Muster hier zeigt, dass die freie Formbarkeit des Pappmaché der skulpturalen Arbeit der Campanas sehr entgegenkommt, auch wenn die Fabrikation nur gewölbte Flächen zulässt.

Objets Trouvés

Fernando & Humberto Campana
chair Stuhl
Martelo (Hammer)
one-off piece Unikat
1989
100×50×50 cm
wood, rubber hammers Holz, Gummihämmer
loan Leihgabe: Robert Wasilewski, São Paulo

A series of solid wooden seats that the Campanas had constructed using thick rubber beams for backrests led to this chair in which they replaced the beams with rubber mallets. This is the first work in which they integrated finished objects and it provided an important trigger for their object collages of the ensuing years.

Aus einer Serie von Sitzen, die die Campanas aus massivem Holz mit dicken Gummibalken als Rückenlehnen gebaut hatten, entstand dieser Stuhl, bei dem sie die Balken durch Gummihämmer ersetzten. Diese erste Arbeit, in die sie fertige Gebrauchsgegenstände integrierten, war eine Initialzündung für ihre Objektcollagen der folgenden Jahre.

Fernando & Humberto Campana
screen Wandschirm
Natureza Morta (Still Life Stillleben)
one-off piece Unikat
1990
193×24×113 cm
charcoal, wood, velvet, aluminium Kohle, Holz, Samt, Aluminium
loan Leihgabe: Estúdio Campana, São Paulo

Traditionally, screens have not only been used as a mobile partitioning of spaces but have also functioned as image carriers. The charcoal that appears here as a sculptural material refers to levels of meaning that one would not typically expect in this context: the shortage of resources, the pollution of the environment, the slash-and-burn clearance of primeval forests. The openings on the sides aid in the transport of the object.

Wandschirme dienen traditionell nicht nur der mobilen Unterteilung von Räumen, sondern auch als Bildträger. Die Kohle, die hier als plastischer Werkstoff auftaucht, verweist auf Bedeutungsebenen, die man in diesem Zusammenhang nicht erwartet: die Knappheit von Ressourcen, Umweltverschmutzung und die Brandrodungen des Urwalds. Die Öffnungen an den Seiten dienen zum Transport des Objekts.

Fernando & Humberto Campana
fruit bowl Fruchtschale
Jabuticaba
one-off piece Unikat
1990
20×43×37 cm
aluminium, jabuticaba wood Aluminium, Jabuticaba-Holz
loan Leihgabe: Adriana Adam, São Paulo

The Campanas have produced a number of objects that manifest an affinity with the *Animali Domestici* (Domestic Animals) of Andrea Branzi. Their individuality and vitality result from the tension between artificial and organic elements, between objet trouvé and construction.

In der Werkstatt der Campanas entstand eine Reihe von Objekten, die den *Animali Domestici* (Haustiere) von Andrea Branzi verwandt sind. Ihre Individualität und Vitalität beziehen sie aus der Spannung zwischen künstlichen und organischen Elementen, zwischen Objet Trouvé und Konstruktion.

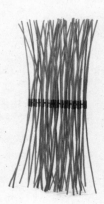

Fernando & Humberto Campana
screen Wandschirm
Cerca II (Fence II Zaun II)
one-off piece Unikat
1994
204×90×36 cm
wicker rods, steel Weidenstöcke, Stahl
loan Leihgabe: Christian Heymes, São Paulo

Fernando & Humberto Campana
chair Stuhl
Taquaral (Bamboo Grove Bambushain)
small series Kleinserie
2000
97×46×60 cm
bamboo, powder-coated steel Bambus, pulverbeschichteter Stahl
loan Leihgabe: Estúdio Campana, São Paulo

Fernando & Humberto Campana
chair Stuhl
3 em 1 (3 in 1)
one-off piece Unikat
1992
101×73×73 cm
wood, aluminium, cotton rope Holz, Aluminium,
Baumwollseile
loan Leihgabe: Estúdio Campana, São Paulo

When the Campanas conceived of a pile of ropes as a metaphor for the chaos of São Paulo,
it gave them the concept for this chair. The end result was not especially coherent, however, as
it united three different elements that were only successful when taken individually: ropes,
wooden discs and wrapped wire. This productive failure eventually spawned a number of later
works, including the *Vermelha* armchair of 1993.
Als die Campanas in einem auseinanderfallenden Haufen Seil eine
Metapher für das Chaos in São Paulo entdeckten, entstand die Idee zu diesem Stuhl, der aber noch kein wirklich schlüssiges Objekt ergab, weil
drei verschiedene Ideen zusammengepackt wurden, die nur separat erfolgreich waren: Seile, Scheiben und gewickelter Draht. Aus diesem pro-
duktiven Scheitern entstand unter anderem 1993 der *Vermelha*-Sessel.

Fernando & Humberto Campana
chair Stuhl
Jenette
serial model Serienmodell:
Edra spa, Perignano
2005
96×56×42 cm
polyurethane, PVC Polyurethan, PVC
loan Leihgabe: Edra spa, Perignano

The broom bristles, which keep a person guessing how far they
can lean back, had to be reinforced for Edra's version of this
chair with a metal plate hidden in the tuft to prevent a backward fall.
Die Besenborsten, die einen im Unklaren lassen,
wie weit man sich an sie lehnen kann, mussten für Edras
Version des Stuhls mit einer in dem Büschel versteckten
Metallplatte verstärkt werden, um der erforderlichen
Sicherheit zu entsprechen und den freien Fall nach hin-
ten zu verhindern.

Fernando & Humberto Campana
armchair Armsessel
Vermelha (Red Rot)
serial model Serienmodell: Edra spa, Perignano
1993
80×80×60 cm
aluminium tube, cotton ropes Alumiumrohr, Baumwollseile
loan Leihgabe: Edra spa, Perignano

After the *3 em 1*, the Campanas explored several intermediate variations before finding their way to this three-legged armchair, which
recalls spaghetti wrapped around a fork or snakes and lianas
in a rainforest. This Motif was first used by the Campanas in a 1991
art art installation and it has since been subjected to numerous
variations.
Vom *3 em 1* fanden die Campanas auf Umwegen zu
diesem dreibeinigen Sessel, der an Spaghetti erinnert,
die auf eine Gabel gewickelt sind, oder an Schlangen und
Lianen im Urwald. In einer Kunstinstallation 1991 verwendeten die Campanas zum ersten Mal dieses Motiv,
das sie seither mehrfach variierten.

Fernando & Humberto Campana
armchair Armsessel
Anemona (Anemone)
serial model Serienmodell: Edra spa, Perignano
2000
73×110×87 cm
PVC, stainless steel PVC, Edelstahl
loan Leihgabe: Estúdio Campana, São Paulo

Marked by transparency and lightness yet suggestive of voluminous
upholstered furniture, the form of this armchair first came to
Humberto Campana in a dream, which has been a source of inspiration for a number of the brothers' designs.
Die Gestalt dieses Sessels, der trotz Transparenz
und Leichtigkeit ein voluminöses Polstermöbel andeutet,
fand Humberto Campana, wie so manch anderen
Entwurf auch, in einem Traum.

Fernando & Humberto Campana
easy chair Sessel
Plastico Bolha (Bubble Wrap Luftpolsterfolie)
small series Kleinserie
1995
104×85×70 cm
chrome-plated steel, bubble wrap verchromter Stahl,
Luftpolsterfolie
loan Leihgabe: Estúdio Campana, São Paulo

As in their *Papelão* series, here the Campanas made use of packaging
material as the upholstery for a piece of furniture. When the
chair was unpacked for a 1998 exhibition at the MoMA, a staff member nearly destroyed it when he assumed that the actual work of
art lay under all the plastic.
So wie in ihrer *Papelão*-Serie verwendeten die Campanas auch hier Verpackungsmaterial als Polsterung eines
Möbels. Als der Stuhl 1998 für eine Ausstellung im MoMA
ausgepackt wurde, hätte ein Mitarbeiter den Sessel
fast zerstört, weil er das eigentliche Kunstwerk unter all
dem Plastik vermutet hatte.

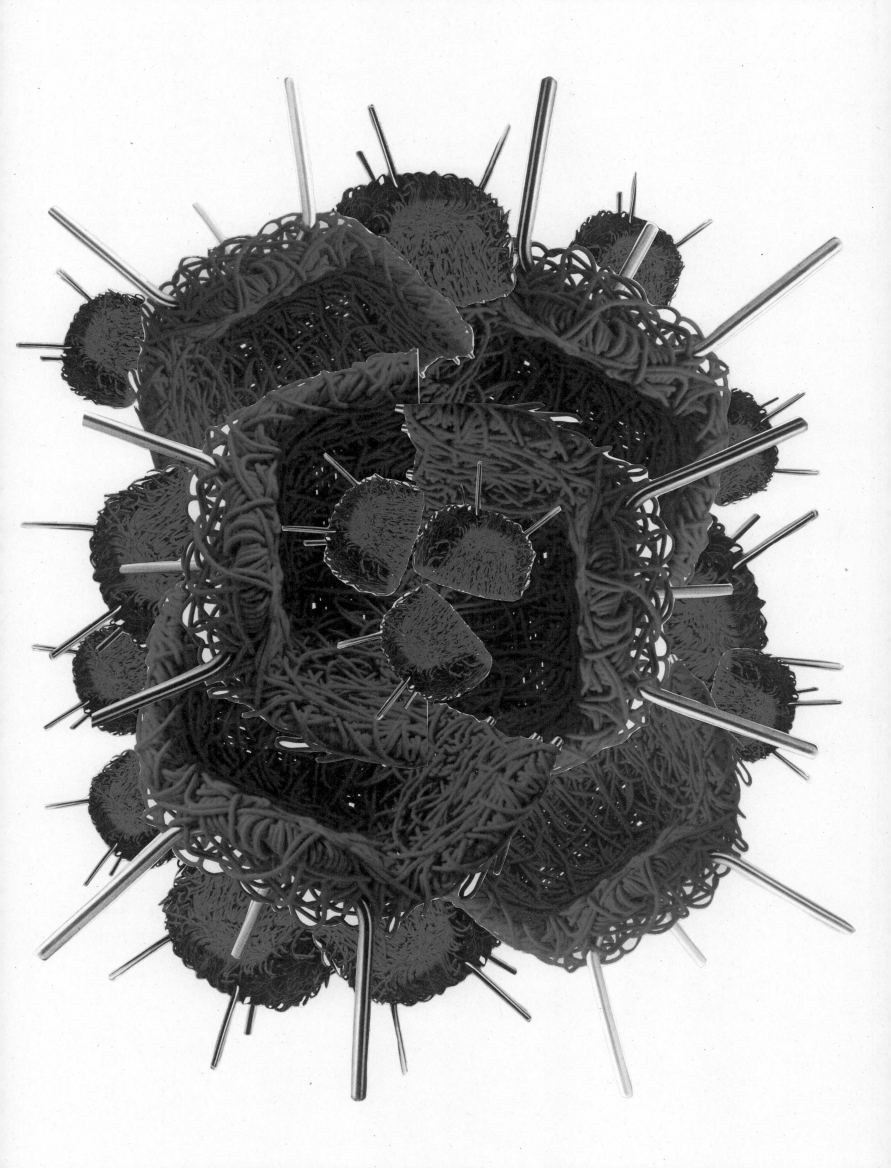

Fernando & Humberto Campana
easy chair Sessel
Jardim (Garden Garten)
small series Kleinserie
1995
90×60×60 cm
chrome-plated steel, plastic garden hose verchromter
Stahl, Gartenschlauch aus Kunststoff
Collection Vitra Design Museum, Weil am Rhein

The garden hose that the Campanas first used as the material for *Jardim* was later utilized in many of their subsequent designs for furniture, accessories, and installations, and even for stage costumes and sets.
Den Gartenschlauch, den die Campanas für den *Jardim* als Werkstoff entdeckten, verwendeten sie später in zahlreichen weiteren Entwürfen von Möbeln, Accessoires und Installationen und sogar für Bühnenkostüme und -requisiten.

Fernando & Humberto Campana
vase Vase
Luva (Glove Handschuh)
small series Kleinserie
1993
36×17×19 cm
steel, rubber glove Stahl, Gummihandschuh
loan Leihgabe: Estúdio Campana, São Paulo

Fernando & Humberto Campana
table Tisch
Tatoo (Tätowierung)
prototype Prototyp
1999
76×153×153 cm
stainless steel, PVC strainers Edelstahl, Kunststoffsiebe
loan Leihgabe: Estúdio Campana, São Paulo

As in many of their designs, here the Campanas ennoble a cheap, unassuming object through its duplication and usage in a new context. An especially ingenious aspect is the shadow projected by the drain strainers, thus creating a patterned carpet on the floor beneath the table.
Wie in vielen ihrer Entwürfe veredeln die Campanas hier ein billiges, unscheinbares Objekt durch dessen Vervielfältigung und Verwendung in neuem Kontext. Besonders raffiniert ist der Schattenwurf der Abflusssiebe, der einen gemusterten Teppich unter den Tisch projiziert.

Fernando & Humberto Campana
side table Beistelltisch
Cobogó (Brick and Concrete Latticework
Backstein- und Zementgitter)
one-off piece Unikat
2008
60×73×62 cm
brick, cement Backstein, Zement
loan Leihgabe: Estúdio Campana, São Paulo

Fernando & Humberto Campana
chandelier Kronleuchter
Prived Oca (Own House Eigenes Haus)
one-off piece for Swarovski's *Crystal Palace* project
Unikat für Swarovskis *Crystal Palace* Projekt
2003
240×100×100 cm
raffia, Swarovski crystals, LED, cabelling Raffiabast,
Swarovski-Kristalle, LED, Verkabelung
loan Leihgabe: Lumsden Limited

The Indian name refers to the dome-shaped huts of Native Brazilians. The raffia and the LED-illuminated crystals that cascade down like tentacles of a jellyfish forge a contrast between simple and precious, genuine and fake.
Der indianische Name *Oca* bezeichnet die kuppelförmigen Hütten brasilianischer Ureinwohner. Das Raffia und die mit LEDs bestückten Kristalle, die wie Tentakel einer Qualle hervorragen, schaffen einen Kontrast aus Einfachem und Kostbarem, Echtem und Falschem.

Fernando & Humberto Campana
architectural model Architekturmodell (1:20)
Untitled Ohne Titel
one-off piece Unikat
2004
101×130×30 cm
raffia, aluminium wire Raffiabast, Aluminiumdraht
loan Leihgabe: Estúdio Campana, São Paulo

The model shows a type of meditation space that the Campanas erected inside their *Ideal House* at the Cologne furniture fair. The original inspiration was provided by the raffia-covered huts of Brazilian Indians.
Das Modell zeigt eine Art Meditationsraum, den die Campanas auf der Kölner Möbelmesse innerhalb ihres *Ideal House* einrichteten. Das Vorbild lieferten die mit Raffia gedeckten Hütten brasilianischer Indios.

Knots
Knoten

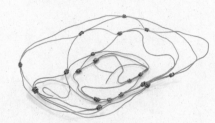

Fernando & Humberto Campana
fruit bowl Fruchtschale
Untitled Ohne Titel
one-off piece Unikat
1993
9×53×40 cm
aluminium wire Aluminiumdraht
loan Leihgabe: Estúdio Campana, São Paulo

Fernando & Humberto Campana
coffee table Couchtisch
Fios (String Schnur)
prototype Prototyp
1990
48×84×95 cm
steel wire Stahldraht
loan Leihgabe: Robert Wasilewski, São Paulo

This initial version of the table comes across as a synthesis between drawings by Giacometti and the wire figures of a Cocteau or a Calder. Together with the *Bob* armchair, it became a forerunner to a whole series of objects that seem to materialize in a state of constant vibration.
Diese erste Fassung des Tisches wirkt wie eine Synthese aus den Zeichnungen Giacomettis und den Draht-figuren eines Cocteau oder Calder. Zusammen mit dem Sessel *Bob* wurde er zum Vorläufer einer ganzen Reihe von Objekten, die sich in ständiger Vibration zu materialisieren scheinen.

Fernando & Humberto Campana
coffee table Couchtisch
Fios (String Schnur)
one-off piece Unikat
1993
47×80×132 cm
aluminium wire, steel, glass Aluminiumdraht, Stahl, Glas
loan Leihgabe: Estúdio Campana, São Paulo

Humberto Campana
armchair Armsessel
Bob
one-off piece Unikat
1990
60×120×80 cm
steel wire Stahldraht
loan Leihgabe: Robert Wasilewski, São Paulo

Dedicated by Humberto to his friend Robert Wasilewski, this arm-chair oscillates between sculpture and furniture, giving the impression of a seismographic recording of a mental state.
Dieser Sessel, den Humberto seinem Freund Robert Wasilewski widmete, oszilliert zwischen Skulptur und Möbel und wirkt so wie die seismografische Auf-zeichnung eines inneren Zustandes.

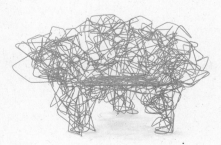

Fernando & Humberto Campana
armchair Armsessel
Yellow Corallo (Gelber Corallo)
one-off piece Unikat
2004
90×100×120 cm
lacquered steel wire lackierter Stahldraht
loan Leihgabe: Mariangela Martinelli, Recife

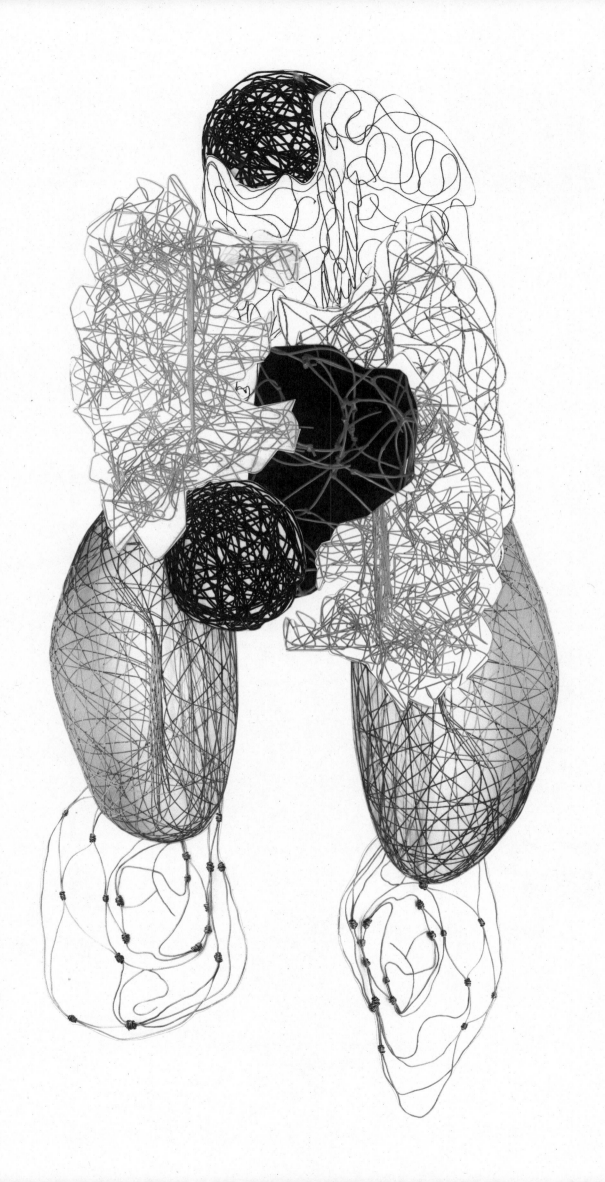

Fernando & Humberto Campana
armchair Armsessel
Corallo
serial model Serienmodell: Edra spa, Perignano
2004
94×144×90 cm
lacquered steel wire lackierter Stahldraht
loan Leihgabe: Alexander von Vegesack, Lessac-Confolens

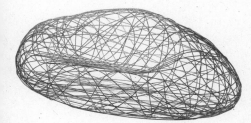

Fernando & Humberto Campana
sofa Sofa
Novelo (Clew Knäuel)
one-off piece Unikat
2003
76×215×120 cm
lacquered steel wire lackierter Stahldraht
loan Leihgabe: Estúdio Campana, São Paulo

Fernando & Humberto Campana
vase Vase
Bola (Beet Rübe)
small series Kleinserie
2001
29×20×20 cm
anodized aluminium wires, PVC tubes Eloxierter Aluminiumdraht, PVC-Schläuche
loan Leihgabe: Estúdio Campana, São Paulo

Fernando Campana
costume Kostüm
Scoubidou
one-off piece Unikat
2006
60×40×30 (variable variabel)
PVC strings PVC-Schnüre
loan Leihgabe; Estúdio Campana, São Paulo

The costume was created for a party held in conjunction with
a workshop given by the Campanas at the Domaine de Boisbuchet. In
the following year, they worked with Frédéric Flamand on the set
design and costumes for a performance of *Métamorphoses* by the
Ballet National de Marseille.
Das Kostüm entstand für eine Party im Rahmen eines
Workshops der Campanas auf der Domaine de
Boisbuchet. Im Jahr darauf arbeiteten sie mit Frédéric
Flamand am Bühnenbild und den Kostümen für
das Stück *Métamorphoses* des Ballet National de
Marseille.

Sticks
Stäbe

Fernando & Humberto Campana
fruit bowl Fruchtschale
Blow up (Explosion)
one-off piece Unikat
2002
19×50×72 cm
steel Stahl
loan Leihgabe: Robert Wasilewski, São Paulo

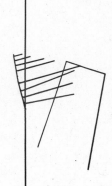

Humberto Campana
sculpture Plastik
Grelha (Grill Rost)
one-off piece Unikat
1987
164×70×110 cm
steel wire Stahldraht
loan Leihgabe: Robert Wasilewski, São Paulo

In the 1980s, Humberto worked primarily on abstract spatial
compositions. One of the works to emerge from this period was this
sculpture, which can be recognized as the frame of a chair – an
initial move towards the experimentations with furniture that began
the following year.
Während der 1980er Jahre arbeitete Humberto vor
allem an abstrakten Raumstudien. Dabei entstand auch
diese Plastik, die das Gerippe eines Stuhls erkennen
lässt – eine erste Annäherung an die ein Jahr später ein-
setzende Beschäftigung mit Möbeln.

Fernando & Humberto Campana
architectural model Architekturmodell (1:20)
Blow Up (Explosion)
2007
84×42×40 cm
PVC, MDF, acetate PVC, MDF, Azetat
loan Leihgabe: Estúdio Campana, São Paulo

With this art installation, the Campanas transferred the explosion motif formulated in earlier works onto a larger scale in the narrow stairwell of the Arte e Arquitectura Building in São Paulo. Viewed from below, the explosion appears frozen in time – just at the moment before the shock wave hits the foyer with its pool of water.
Mit dieser Kunstinstallation übertrugen die Campanas das schon früher formulierte Explosionsmotiv in vergrößertem Maßstab in das beengte Treppenhaus des Arte e Arquitectura Building in São Paulo. Von unten betrachtet, erscheint die Explosion wie eingefroren – gerade bevor die Druckwelle das Foyer mit dem Wasserbecken erreicht.

Fernando & Humberto Campana
screen Wandschirm
Escultura (Sculpture Plastik)
small series Kleinserie
1993
206×220×62 cm
aluminium Aluminium
loan Leihgabe: José Roberto Moreira do Valle, São Paulo

With good reason, the Campanas have designed an unusually large number of fruit dishes and screens. With their modest functional requirements, these objects present an ideal media for the execution of an artistic approach to design.
Die Campanas haben aus gutem Grund ungewöhnlich viele Obstschalen und Wandschirme entworfen: Beide Gegenstände sind wegen ihrer geringen funktionalen Anforderungen ideale Medien für eine künstlerische Herangehensweise.

Fernando & Humberto Campana
armchair Armsessel
Black Iron Chair (Schwarzer Stahlstuhl)
one-off piece Unikat
2004
78×120×87 cm
lacquered steel wire lackierter Stahldraht
loan Leihgabe: Estúdio Campana, São Paulo

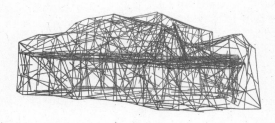

Fernando & Humberto Campana
bench Sitzbank
Pedra (Rock Fels)
limited edition of 10 copies (prototype) limitierte Auflage von 10 Exemplaren (Prototyp)
2004
80×301×190 cm
lacquered steel wire lackierter Stahldraht
loan Leihgabe: Robert Wasilewski, São Paulo

Fernando & Humberto Campana
chair Stuhl
Pedra Azul (Blue Rock Blauer Fels)
limited edition of 12 copies (prototype) limitierte Auflage von 12 Exemplaren (Prototyp)
2004
82×55×82 cm
lacquered steel wire lackierter Stahldraht
loan Leihgabe: Estúdio Campana, São Paulo

Fernando & Humberto Campana
vase Vase
Batuque (Drummer Trommler)
small series Kleinserie: Cappellini spa, Arosio
2000
70×60×50 cm
glass Glas
loan Leihgabe: Estúdio Campana, São Paulo

Fernando & Humberto Campana
vase Vase
Batuque (Drummer Trommler)
one-off piece Unikat
2000
169×60×67 cm
glass Glas
loan Leihgabe: Estúdio Campana, São Paulo

Fernando & Humberto Campana
clothing rack **Kleiderständer**
Alvo (Target **Zielscheibe**)
small series **Kleinserie**
1990
155×49×46 cm
steel **Stahl**
loan **Leihgabe: Estúdio Campana, São Paulo**

Fernando & Humberto Campana
mirror **Spiegel**
Untitled **Ohne Titel**
one-off piece **Unikat**
2008
ø 150 cm
mirror glass, scotch tape **Spiegelglas, Klebeband**
loan **Leihgabe: Estúdio Campana, São Paulo**

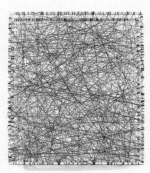

Fernando & Humberto Campana
relief **Relief**
Untitled **Ohne Titel**
one-off piece **Unikat**
2005
300×250×35 cm
plastic, powder-coated tubular steel **Kunststoff, pulverbeschichtetes Stahlrohr**
loan **Leihgabe: Alexander von Vegesack, Lessac-Confolens**

A work that Humberto and Fernando Campana produced upon commission during one of their workshops at the Domaine de Boisbuchet.
Eine Auftragsarbeit, die Humberto und Fernando Campana während eines ihrer Workshops für die Domaine de Boisbuchet anfertigten.

Hybrids
Hybride

Fernando & Humberto Campana
easy chair **Sessel**
Shark (Hai)
small series **Kleinserie**
2000
75×91×77 cm
stainless steel, polycarbonate, cane **Edelstahl, Polycarbonat, Rattan**
loan **Leihgabe: Estúdio Campana, São Paulo**

Long before Fernando and Humberto Campana began collaborating, Humberto had woven trays and baskets. With *Shark*, a precursor to the *Transplastics* series, the Campanas returned to this artisanal technique and made use of it in a unique manner for connecting the frame to the seat and backrest.
Lange bevor Fernando und Humberto Campana zusammenarbeiteten, hatte Humberto Tabletts und Körbe geflochten. Mit dem *Shark*, einem Vorläufer der *Transplastics*-Serie, kamen die Campanas auf dieses Handwerk zurück und nutzten es in einzigartiger Weise für eine Verbindung zwischen Gestell und Sitz- und Rückenfläche.

Fernando & Humberto Campana
child's armchair **Kindersessel**
Café Chair (Caféhausstuhl)
one-off piece **Unikat**
2007
61×53×61 cm
polypropylene, rattan **Polypropylen, Rattan**
loan **Leihgabe: Estúdio Campana, São Paulo**

The entire œuvre of the Campanas can be understood as an appropriation of a contradictory environment in a quasi-immunological process. The *Transplastics* series originated in a vision in which they imagined: 'What if one day the earth was covered in plastic? Plants would have to adapt to this plastic soil.' Thus, in this object, the contrasts have been reconciled in a functional and aesthetic symbiosis.
Die gesamte Arbeit der Campanas lässt sich als Aneignung einer widersprüchlichen Umwelt in einem quasi immunologischen Prozess verstehen. Die *Transplastics*-Serie entstammt einer Phantasie, in der sie sich vorstellten: »Wie wäre es, wenn die Erde eines Tages mit Plastik bedeckt wäre? Die Pflanzen würden sich dem Kunststoffboden anpassen müssen.« So haben sich auch in diesem Objekt die Gegensätze in einer funktionalen und ästhetischen Symbiose miteinander versöhnt.

Fernando & Humberto Campana
suite Sitzgruppe
Una Famiglia (One Family Eine Familie)
one-off piece Unikat
2006
140×87×78 cm
polypropylene chairs, iron structure, rattan Polypropylen-
stühle, Eisenstruktur, Rattan
loan Leihgabe: Beth Rudin DeWoody

Fernando & Humberto Campana
seating landscape Sitzlandschaft
Diamantina III
one-off piece Unikat (commissioned by Design Miami, on the occasion
of the Designer of the Year Award, 2008 Auftragsarbeit für Design
Miami, anlässlich der Auszeichnung als Designer des
Jahres 2008)
2008
466×206×175 cm
iron structure, rattan, amethysts Eisenstruktur, Rattan, Amethyste
loan Leihgabe: Design Miami & Craig Robins, Miami

Named after a small town in the Brazilian highlands, which has been
an important diamond mining site since the seventeenth century, the
piece symbolizes the many hidden and endangered natural treasures
of Brazil.
Der Name ist einer Kleinstadt im brasilianischen Bergland entlehnt, die seit dem 17. Jahrhundert ein
bedeutender Fundort von Diamanten ist, und steht hier
für die vielen verborgenen und bedrohten Kostbarkeiten der Natur in Brasilien.

Fernando & Humberto Campana
floor lamp Bodenleuchte
Gallon Lamp 6 (Kanister-Leuchte 6)
one-off piece Unikat
2007
108×108×29 cm
plastic canisters, rattan, light bulbs, cabelling Kunststoffkanister,
Rattan, Leuchtmittel, Verkabelung
loan Leihgabe: Estúdio Campana, São Paulo

Fernando & Humberto Campana
ceiling lamp Deckenleuchte
Transcloud
one-off piece Unikat
2008
70×330×70 cm
steel, rattan, polypropylene, light bulb, cabelling Stahl,
Rattan, Polypropylen, Leuchtmittel, Verkabelung
loan Leihgabe: Alexander von Vegesack, Lessac-
Confolens

Ever since the Renaissance, the self-sculpting quality of clouds
has been a continual source of inspiration for artists – a fascination
shared by Fernando and Humberto Campana.
Spätestens seit der Renaissance hat die eigenbild-
nerische Qualität von Wolken die Künstler immer
wieder inspiriert – Fernando und Humberto Campana
teilen diese Faszination.

Fernando & Humberto Campana
ceiling lamp Deckenleuchte
Transcloud
one-off piece Unikat
2007
45×210×170 cm
steel, rattan, polypropylene, light bulb, cabelling Stahl,
Rattan, Polypropylen, Leuchtmittel, Verkabelung
loan Leihgabe: Albion Gallery, London

Fernando & Humberto Campana
panel Tafel
OSB Masisa Campana, Stuffed Toys (Plüschtiere)
prototype Prototyp
2003
185×123×4 cm
OSB board, synthetic plush bears OSB-Platte, Plüschbären
aus Synthetik
loan Leihgabe: Estúdio Campana, São Paulo

Fernando & Humberto Campana
panel Tafel
OSB Masisa Campana, Esperança Dolls
(Esperança-Puppen)
prototype Prototyp
2003
122×244×3 cm
OSB board, cotton dolls OSB-Platte, Puppen aus
Baumwolle
loan Leihgabe: Estúdio Campana, São Paulo

In this study, the Campanas experimented with implanting a
motif directly into a material. They threw the rag dolls into the press-
board machine shortly before the press sequence. The result is a
perplexing ambivalence of image and object.
In dieser Studie experimentierten die Campanas mit dem
Implantieren eines Motivs direkt in den Baustoff:
Sie warfen die Stoffpuppen in die laufende Maschine zur
Produktion von Pressspanplatten kurz vor dem Press-
vorgang. Das Ergebnis ist eine verblüffende Ambivalenz
von Bild und Objekt.

Fernando & Humberto Campana
carpet Teppich
Animado (Animated Belebt)
one-off piece Unikat
1997
250×100 cm
artificial grass mat, cow hide, rubber Kunstrasen, Kuhfell, Gummi
loan Leihgabe: Estúdio Campana, São Paulo

Fernando & Humberto Campana
panel Tafel
Untitled Ohne Titel
study Studie
2005
102×61×13 cm
glass, amethysts Glas, Amethyste
loan Leihgabe: Estúdio Campana, São Paulo

Picture credits Bildnachweis

The Copyright of all pictures is exclusively with Estúdio Campana, São Paulo, except for the following ones (listed by pages):
Das Copyright sämtlicher Abbildungen liegt exklusiv beim Estúdio Campana, São Paulo, bis auf die folgenden (nach Seiten aufgeführt):

Fernando Laszlo: 4, 6, 7, 8, 9, 11, 12, 13, 14, 20 (above oben), 25 (above oben), 35, 36, 37, 40, 41, 42, 44, 46, 57, 60/61, 62, 63, 64, 68, 70 (below unten), 71, 73, 74, 75, 76, 77, 81, 82, 95 (all alle), 96 (all, except picture at bottom alle, bis auf das unterste Bild), 98 (all, except picture at top alle, bis auf das oberste Bild), 99 (all alle), 101 (all, except 2nd picture from top alle, bis auf 2. Bild von oben), 102 (all alle), 103 (all, except picture at top alle, bis auf oberstes Bild), 104 (all, except picture at bottom right and 4th picture from top alle, bis auf Bild unten rechts und 4. Bild von oben), 105 (all, except 4th picture from top alle, bis auf 4. Bild von oben), 106 (all, except picture at top and 3rd picture from top alle, bis auf oberstes Bild und 3. Bild von oben), 108 (all alle), 109 (all, except 4th picture from top alle, bis auf 4. Bild von oben), 111 (all, except 2nd and 3rd picture from top alle, bis auf 2. und 3. Bild von oben), 112 (2nd, 4th, and 5th picture from top 2., 4. und 5. Bild von oben), 114 (all, except 2nd picture from bottom alle, bis auf 2. Bild von unten), 115 (all, except picture at top alle, bis auf oberstes Bild), 116 (top and 2nd picture from top oben und 2. Bild von oben), 118 (2nd, 3rd, and 4th picture from top 2., 3. und 4. Bild von oben), 119 (all, except 4th and 5th picture from top alle, bis auf 4. und 5. Bild von oben), 121 (3rd and 4th picture from top 3. und 4. Bild von oben), 122 (1st and 2nd picture from top 1. und 2. Bild von oben), 124 (2nd, 3rd, and 5th picture from top 2., 3. und 5. Bild von oben), 125 (2nd, 3rd, and 4th picture from top 2., 3. und 4. Bild von oben), 127 (1st, 2nd, and 4th picture from top 1., 2. und 4. Bild von oben), 128.
Andréas Heiniger: 20 (below unten), 23 (below unten), 24, 28, 32 (below unten).
Andrés Otero: 19, 23 (above oben).
Dudu Cavalcanti (N Imagens): 21 (above oben).
Vitra Design Museum: 22 (above oben), 125 (bottom unten).
Milton Guran: 22 (below unten).
Studio Andrea Branzi: 31.
Nair Benedicto (N Imagens): 32 (above oben).
David R. Ingham: 33 (above oben).
Cooper-Hewitt National Design Museum/Andrew Garn: 33 (below unten).
Edra spa/Emilio Tremolada: 38/39, 48, 50, 51 (above and below oben und unten), 52, 53, 58 (above oben), 98 (picture at top oberstes Bild), 106 (top and 3rd picture from top oberstes Bild und 3. Bild von oben), 112 (top oben), 116 (3rd, 4th, and 5th picture from top 3., 4. und 5. Bild von oben).
Vitra Design Museum/Andreas Sütterlin: 43, 59, 87 (below unten), 112 (3rd and 6th picture from top 3. und 6. Bild von unten), 114 (2nd picture from bottom 2. Bild von unten), 115 (top oben), 118 (top oben), 121 (top oben).
Bernardaud, Paris: 45, 101 (2. von oben).
Massimo Morozzi: 53 (below unten).
Mathias Schwartz-Clauss: 29, 72, 87 (above oben), 88 (above oben), 90.
Moss Gallery: 78.
Albion Gallery: 79, 125 (top oben).
Phillips de Pury & Company: 80, 118 (bottom unten).
Mariana Chama: 84.
Titus Riedl: 86.
Isabel Gouvea: 88 (below unten).
Celso Brandão: 89 (above oben).
Fabiana Figueiredo (N Imagens): 89 (below unten).
Rita Toledo Piza: 91 (above oben).
TT Leal/Pedro Lobo: 91 (below unten).
André Soares de Albuquerque: 92.
Pino Pipitone: 96 (picture at bottom unterstes Bild).
Hans-Jörg Walter: 105 (4th picture from top 4. Bild von oben).
Cappellini spa: 122 (2nd picture from bottom 2. Bild von unten).
Christine Kromer: 125 (bottom unten).

Catalogue Katalog

General Editors Herausgeber
Alexander von Vegesack,
Mathias Schwartz-Clauss

Editor Redaktion
Mathias Schwartz-Clauss

Photo Editor Bildredaktion
Daniel Kern

Translations Übersetzungen
Julia Thorson
(German › English Deutsch › Englisch)
CLS Communication AG, Zürich
(Portuguese › German Portugiesisch › Deutsch)
Paula V. de Almeida Klop
(Portuguese › English Portugiesisch › Englisch)
Carolien Gutberlet
(Italian › German Italienisch › Deutsch)
Barbara Fisher
(Italian › English Italienisch › Englisch)

Copy Editors Lektorat
Kirsten Thietz (German Deutsch)
Ariel Krill (English Englisch)

Graphic Design Gestaltung
groenlandbasel, Basel:
Dorothea Weishaupt und Matthias Huber

Lithography Lithografie
Andreas Muster, Basel

Printing Druck
DZA Druckerei zu Altenburg GmbH

Made out of 100% deinked recovered paper.
Hergestellt aus 100% entfärbtem Altpapier.

The Deutsche Bibliothek has registered this publication in the Deutsche Nationalbibliografie; detailed bibliographical information can be found on the internet at http://dnb.ddb.de.
Die Deutsche Bibliothek verzeichnet diese Publikation in der Deutschen Nationalbibliografie; detaillierte bibliografische Daten sind im Internet über http://dnb.ddb.de abrufbar.

ISBN 978-3-931936-47-1
Artikelno. 200 803 01
Printed in Germany

© 2009 Vitra Design Stiftung gGmbH
and the authors und Autoren;
Charles-Eames-Str. 2,
D-79576 Weil am Rhein
First edition Erste Auflage 2009

The collages accompanying the list of exhibited works were produced by Fernando and Humberto Campana especially for this purpose. The originals are shown in the *Antibodies* exhibition with a limited edition of lithograph prints available from the Vitra Design Museum. Die Collagen, die das Verzeichnis der ausgestellten Werke begleiten, wurden von Fernando und Humberto Campana eigens für diesen Zweck angefertigt. Die Originale werden in der *Antibodies*-Ausstellung gezeigt und Lithografien davon sind in einer limitierten Auflage über das Vitra Design Museum erhältlich.

With the support of Mit Unterstützung von **vitra.**

Exhibition Ausstellung

Curator Kurator
Mathias Schwartz-Clauss

Assistant Curator Kuratorische Assistenz
Daniel Kern

Project Development at the Estúdio Campana
Projektentwicklung im Estúdio Campana
Lélia Arruda, Leo Kim, Luiza Albuquerque,
Eduardo Wolk

Exhibition Design Ausstellungsgestaltung
groenlandbasel, Basel:
Matthias Schnegg, Bernhard Schweizer

Graphics Grafik
groenlandbasel, Basel:
Dorothea Weishaupt, Matthias Huber,
Daniela Stolpp

Technical Management Technische Leitung
Stefani Fricker

Audio-Visual Designs and Technical Drawings
Audiovisuelle Gestaltung und technische Zeichnungen
Gregor Bielser

Logistics Logistik
Bogusław Ubik-Perski

Restoration Restaurierung
Richard Adler

Administration and Finance
Verwaltung und Finanzen
Harry Schöpflin, Jörn Strüker

Tour Organization Tourneeorganisation
Reiner Packeiser, Isabel Serbeto

Press Relations Pressearbeit
Gabriella Gianoli PR, Alexa Tepen

Events Veranstaltungen
Alexa Tepen, Esmeralda Hernandez,
Kilian Jost

Visitor Service Besucherservice
Anneliese Gastel

Products Produkte
Marine Gallian

The *Zig Zag* screen, designed for Edra in 2001, as it stands today in Fernando Campana's living room, loaded with all kinds of finds and souvenirs – like an American Indian's dreamcatcher.
Der Wandschirm *Zig Zag*, 2001 für Edra entworfen, aus Fernando Campanas Wohnzimmer. Dort steht er wie ein indianischer Traumfänger – beladen mit allerlei Souvenirs und Fundsachen.

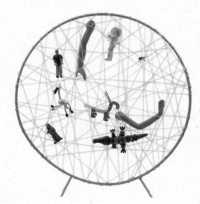